CHRISTIANITY AND THE ROMAN EMPIRE

From Nero to Theodosius

T0327061

Christianity and the Roman Empire

From Nero to Theodosius

By

PAUL ALLARD

Seventh Edition

Translated from the French
by
ANTHONY P. GYTHIEL

ST VLADIMIR'S SEMINARY PRESS
YONKERS, NEW YORK
2017

Library of Congress Cataloging-in-Publication Data

Names: Allard, Paul, 1841–1916, author. | Gythiel, Anthony P., 1930– translator.
Title: Christianity and the Roman Empire from Nero to Theodosius / by Paul Allard
; translated from the French by Anthony P. Gythiel.
Other titles: Christianisme et l'empire romain, de Néron à Théodose. English
Description: Seventh edition. | Yonkers, New York : St Vladimir's Seminary
Press, 2016. | "A translation of Paul Allard, Le Christianisme et l'Empire
Romain de Néron à Théodose, Paris, Librairie Victor Lecoffre, 1908." | Includes
bibliographical references and index.
Identifiers: LCCN 2016059138 (print) | LCCN 2016059733 (ebook) | ISBN
9780881415629 (alk. paper) | ISBN 9780881415636 ()
Subjects: LCSH: Church history—Primitive and early church, ca. 30–600.
Classification: LCC BR170 .A413 2016 (print) | LCC BR170 (ebook) | DDC
270.1—dc23
LC record available at https://lccn.loc.gov/2016059138

Copyright © 2017
St Vladimir's Seminary Press
575 Scarsdale Road, Yonkers, NY 10707
1–800–204–2665
www.svspress.com

ISBN (print) 978–0–88141–562–9
ISBN (electronic) 978–0–88141–563–6

A translation of Paul Allard,
Le Christianisme et l'Empire Romain de Néron à Théodose
Paris, Librairie Victor Lecoffre, 1908.

Table of Contents

Foreword

Paul Allard was one of his generation's greatest scholars of Christianity in the Roman Empire. He was born at Rouen in France in 1841 and studied law, rising through the profession to become a judge in the civil courts. He died in 1916. His voracious reading and innate intelligence led him, in the hours he had free from his legal work, into the depths of research on Roman imperial affairs and, once there in the classics section of the library, he never emerged, changing career tracks to become a world-class historian and theologian. In 1874 he translated and expanded Northcote and Brownlow's seminal study on the Roman Catacombs (*Rome souterraine*) and embarked on a lifelong interest in the primitive Church in its Roman imperial context. He gained a deep and first hand knowledge of the Roman catacombs himself, becoming a world expert on epigraphy, and this spurred him to produce what was to be the *leitmotif* of his historical work, a study of the imperial persecutions of Christianity in several volumes.[1] In all of this work he brought together a profound archaeological knowledge with a theological sensitivity and a very full understanding of the principles of Roman jurisprudence. Assessing the persecutions, he followed a largely theological, line as already established by the great theologian lawyer Tertullian, and stressed throughout his painstakingly detailed work that the persecutions were intrinsically unjust, out of proportion to the threat the authorities had perceived, and generally animated by deeply unworthy motives. His clear catholic sympathy with the notion of persecution as the early fathers had interpreted it—that is as an eschatological sign of the spirit of the world being opposed to the Bride of the Lamb—caused his generation of more secularized historians (who as usual deluded themselves that they commanded the heights

---

[1] *Histoire des persecutions pendant la premiere moitié du troisième siècle* (Paris, 1881); *La persecution de Diocletien et le triomphe de l'Église*, 2 vols. (Paris, 1890); and *Histoire des persécutions pendant les deux premiers siècles*. 2nd ed. (Paris, 1892).

7

of objectivity and detachment) to regard his work as the enthusiasm of an amateur, a criticism that is still aimed at him by ideologues who think history has no place in it for theology.

His studies of the persecutions attracted the catcalls of the anti-clerical academy of his day. A certain readiness to accept many of the details of the martyrologies as legends that always had within them some basis in fact—when his contemporaries wanted to put them all in the basket of historical irrelevances—laid him open to critical attack. Some of it was basic hostility against his conservative catholic outlook, but a real part of it was ideological in character: accusing Allard of sinning against their very heartfelt premise that an historian is an independent god in his or her own right, and ought to be above and apart from all religious pieties. As Allard saw it, however, the history of Christ's Church is inescapably a theological matter, not merely an issue of *wissenschaftliche* religious history but rather a claim (as long as Christ's *ekklēsia* will endure) that the record of the Church's existence on earth is not merely a question of its sociological imprint or its political structures, but more so a matter of intrinsic moral and eschatological significance: the claim to be the Covenant community of the New Age, wrestling with the world order as either the field of its mission or its martyrdom. Allard's work embarrassed many of his secular contemporaries, and they tried to dismiss him as not a "properly trained" historian; but they could not cover up the evidence that here was a polymath who had read voraciously. His next labor was equally monumental—a study of Roman slavery (*Les esclaves Chrétiens depuis les premiers temps de L'Église jusqu'a la fin de la domination romaine en occident*) issued in Paris in 1876. His study on the Christian Empire (*Le Christianisme et l'empire romain de Neron à Théodose*) appeared in 1896; followed by works on St Basil the Great (1899) and Julian the Apostate (1900). He would also produce works on archaeology (1898), Roman pagan art (1879), Sidonius Apollinaris (1910), and on the spectacular ancient house church of San Giovanni e Paolo on the Caelian hill (1900), where the present writer, as a young deacon, once served as guide to the Roman *scavi*.

In this advancing labor of scholarly publication, Allard's histori-cal-critical skills were clearly being sharpened to a fine blade, and his readiness to take on the grand themes with heroic commitments to research reading were evident. In his studies, he presented honestly and clearly the mass of detailed data he acquired, which make of his works a treatment that has still not been matched for depth of cover-age. As is the case with the *sophiste* Gibbon, in his *Decline and Fall of the Roman Empire*, one may demur from this or that interpretation placed upon the evidence (indeed Gibbon's drivenness by ideological constructs far exceeds that of Allard), but in each instance, with both Gibbon and Allard, when one "checks up on their references," it invari-ably turns out that they have closely read the primary sources. Their mindset was formed by immersion into the vastness of the ancient evidences. It is this close familiarity with a wealth of classical knowl-edge of all aspects of the imperial past that gives Allard's work on the Roman Empire to the time of Theodosius an enduring and valuable character.

It has been the case for too long that students of the New Testament and the Fathers of the Church tended to read their texts in bubbles of disconnectedness. The Scriptures were approached as self-contained with hardly a nod to the ancient contexts, except for the history of ideas; and the Fathers' writings were habitually smashed apart and mined for doctrinal propositions or canons. This destructively reductionist way of reading enslaved the ancient texts to contemporary modes of think-ing—and so has always proved popular. Of late the New Testament has been creatively repositioned in a much more conscious historical narrative. This widening sense of what life was like in antiquity has started to lead us away from some of the more ridiculously narrow foolishness of earlier studies that, having once found out a stunningly "new" historical perspective (such as the thought that Jesus was a Jew, or that the title Son of Man had been used by some sectarians to con-note the Angel of the End Time) it obsessed them to the point of the exclusion of all else. The Christologies, or should we say Jesus-ologies, of the school of Historical Jesus Criticism (the so-called "Quests") is a case in point. Often it seemed that the smaller the evidential point, the larger it was going to be written up as the "true version" of events; the only valid perspectival point obscured by too many generations of fideist theologians. All this overheated work led, via a post-Marxian "hermeneutic of suspicion," to the wave of studies of the end of the last century (still continuing unabated in the popular media) that were little short of paranoid fictional re-imaginings of the alleged life and character of Christ. In terms of patristic reception the slicing and dicing of the early theologians, so as to make them post-Reformation apologists bent on "proving dogmatic cases," led to a terribly dry-as-dust reductionism. Patristics was languishing. This field too has been renovated of late by setting the work of the fathers back into the larger frameworks of Late Antique philosophy, rhetoric, metaphysics, and mysticism. They have emerged once more as intellectual giants who refused (like many of their contemporaries, and ours) to keep these correlate insights in separate boxes, but strove rather for the organic synthesis that uses all these approaches as means to an end (a *telos*) not as exploded and separate ends in themselves.

The modern Academy is today groaning under the separateness of its scholastic subdivisions of studies that make a Great Divide between science and humanities and produce ever more specialized geniuses in various fields who are embarrassingly ignorant of the very basics of another: an ignorance that emerges painfully when they leave the empirical domain and start to emit philosophical meta-narrative based upon their primary subject. This tendency to make "subject islands" to themselves is reaching alarming proportions today and places the whole University artifice of the last three hundred years in a certain state of crisis.

This is partly why it is a pleasure to read an "old school" scholar. Allard is a prime example of one of those scholarly minds that was disciplined by prolonged immersion in the fundamental sources, so as to be formed in a holistic perspective. In worlds of discourse that prefer tangents and reductions and mere ideological parts, he seems a very "old world" type of scholar: but his witness remains of enduring worth to all those who value history primarily as a quest for truth: a quest that refuses to be put off by the sardonic retort of the many

Pilates who remain among us (Jn 18.38). He stands for a value that sets a course for a Churchly sense of Church History, one that knows that its historical study is also a theological concern: where historical truth and theology are not incompatibles, and where the ministry of history serves the Church to great effect with its adage: "Never put the ideology before the evidence." Allard cannot be faulted on the magisterial way he allowed the evidence to inform and furnish his mind. In his case it nurtured his spirit and rendered him a model of a learned and deeply spiritual historian.

The translator and St Vladimir's Press are to be warmly congratulated for bringing this splendid volume back to life. It will open the eyes of new generations of students to the great complexity of the context of the birth of the Church's fundamental structures, and offer many instructive parallels with the way the early Christian's adopted and adapted what was offered to them in their surrounding political and intellectual culture. It will also serve to show them, in Allard, a model of a man who followed the dictum of St Gregory the Theologian, and had put his *logos* (that is his spirit and intellectual energies) in the service of the *Logos*, a man who thought it no sin to be an honest historian and a devout Christian.

Archpriest John A McGuckin, PhD, DD, DLitt., FRHistSoc.

Preface

This book spans four centuries, from the day Christianity made its first appearance in the Roman Empire until it became the empire's sole recognized religion. During the first three hundred years Christianity defended itself against paganism, which was supported by the imperial power; during the last hundred years, it used this same power to end idolatry. Over the course of these two unequal epochs, a complete reversal of roles occurred, with one major difference, however. Christianity was persecuted until it bled, while paganism disappeared partly through persuasion and partly through force of law. Its adherents were never ill-treated.

The reader will understand that this book, with its very narrow scope, does not attempt to cover such a wide-ranging history. Several volumes would be needed. Not long ago [in 1900, 1903, 1905 and 1906, in *Histoire des persécutions pendant la première partie du troisième siècle (Septime Sévère, Maximin, Dèce)*—a work recognized by the Prix Thiers of the French Academy], I devoted five volumes to the persecutions undergone by the Christians. Several years later, six volumes were required by Duke de Broglie to describe, in masterful fashion, the relationship between Church and state during the fourth century. The pages that follow have no purpose other than to set forth, in as precise a manner as possible, the results that seem to have been definitely acquired by the science of history on this twofold subject. Consequently, these pages will not excuse the reader eager for details from referring to the original documents and to the works from which we have tried to draw a complete picture. They will, however, serve as a preparation for a new study of the questions with which they are concerned, and as a summary of the earlier works to which these questions have given rise.

I have made an effort to omit nothing essential, bringing the major outlines of this history into full relief. Nor do I pretend to have read everything, because the literature on the subject is vast.

It is my hope that I consult every source that deserves to be called a source. These are, first of all, the original texts that are irreplaceable: the work of ancient historians, panegyrists, orators, and Church fathers; saints' lives; acts of the martyrs; collections of laws inscriptions; and collections of councils. Then follow secondary or derivative sources, including modern authors in French, German, English, and Italian, who treated with competence some aspects of the subject studied here. Deliberately concise with my notes, I did not attempt to indicate all of these sources at the end of each chapter. The bibliographical index at the end of the volume facilitates an acquaintance with the most important French and English sources. Learned readers will recognize that the most significant sources, at least, have been examined, and that the substance of these texts has become part of my book.

The reader will also recognize that in this book, written by a Christian, the lights and shadows have been distributed with neither hatred nor complacency, and without deviating from the most rigorous historical impartiality. The author neither tried to impose nor to formulate any pre-conceived conclusions. If apology has earned the right to lean on history, where it sometimes finds its most solid foundation, history, in turn, need not be considered an apology. The facts speak for themselves. If any conclusions are to be derived, only the reader can draw them.

November 1896.

Note to the Third Edition

A selection of primary texts dealing with the relationship between Roman emperors and Christians until the reign of Constantine the Great (A.D. 306–337), has been inserted at the end of this volume. These documents illustrate in a very precise fashion the variations in imperial policy with respect to Christianity. Some passages are found in the endnotes; it may be useful to see them all gathered together.

CHAPTER ONE
Christians and the Emperors
of the First Century

1. Roman Religions

The religion of ancient Rome was very simple. The Latin gods were nothing more than forces of nature, personified by the imagination of an agricultural and warlike people. Little by little this primitive pantheon was expanded. Conquest ushered in new deities. The Romans believed that all national religions were true. They hurried to appropriate the divinities of the peoples they vanquished and thereby transform enemies into protectors. In this fashion they added to the gods of Latium those of the various regions of Italy, one after the other. Any enlargement of the territory of primitive Rome was at the same time an enlargement of its religion. Other causes successively enriched it. Lacking any concept of a universal religion, the ancients, in times of public calamity, were inclined to address themselves to foreign gods whom they deemed able to push aside the scourges from which their native gods had been unable to protect them. In this way, through the influence of the Sibylline Oracles, the main gods of Greece were gradually introduced to Rome. As Roman power extended to the East, however, other religious forms were revealed to the conquering people. The troubling and sensual mysticism of the East awakened new needs in the soul. The deities of Egypt and Asia had their priests in Rome and found devotees among those whose religious aspirations were no longer satisfied by the rough simplicity of the Italic religions, nor the too-human mythology of Hellenism.

These diverse cults did not immediately gain equal acceptance. Some remained relegated for a time outside the confines of Rome, while others received citizenship at once. Some cults were rejected at first, even forbidden on several occasions, and finally introduced by an irresistible surge in popular sentiment. Many saw their admission advanced by an accidental resemblance between their gods and those of Rome; these were quickly identified. Thus arose gradually a religion of successive annexations, assimilations, and compromise, as we see at the beginning of the Roman Empire after the reforms of Augustus. Most gods of the state were nothing more than hybrids wherein Latin, Italian, Greek, and Asiatic elements were combined, with Greece nearly always imposing the perfection of its malleable form. The small number of foreign divinities that proved recalcitrant to this fusion found no place in the official religion. However, as the object of private devotions, they continued to enjoy wide tolerance. This tolerance for every form of piety and superstition would be suspended in only two cases: when the state believed it must intervene in the name of the public interest or morality, and when a religion claimed exclusive dominion over minds and wills.

It would be a mistake to ascribe the intolerance shown by the Roman state in the second instance to some metaphysical theory. The state religion was not doctrinal. As we have seen, it was an assemblage of pieces of varied origin, a heterogeneous mosaic to which time, custom, poetics, and popular instinct lent an apparent cohesion and harmony. Throughout history, the Roman mind maintained an outlook that was fortified, rather than weakened, by an almost uninterrupted series of victories and conquests. Rome's fortune seemed to be linked to its religion. The most refined contemporaries of Augustus and Tiberius were no less imbued with this idea than were the coarse inhabitants of the primitive towns of the Palatinate. They cared little about the foundation of this religion, its absolute certainty, or its historical origins. More than one adherent would have readily echoed the indifferent or disheartened words of Pilate: "What is truth?" However, political interest and an all-powerful superstition, which even the most skeptical did not try to deny, made the national gods sacred to them. Even those of another nationality, whose adoption was recent, found themselves aligned to the secular foundations of the state by a widely accepted fiction. Praying to other gods was allowed, but professing that they alone deserved worship, that they alone existed and possessed an absolute truth, seemed like an attack on Roman authority. The people believed that this power would be weakened the day Rome's traditional religion crumbled. This concept was so inherent to Roman paganism that it would remain unchanged among paganism's last adherents, the contemporaries of St Ambrose and St Augustine.

Among the foreign religions that existed before the advent of Christianity, none appeared likely to call down the wrath of the civil authorities. In honoring his favorite god, the follower of Isis or Mithras never entertained the idea of refusing homage to the sacred personages publicly adored in Rome. Even less would he have considered contesting their divine character. Later, when exotic cults had become popular and numbered among their adherents important members of the aristocracy, we see them simultaneously endowed with official priesthoods and invested with the most bizarre titles of the eastern devotions. The situation of Judaism was entirely different. This religion was essentially monotheistic, and therefore exclusive. In its eyes no gods exist other than its own. For Judaism, the gods of the nations either had no reality, or they were harmful demons. It either mocked or hated them. This trait of the Jews was noted by the ancient historians. The Jews, they tell us, are a race famous for its scorn of the gods, considering profane everything which among us is sacred.[1] This characteristic of Judaism was made even worse by the spirit of proselytizing that it had in common with other eastern religions, but which in Judaism became particularly injurious, since it detached from every other belief those whom it attracted to its own.[2]

At no time, however, did Rome consider banning the Jewish religion. As long as its followers remained the body of a nation—a weakened, mutilated body, but preserving a remnant of life—such tolerance is easily explained. The Romans always respected national religions. Augustus and his family showered the temple of Jerusalem with gifts. After the Jewish nation perished in the year AD 70, leaving

---

[1] Pliny, *Nat. hist.*. XIII, 4; Tacitus, *Hist.*, v, 2, 5, 13. [Notes follow the format used in Allard's original citations (titles of texts in Latin, with textual divisions often given in Roman numerals).—*Ed.*]

[2] Tacitus, *Hist.*, v, 5.

only religion and race still standing, Rome supported a cult that was its natural enemy with the same patience. Rome continued to bend laws directed against associations so as to benefit the synagogue, and exempted the Jews from any obligations contrary to their conscience.[3] Only proselytism was more or less forbidden them.[4] This tolerance, barely interrupted by some police measures more violent than sustainable,[5] seems surprising at first, but can be explained upon reflection. Due to the very fact that religion, with the Jews, was linked to race and seemed to merge with it, a universal empire like Rome had nothing to fear. This base was too narrow to hold the peoples of every background upon whom hung the Roman eagle. A monotheism fraught with minute requirements that formed around it like a hedge of thorns was too gloomy to seduce them. Imperial policy thus took care not to resort to useless severities that would have awakened a barely slumbering fanaticism and needlessly imperiled the public peace.

Rome's intolerance was reserved for insubordinates more gentle and, from its point of view, more dangerous. As the Jewish religion had done, Christianity taught people the worship of the true God. Unlike the Jewish religion, whose demands were too great and whose national character was too pronounced to attract many lasting converts, Christianity asked of its followers no other sacrifice than that of their errors and vices. Its simple rituals and a morality free of peculiarities appealed to all without any distinction as to nationality or race. One could become a Christian without ceasing to be Roman. Seemingly, this should have led to lenient policies toward Christianity. On the contrary, it was the cause of their severity. By preaching and making a universal religion possible, Christianity seemed to pose a direct threat to the religion of the state, as the empire professed it. Its success would be the ruin of official paganism. Since they believed the survival of paganism to be inseparable from that of Rome, the politicians tried to stop the spread of the new religion by any means. The best emperors—those most concerned with the public interest and most imbued

---

[3] *Digest*, L, ii, 2, 3.

[4] Paul, Sent., v, xxiii, 3, 4; *Digest*, xlviii, viii, 11; Spartian, *Severus*, 17.

[5] Tacitus, *Ann.*, II, 85; Josephus, *Ant. Jud.* xviii, 3, 4; Philo, *Adv. Flaccum; Legat. Ad Caium;* Suetonius, *Claudius*, 25; *Act. Apost.* xviii, 2; Dio Cassius, lx, 6.

with Roman prejudices—would for that reason prove to be among Christianity's most ardent persecutors.

Christianity was born long enough ago, before the empire was concerned with it. At the beginning it was hardly distinguishable from Judaism. As Tertullian has said, Christianity grew up in the shadow of this tolerated religion.[6] The persecutions to which Christianity was subjected by Judaism seemed to Roman statesmen at first as conflicts between Jewish sects of differing tendencies.[7] In the accusations directed against Paul and the first missionaries of the gospel, they saw only quarrels over words, or discussions of discipline and doctrine of which the civil authority had no knowledge.[8] They received the denouncers with a barely concealed ill humor. If Paul was led to Rome to be presented at the court of the emperor, it was only because he had rendered this procedure inevitable by his appeal to Caesar; Festus, the procurator, had wanted to dismiss him without judgment.[9] The tendency of the Roman authorities was rather to protect an oppressed minority against the boisterousness of the Jews.[10]

The Jews, however, concentrated with malice and perseverance on bringing to light not only the features that separated them from nascent Christianity, but also motives the Roman authorities could hold against them. Their hatred renewed against the Church the tactic used against Jesus. Just as during the days of the Passion they were shown to be more Caesarean than Pilate himself, they now seemed more sensitive to the interests of Rome than its own magistrates. At Thessalonica, they charged Paul and Silas with breaking the laws of the empire and recognizing a king other than Caesar.[11] At Caesarea, they joined to their grievances accusations of the same type, for Paul defended himself by saying: "I have committed no offence whatever against either Jewish law, or the temple, or Caesar."[12] If the facts con-

---

[6] *Sub umbraculo religionis insignissimae, certe licitae.* Apol., 21.
[7] Suetonius, *Claudius, 25;* Dio Cassius, LX, 6; *Act. Apost.* xviii, 2.
[8] *Act. Apost.* xviii, 14, 15; xxiv, 1–27; xxv, 19.
[9] Ibid., xxvi, 31, 32
[10] *Ibid.,* xviii, 16; xxi, 32.
[11] Ibid., xvii, 7.
[12] *Ibid.,* xxv, 8.

tradicted such slander, they confirmed at the same time the distinction that the Jews tried hard to accredit. We see the missionaries of the new faith part with the synagogues in order to gather their members around them in private houses.[13] So numerous were they, and the name of Christ so well known, that at Antioch they were no longer called by any name other than Christians.[14] This word was now freely uttered in Asia, even by principes and governors.[15] In Europe the confusion probably lasted longer, for at Philippi of Macedonia Paul and Silas were prosecuted as Jews.[16] In Rome under Claudius, the Jews were not yet clearly distinguished from the Christians, although the name of Christ, written more or less correctly, was known to the public authorities.[17] But by the time of Nero the populace of Rome could speak of Christians.[18] Around the same time, probably, an unknown hand wrote "*christianos*" on a wall at Pompeii.[19]

The circumstances of Christianity's introduction to Rome have remained obscure. It was likely carried there the day after Pentecost by some Roman converts who had heard the preaching by the apostles at Jerusalem, fruitful in conversions.[20] The Jewish element was certainly numerous in the first Christian community of Rome, and this community probably first developed in the quarters inhabited by the Jews.[21] However, other parts of the city received the gospel early, since St Peter seems to have baptized on the *via Nomentana* or the *via Salaria*,[22] in the vicinity of the praetorian camp, and St Paul also preached in the same region.[23] After the year 57, the Roman faithful acquired a famous recruit if, as the facts lead us to suppose, the change of religion of Pomponia Graecina, reported by Tacitus, is to be understood as a

[13]*Ibid.*, xviii, 6, 7.
[14]Ibid., xi, 26.
[15]Ibid., xxvi, 28.
[16]*Ibid.*, xvi, 20.
[17]Suetonius, *Claudius*, 25.
[18]Tacitus, Ann., xv, 44.
[19]De Rossi, *Bull. di arch. crist.*, 1864, p. 69; *Corp. inscr. lat.*, Vol. iv, 679.
[20]Act. Apost., II, 10, 41.
[21]Suetonius, *Claudius* 25; *Act. Apost.*, xviii, 2.
[22]De Rossi, *Roma sotterranea*, vol. I, p. 179; *Bull. di arch. crist.*, 1867, p. 30; Marucchi, *Nuovo Bull. di arch. crist.*, 1901, p. 71–111, and 277–290.
[23]Act. Apost., xxviii, 16, 30, 31; Philipp. 1:13.

conversion to Christianity.[24] The Christians named in the salutations that conclude the letter written around 58 by St Paul to the Romans are of a more humble rank. Some of them were apparently enslaved, but for the most part they bore Roman, rather than Jewish, names.[25] Consequently, it appears that the primitive Church of the eternal city included two elements whose proportions are impossible to determine, and may have been formed of Jews and Gentile converts.

The Acts of the Apostles relate that in 61, at the time of Paul's arrival as a prisoner, the "brothers" came to meet him at several miles from Rome.[26] This seems to indicate that the city's Christian community was not yet very large. Nor did it give offense to the government, which for two years allowed Paul, guarded by only one soldier, to receive whom he wished in his house, and to preach the word of God there and outside.[27] This preaching probably bore fruit rapidly, for Tacitus tells us that in 64 the Christians of Rome already formed "a large multitude."[28] But with the public attention attracted by their numbers, mistrust and slander quickly arose against them. An opinion widespread since the first centuries attributed to the "jealousy" of the Jews the evil rumors about the Christians, which did not take long to circulate.[29] Soon "the most atrocious and the most shameful" crimes were attributed to them.[30] Their secluded life, their secret meetings, the mystery with which, for fear of profanation, they surrounded their religious practices, the division that conversions often brought to families, and the communication between the early faithful and the slaves, who were easily won to the faith, seemed to encourage every suspicion. In the pastoral epistles of St Paul and the first letter of St Peter, we see the concerned apostles recommending against any imprudence that might give rise to such rumors, making it a law for every Christian

[24]Tacitus, *Ann.*, xiii, 32; De Rossi, *Rom. sott.*, vol. ii, p. 363.

[25]St Paul, *Rom.* xvi, 3, 16. Cf. Lightfoot, *Philippians*, p. 171ff. I rule out the hypothesis that views this last chapter as the proper finale to the copy destined for the Ephesians.

[26]*Act. Apost.*, xxviii, 15.

[27]*Ibid.*, 30, 31.

[28]Tacitus, *Ann.*, xv, 44

[29]Tertullian, *Apolog.*, 21. Cf. St. Clement, *Cor.*, 6.

[30]Tacitus, *Ann.*, xv, 44.

to obey the agents of authority, be they domestic or political.[31] Slaves in particular were to respect their pagan masters[32] and wives to show submission to their husbands, "so that the message of God is not disgraced."[33] Even the most prudent conduct and irreproachable virtue, however, does not always suffice to disarm prejudice. Even in the eyes of enlightened people who held themselves above popular rumor, the care with which the faithful abstained from pagan feasts, their hatred of spectacles, their voluntary distance from public offices, which were often tainted by idolatry, led to a charge as formidable as it was vague. In the case of Pomponia Graecina, it was precisely the harshness and apparent sadness of her life, "her lugubrious habits," that betrayed her conversion and compelled her husband, following ancient custom, to bring her before a domestic tribunal. They thus saw in the Christians a people of a distinct species, and those who did not charge them with hidden murder or secret debauchery accused them, at the very least, with "hatred of mankind."[34]

2. Nero and the Christians (64–68)

Nero profitably exploited this unfavorable disposition of public opinion when, in 64, he tried to divert suspicions linked to himself to the Christians after the fire of Rome. He succeeded only imperfectly. The people believed the Christians were capable of every crime; worldly people viewed them as natural adversaries and a living condemnation of a corrupt society. The hand of Nero and his associates appeared too visibly in the disaster that dismayed Rome for the diversion to have any chance of complete success, however. Nonetheless, the trial followed its course. Through the often obscure story told by Tacitus, we can follow its various phases.[35] First, certain individuals were arrested and admitted they were Christians. Indications collected during their

---

[31]St Peter, I *Ep.*, II, 13, 11.
[32]St Paul, I *Tim.*, vi, 1.
[33]St Paul, *Tit.*, II, 5. Cf. St. Peter, I *Ep.*, III, 1.
[34]Tacitus, *Ann.*, xv, 44.
[35]Tacitus, *loco cit.* The various events of the trial, and the translation difficulties that certain expressions of Tacitus present, are clearly elucidated by Ramsay, *The Church in the Roman Empire*, 1894, p. 232ff.

interrogation led to their fellow believers, and soon the number of detainees became quite large. But the trial deviated at once. For those arrested first, perhaps the charge of arson was allowed to stand; as for the multitude of the accused that joined them, it was not as arsonists but as "enemies of the human race" that they were condemned to various tortures. What Nero wanted was less to punish an imaginary crime than to appease the anger of the crowd by giving it victims. This effect, he thought, would surely be produced if pleasure were added to vengeance and torture transformed into a spectacle. Hence those horrible celebrations in which the circus and the gardens of the Vatican were the theater, and which Tacitus, according to contemporary documents, and St Clement, perhaps an eyewitness, describe: Christians covered with skins and chased by dogs, like prey; Christian women exposed to beasts in mythological disguises; crucified people coated with pitch and lighted like torches.[36] Nero's cruelty, however, exceeded its goal. As carefully noted by Tacitus, the Roman crowd felt a wave of pity even for the Christians, who were objects of popular loathing but obviously innocent of the fire.

Such was the first act of persecution directed against the worshipers of Christ. It would be difficult to see anything else in the tortures of 64. If Nero made an effort to change public opinion by pursuing the so-called arsonists, he sought for the accused in a group of people already known to the people under the name of Christians. The first charge rapidly gave way to another, and the condemned were sent to death as enemies of the human race, that is, as resistant to Roman civilization and religion. The character of the proceedings, which began with the occasion of an accidental act, then became general and rather vague so as to include men who had no other tie than their religion, made plausible the oft-contested opinion that the persecution begun in Rome extended from there to the provinces, and lasted as long as Nero's reign.

This opinion is confirmed by a short but very significant sentence from Suetonius. When reading Tacitus, we are led to believe that Nero's conduct towards the Christians was a consequence of the fire of Rome.

[36]Tacitus, *Ann.*, xv, 44; St Clement, *Cor.* 6.

What the great historian says of the ease with which the accusation changed its object allows us to infer that, from then on, imperial policy had other grievances against them. The biographer of the emperors demonstrates this more clearly. According to him, any special local character disappeared. There were no more links between the fire and the persecution. Suetonius speaks of the latter at one point in the Life of Nero, and only tells of the fire much later. According to this reading, the persecution appears to be independent of the calamity. Less concerned than Tacitus with highlighting and, so to speak, finishing with one last brush stroke the portrait of Nero's crimes, his disregard of the accident allows us to grasp the full scope of the measure. "The Christians," he says, "people of a new and harmful superstition, were struck with various torments."[37] These words accord with a permanent, systematic repression having as its motive the "newness" and "harmful" character of the Christian "superstition." The context reinforces this meaning, because the phrase we have just quoted appears in the midst of a long enumeration of measures destined to endure: rules, laws, and edicts having as their object the suppression of abuses and the assurance of public order.

Alongside this text, a contemporary document assumes historical validity: the First Epistle of St Peter. The most fitting date for it is after the events of 64, at the time when the persecution began to reach the provinces. Writing from Rome—designated by the symbolic name Babylon[38]—to the Christians of Pontus, Cappadocia, Asia, and Bithynia, the apostle advises them with a view to the "new" calamity[39] about to befall them, or which may have already reached them. He recommends that they guard themselves more than ever against anything contrary to law or morality. "None of you ever deserve to

[37]Suetonius, Nero, 16.

[38]Critics today understand Babylon, in the penultimate verse of the First Epistle of Peter, to be Rome (as it was designated in the secret style of the Jews and Christians) and not as the city in Chaldea, which perhaps no longer existed in the first century and where Peter never preached. On p. 236, Ramsey insists on the essentially *Roman* character of the letter of Peter; but on p. 288 gives not very solid reasons for prolonging the life of Peter and allowing his letter to extend to the time of the Flavians. Cf. Harnack, *Geschichte der altchr. Lit.*, vol. II (1897) p. 451.

[39]St Peter, I *Ep.*, iv, 12.

suffer for being a murderer, a thief, a criminal, or greedy for another's goods."[40] However, he reminds them that their very innocence will not protect them from prosecution. "If any of you should suffer from being a Christian, then there must be no shame, but thanksgiving to God for bearing this name."[41] So the Christians of the provinces were punished, and their religion alone, apart from any charge under common law, could be for them a cause of condemnation.

3. The Persecution of Domitian (*c.* 95–96)

The names of the victims of the first persecution are not known with certainty with the exception of Saints Peter and Paul, whose martyrdom at Rome is evidenced by documents of the first and second century.[42] An almost unanimous tradition states that they perished under Nero. After the death of this princeps, the Christians had a long interval of peace, but their legal situation and the nature of the crimes pronounced against them was not modified. In the rescission of Nero's acts, only this "Neronian institution" survived.[43] The tranquility they enjoyed under his three ephemeral successors, then under the first two Flavians, remained precarious, at the mercy of any hint of suspicion or fanaticism. Their existence was now well known. They were viewed as brothers of the Jews, but enemy brothers,[44] so much that they shared the unpopularity of the latter, which further increased at the time of the Flavians due to the terrible revolt that obliterated their nationality. They no longer had the means to take shelter under the tolerance which still protected Judaism, as a religion. The persecution that broke out anew against the Christians at the end of Domitian's reign afflicted yet did not surprise them. During twenty-seven years of unstable peace, they never ceased to be exposed. To subjugate them

---

[40] *Ibid.,* 15.

[41] *Ibid.,* 16.

[42] St Clement, *Cor.* 5, 6; St Dionysius of Corinth, in Eusebius, *Hist. Eccles.* II, 25, 8. Cf. St Ignatius, *Rom.,* 4; Origen, in Eusebius, *Hist. Eccl.,* III, 1, 2; Tertullian, *De Praescr.,* 36; *Scorp.,* 15; Caius, in Eusebius, *Hist. Eccl.,* ii, 25, 7.

[43] *Permansit, erasis omnibus, hoc solum institutum neronianum.* Tertullian, *Ad nat.,* I, 7.

[44] See the discourse of Titus to his officers during the siege of Jerusalem, in Septimius Severus, II, 30, probably reproducing a lost passage of Tacitus.

again required no change in the laws, nor in the general policy of the Roman Empire.

We have considered what might plausibly have occasioned this new harshness in Domitian's relations with the Jews. By demanding more fiercely than Vespasian and Titus the tax of the didrachma—formerly a voluntary tax for the temple at Jerusalem, now a forced tribute for the temples at the Capitol—the greedy emperor perhaps wished to subjugate Jewish converts to Christianity, or even believers of pagan origin for whom the estrangement from idolatry created the impression of "leading a Jewish life," according to an expression of the time.[45] Their refusal may have excited the tyrant's anger and, when repeated by large numbers, have revealed to his distrustful eye the progress made by the Christian population in a quarter of a century. This origin of Domitian's persecution seems to be indicated by the twofold reproach addressed to many of its victims: the adoption of Jewish morals, and atheism.[46] Following Jewish morals was not punishable, but rejecting the official religion of Rome (without the excuse of following the tolerated religion of the Jews) was properly considered atheism. At the end of the first century, this abbreviated formula seems to have summarized every grievance of the governors and the people against the Christians.

At the very least, this is what seems to emerge from the history of Dio Cassius. Concerning the "the same year" of 95, he says,

> Domitian put to death, besides many others, his cousin Flavius Clemens, who was then consul, and the wife of Flavius, Flavia Domitilla, who was his own relative. The crime charged against both was atheism. On this same charge many who had adopted Jewish customs were condemned. Some were put to death, others had their property confiscated. Domitilla was exiled alone on Pandataria.[47]

[45]Suetonius, *Domit.*, 12.

[46]Dio Cassius, LXVII, 4.

[47]Regarding a second Domitilla, a niece of Clemens and relegated as a Christian to the island of Pontia, see Eusebius, *Chron. ad Olymp.* 218; St Jerome, *Ep.* 108. M. de Rossi (*Bull. di arch. crist.*, 1865, pp. 17–24 and 1875, pp. 69–77) has defended, with reason in my opinion, the distinction between the two Domitillas, which is contested today by numerous critics.

The emperor also executed Glabrio, who had been consul; he was accused of the same crime as the others.[48] Suetonius also writes about the execution of Clemens and Glabrio, but in somewhat different terms.[49] He says that Clemens was despised because of his inertia, a rebuke often addressed to the faithful, who were charged with taking no interest in public affairs. But he adds that Clemens was condemned "on a very slight suspicion," which leads us to suppose that political distrust may have born some relation to his death. According to Suetonius, Acilius Glabrio was also described as "contriving new things," *molitor novarum rerum.* This expression is compatible with the spite attached to the Christians, who were seen as "enemies of the human race," that is to say, adversaries of the established order. The more elevated their rank, the more likely accusations of this type were to arise. At any rate, the religion of the personages cited by Dio is beyond doubt. Apart from the terms used by him, which are transparent enough from an author who systematically avoided naming the Christians, we know that a catacomb was dug in a plot belonging to Domitilla at the time of the Flavian dynasty, while the funerary vault of the Acilii existed in another catacomb at the same time.[50]

At first glace, it is tempting to consider the executions of noble Christians as a chapter in the struggle of Domitian against the aristocracy. Throughout his reign he encountered strong opposition, to which he responded with numerous trials, bringing before the senate trembling informers in the pay of the princeps. He did not spare the intellectual aristocracy, which showed severity toward his vices, any more than he did the hereditary aristocrats. Domitian had many Stoics killed and even outlawed philosophers, in a general way. He showed no mercy towards men and women of noble birth who had embraced Christianity. His worried eye saw conspiracies everywhere, and perhaps nowhere more than in the ranks of Christian nobility. Suetonius makes this clear by insisting on the futility of these suspicions. The caliber of these converts may have surprised and alarmed the tyrant. It

[48]Dio Cassius, LXVII, 4.
[49]Suetonius, *Domit.,* 15.
[50]De Rossi, *Bull.di arch. crist.* 1805, 40ff; 1873, 30ff.: 1888–1889, pp. 15–66 and 103–133.

revealed, in an unexpected way, the importance of the conquests made by Christianity. The social rank of its adherents, beyond the numbers alone, was striking. Without ceasing to recruit among the peasants, Christians now came from the most illustrious houses, from senatorial families and those of the consuls. This discovery may perhaps have been a factor in the harshness of Domitian towards the faithful. However, we should not allow the nobility of the condemned, as indicated by Dio and Suetonius, to delude us. Domitian's persecution not only reached the aristocrats, but extended to believers of every status and country.

Rome's Christian community was tested to the point that only around 96 did Pope Clement regain the leisure and freedom of mind necessary to respond to a letter received some time ago from the church of Corinth. "The misfortunes, the unforeseen catastrophes which have overwhelmed us the one after the other, are the cause of this delay."[51] A writing of a different kind altogether bears the marks of the persecution even more vividly. St John himself had suffered for Christ before being exiled to Patmos.[52] He saw Rome—or, as he says, Babylon the Great—drunk with the blood of the martyrs.[53] He knew those who were beheaded for bearing witnesses to Jesus.[54] He wrote his Apocalypse in the midst of the turmoil, when many Christians had already perished and many were yet to die.[55] Among the churches he addressed in Asia is Smyrna, where several believers would be sent to prison,[56] and another, Pergamum, which already had a martyr.[57] "He was killed among you, where Satan lives," John says to the Christians of this city, speaking of Antipas.

---

[51]St Clement, *Cor.*, 4.

[52]*Apocalypse,* I, 9. St. Irenaeus, *Haeres.,* V, 30, states that St John wrote the *Apocalypse* at the end of the reign of Domitian. The theory that places the *Apocalypse* in the days following the persecution by Nero is almost entirely rejected today. See von Harnack, *Gesch. der altchr. Lit.,* Vol II, p. 245.

[53]*Ibid.,* xvii, 5, 6.

[54]*Ibid.,* xx, 4.

[55]*Ibid.,* vi, 11.

[56]*Ibid.,* ii, 10.

[57]*Ibid.,* 13.

This passage is notable, for Pergamum was the first city of the Asian province where flattery, encouraged by politics, had erected a temple to Rome and Augustus.[58] At the time St John wrote, Pergamum was the primary center of the imperial cult, just as Nicomedia was for Bithynia. Although scarcely more than a hundred years old, this cult was widespread and very popular. It consecrated the union between the provincials and Rome and, by means of the double attraction of religion and spectacle, attached them to the empire to the extent that the emperor's person had become a visible god. It seems to follow from the Apocalypse that participation at these feasts, during the time of Domitian, had become a test for eastern Christians. Those who obeyed were cleared of the accusation of atheism. But "those who did not worship the Beast and its image were put to death."[59] The tone with which the apostle, in many passages,[60] speaks of "the Beast"—that is to say, the homicidal and idolatrous empire—and of "its image"—meaning, apparently, the emperor—we sense a full-scale persecution. We are already far removed from the time when St Paul entertained friendly relations at Ephesus with the Asiarchs, the provincial priests in charge of Asia's imperial cult.[61] Then, the Christians were ignored or tolerated, and no one dreamed of putting them to the test. Now, persecution was a frequent stumbling block for them. The Apocalypse's author needed to support or reawaken their courage by prophesying, in vivid colors, the downfall of the empire that desired their worship, this Rome that "has made the world drunk with the wine of its impurity and soaks her robe in their blood."[62]

These inflammatory words, crafted for the faithful of Asia and the particular type of trials to which they were exposed, do not correspond exactly to the state of mind of Christians living at the center of the Roman world. Less concerned with the future than the present, they did not despair, even in the midst of the most cruel treatment, of one day arriving at an understanding with the persecutor-state.

[58]Dio Cassius, LI, 20.
[59]*Apocalypse*, xiii, 15.
[60]*Ibid.*, xiii, 7, 8, 11–17; xiv, 9,11; xvi, 2.
[61]*Act. Apost.*, xix, 31.
[62]*Apocal.*, xvii, 2, 6; xviii, 24.

Furthermore, in their language, attitudes, and even feelings, they persisted in showing themselves to be loyal subjects of the empire. In keeping with the recommendations of St Paul, they made a place in the liturgy for prayers for the sovereign. In a magnificent prayer preserved for us by Clement of Rome, they asked peace and stability for their princepes and magistrates, praying to God to direct their counsel according to what is good, so that they would administer in peace and clemency the authority given to them.[63] The church of Rome, to which from the outset God had given a sense of the politics and spirit of government, was already heralding ideas that the second-century apologists would seek to promote.

[63]St Clement, *Cor.*, 61.

CHAPTER TWO

Christianity and the Empire in the Age of the Antonines

1. The Rescript of Trajan (*c.* 112)

At first glance, it appears that an understanding could have been reached between the empire and Christianity in the second century. Rome at that time saw a succession of rulers superior in intelligence and decency to the two preceding dynasties. The age of the Antonines marks the high point of the imperial regime. Four sovereigns of outstanding intelligence and an equal aptitude for business, succeeding one another not randomly through heredity but by means of carefully considered adoptions, governed the civilized world with a moderation unparalleled until then. Through the seriousness of his politics and the continuity of his intentions, Trajan renewed ancient Roman tradition. Hadrian's levity and skepticism had little effect upon his public conduct and did not prevent him from fulfilling his obligations as sovereign. Antoninus was simple, hard-working, and good. Marcus Aurelius brought to the throne the virtues of a philosopher. Before principes so capable of understanding, the Christian religion (in which every social class was now represented) did not remain without its defenders. It had ventured out of the shadows and now felt strong enough to directly address the opinions of reasonable people. Learned men and convert philosophers pled its cause. They were less concerned with dissipating the prejudices of the common people than with enlightening the minds of the emperors. The latter, after reading their writings, would be convinced of the innocence and political loyalty of the Christians. Other voices, more discreet and more timid, were raised at the same time in their favor. Without interceding directly on their behalf, high-placed magistrates let it be understood that there might be some degree of excess or injustice in the manner in which they were treated. From all sides it appeared that a reconciliation was imminent. Such reconciliation, however, would not occur at any point in the second century. Neither Trajan nor Hadrian, nor Antoninus, nor Marcus Aurelius, was receptive to such overtures. Out of these apparently favorable efforts and circumstances came one outcome, due less to any effort or circumstance than to the political mind of the sovereigns: a greater clarity and precision in the criminal proceedings applied to subjects of the empire accused of Christianity.

It is said that Domitian, at the very end of his reign, halted the persecution directed against the Church.[1] This does not mean that he expunged the principle posited under Nero, according to which one could "be punished like a Christian,"[2] for the profession of Christianity in itself constituted a criminal act even without being accompanied by another crime. Domitian put an end to the persecution in the sense that he probably renounced searching out Christians, or submitting people suspected of having embraced the new religion to a test such as forced participation in the cult of Rome and Augustus. But the general proscription enacted against the worshippers of Christ continued, as a sort of legal axiom: according to the circumstances, magistrates invested with the *ius gladii* ["right of the sword," i.e., the right of decision over life and death—*Ed.*] were at liberty to condemn a Christian because of his religion, just as they could also allow believers to live disturbed.

An episode contemporaneous with Trajan sheds light on this legal situation. Trajan certainly promulgated no edict against the Christians; Pliny's letter addressing this question, written about 112, makes this clear. However, an act of martyrdom was reported during his reign.[3] It involved the condemnation of the bishop of Antioch, St Ignatius, who was sent from that city to Rome to suffer in the amphitheater, and "to be ground by the teeth of the lions, to become God's wheat," according

---

[1] Hegesippus, in Eusebius, *Hist. Eccl.*, III, 20, 5; Tertullian, *Apol.*, 8.
[2] St Peter, I *Ep.*, IV, 16.
[3] The traditional date is 107 (Eusebius, *Chron.*; Ruinart, *Acta sincera*, 1689, p. 606, 707; cf. De Rossi, *Inscr. christ.*. vol. I, p. 6). Lightfoot, *S. Ignatius and S. Polycarp*, 1889, vol. II, p. 472, lets it vary between 100 and 118.

to his admirable expression.[4] The history of his journey, as set forth in his correspondence, tells us much about conditions among the Christians. In the Asiatic cities traversed by the condemned man and his escort, bishops, priests, and believers—either from these same places or sent by their churches—came to pay him tribute.[5] Their approach could not have taken place in secret, since Ignatius was accompanied by a group of ten soldiers who held him with a chain,[6] yet none of the numerous visitors was punished, and only two Christians, Zosima and Rufus, who were probably arrested at Antioch at the same time as Ignatius, shared his fate. Nothing more clearly highlights the legal position of the disciples of the gospel: the sword remained suspended over all, but struck only the few who incurred the severity of the magistrates through special circumstances, such as popular sentiment or their personal importance.

Another episode, which gave Trajan an occasion to concern himself personally with Christians, sheds further light on the situation. Around the year 111, Pliny the Younger was charged with the government of Bithynia, which had become an imperial province. It was a matter of restoring order to a large territory ineffectually administered until then by proconsuls in the senate's name. The nature of this mission, perhaps no less than Pliny's personal character, obliged the new legate to frequently defer to the emperor and follow his advice in all matters of importance. Among these the Christian question did not come up right away, but rather in the second year of his governance, stemming from a long communication to which Trajan gave a brief answer.[7]

During the course of a trip he undertook around this time in the eastern part of the province, Pliny received complaints about the Christians, which showed him that Christianity had already grown deep and numerous roots in Bithynia. Evangelical propaganda had

---

[4]St Ignatius, *Rom.*, 4.

[5]St Ignatius, *Ephes.*, 1, 2, 5, 6, 21; *Magn.*, 15; Smyrn., 10, 12, 13; *Trall.*, 13; *Rom.* 10; *Ad Polyc.*, 1, 7, 8.

[6]*Rom.*, 4.

[7]Pliny, Ep., X, 97, 98. The authenticity of Pliny's letter and of Trajan's rescript, contested not long ago by some critics, is no longer in serious doubt.

had enough success in these areas to rapidly modify the social order and even alarm, on certain points, the material interests. Not only was the religion practiced in the cities, the usual center of its action, but from there it had spread to the market towns and even into the countryside, recruiting numerous adherents. The numerical balance between the followers of the two religions had already changed so considerably that the temples were deserted, to the point that the public cult seemed to be interrupted, and the people who lived off commerce in animals destined for sacrifice complained of only rarely finding buyers. Christians, probably the most influential and visible group, were referred to the legate as the authors of this evil. In his career as lawyer and magistrate, Pliny had never assisted in religious trials; these probably fell outside the jurisdiction of ordinary tribunals and were tried instead by the emperor or his direct representatives. He was ignorant as to whether these proceedings against the Christians, carried out at Rome or elsewhere, had revealed reprehensible acts. He only knew, in a general way, that Christianity was forbidden and, consequently, its followers could be punished. This was enough to dictate his conduct. On three occasions he interrogated the accused, asking them whether they were Christians. Those who responded affirmatively he judged guilty. Without seeking to establish whether or not they had committed some secondary crime while practicing their worship, he reckoned that the very fact of being a Christian was considered illegal, and one could not persevere in this without criminal obstinacy. He thus ordered that anyone who confessed to being a Christian be led away for torture with the exception of those who, having declared themselves Roman citizens, must be judged at Rome.

If the question had always arisen in this way, Pliny would perhaps never have considered seeking the advice of the princeps. His duties as judge seemed well defined, but his humanity groaned at sending people to death who were merely guilty of a rather theoretical infraction, when no act of dishonesty, immorality, or cruelty had been raised against them. In writing to the emperor on this subject, he probably would have been satisfied to ask Trajan whether age, sex, or weakness of body and mind could be taken into consideration and, depending on the case, become extenuating circumstances.

However, the affair rapidly widened and in no time assumed vast proportions. As often happened a first act of severity, by impacting public opinion, aroused the attention and passions of the people and led to new denunciations. Pliny was alarmed by the large number of people already accused or on the brink of being indicted. They were of every age, sex, and rank. Not every accusation had been made openly; the legate received an anonymous list containing many names of real or purported Christians. Pliny could not send everyone to torture without examination. He first had to make certain of the truth of the charge. To this end, he submitted the accused to meticulous interrogation. He began by asking them if they were Christians. For those who confessed without hesitation, the outcome of the trial was never in doubt, since Pliny himself had previously established the procedures to follow. For those who denied it, however, the situation became complicated.

To the question "Are you a Christian?" many, indeed, answered negatively. Some denied ever having been so, others said that they had ceased being Christian several years ago, some as many as twenty-five years ago. The sincerity of their answers was put to the test by obliging them to worship the statues of the gods and curse Christ, which they did without difficulty. But a new question arose concerning those who declared that they had been Christians but had renounced Christianity many years ago. Did the name "Christian" conceal some common crime, some immoral act, inherent to the practice of that religion? In this case, apostasy itself need not disarm justice, and those who had renounced Christianity still remained responsible for criminal acts committed when they were practicing the religion. Pliny strove above all to discover whether such acts had been committed. Upon being interrogated, the apostates replied that their error consisted only in meeting before sunrise on a fixed day to sing the praises of Christ; to promise by oath not to commit any crime, theft, robbery, adultery, or betrayal of trust; and to meet a second time to take a harmless meal, a practice abandoned since an edict from the governor forbade associations. Two female slaves, who had the rank of deaconesses among the

Christians, were tortured and confirmed through their testimony the declarations of the apostates.

One thing was confirmed by these consistent responses: those who formerly had been Christians shared "an excessive, evil superstition," to use Pliny's expression, without any more serious reproach being addressed to them. This consideration, in concert with the great number of the accused, present as well as future, convinced Pliny to suspend the trials and consult the emperor. He submitted to him this question: Was the name "Christian" alone punishable, or the crimes committed under this name? Pliny himself had already prejudged the answer by sending to death people who persisted in calling themselves Christians, although no accessory act had been charged against them. But the situation of the apostates, against whom no common crime had been brought out, was entirely different. Should they be punished because a short time ago they bore the name Christian, without their apostasy benefiting them today? Or, on the contrary, should repentance pardon and absolve those who, having been Christian, had stopped or were willing to stop? Pliny did not conceal from the emperor that he was inclined toward the latter course of action, for in it he saw a means of pacifying the province, from a religious standpoint, by bringing back many of those gone astray.

Trajan's answer contained an endorsement of Pliny's conduct, without reservations. The emperor declared that a uniform rule could not be applied to every case. He added that the Christians were not to be hunted down, but if they were brought before the judge and convicted, they must be punished. An exception was to be made for those who declared that they were not Christians and proved it by worshiping the gods; even though they had been Christians in the past, they must be pardoned because of their repentance. But the emperor insisted on one point, rather lightly touched upon by Pliny: anonymous accusations must play no part whatsoever. "They create the worst sort of precedent and are quite out of keeping with the spirit of our age."

This rescript is what we might expect from Trajan, who was a scrupulous guardian of Roman legislation but politically sensible. He maintained the fundamental crime of Christianity, as laid down in 64 by an act of Nero. However, he did not believe the Christians dangerous enough to order that they be officially prosecuted, as would occur with revolutionaries or bandits, nor to receive anonymous denunciations against them in disregard of common law and to the detriment of public order. Christianity was, in effect, an abstract crime, manifesting itself only by innocent acts, as Pliny's investigation proved; the name itself was criminal, but no crimes were concealed under this name. For this reason anyone who renounced it must be pardoned; the name, once erased, left behind no guilty past of which justice must render account.

Here we find an indirect tribute to the innocence of Christian morals, which were often slandered at the time. Pliny points to this with the moderate tone of his letter, wherein some pity may be detected, and in which he shows himself to be a more or less conscious apologist. But the rescript's goal is not to avenge the faithful against unjust attacks, nor to soften their legal situation. Its imperial redactor intends only three things: to make the situation quite clear by dispelling doubts that remained in the minds of certain magistrates on the question of whether the name alone—that is to say, the mere profession of Christianity—was sufficient to constitute a crime; to ensure public tranquility by attacking anonymous accusations as invalid; and, above all, to make it easier for Christians to return to the cult of the gods by guaranteeing immunity to apostates. These principles would dominate the emperors' religious policies during the second century, and on several occasions they would find opportunity to call them to mind.

2. The Rescripts of Hadrian (*c.* 126) and Antoninus (*c.* 160)

The circumstances in which Hadrian acted were rather unusual. In spite of Pliny's testimony and the implicit advice of Trajan, Christian morals had not ceased to be maligned. Particularly in the East, the populace fancied the assemblies of the worshippers of Christ to be criminal orgies where debauchery mingled with murder. From the gullible masses arose cries of anger, shouting, and threatening prayers asking for—even demanding—the condemnation of the Christians.

Several magistrates readily yielded to such pressure while others, more conscientious, became indignant and took the side of the unjustly persecuted innocents. On this subject, Hadrian received letters and reports from "many" governors.[8] Among these was Licinius Granianus, a proconsul of Asia, who appears to have written with particular insistence. As far as we can judge from the brief summary that Eusebius has left us, his letter complained not only about the furor of the people and the blood too easily shed to appease it, but went so far as to discreetly claim opposition to the principle followed in the trials of the Christians, doubting "that it was just to condemn people because of their name and their sect, without any other crime."[9] This was very nearly a request for a revision of Trajan's rescript. Hadrian seems to have experienced some hesitation, for he did not answer at once, and his answer was addressed not to Granianus but to his successor, Minicius Fundanus.[10]

Hadrian's new rescript had none of the *imperatoria brevitas* of that of Trajan; rather, the less clear reasoning of this changeable and wavering emperor conveyed a sense of indecision. Hadrian's order may be reduced to two main headings. Like his predecessor, he forbade any accusations that did not take regular form; his aim was not so much anonymous libel (the use of which had probably disappeared) as the tumultuous "prayers and acclamations" with which crowds hostile to the Christians would besiege the governors. What worried the emperor was the fear that "slanderous informers be afforded an opportunity for plunder." Here, evidently, it is not Christians that Hadrian was trying to protect; he feared giving private hatreds free reign and, by means of clamorous demands, allowing "innocents," i.e., people wrongly accused of Christianity, to be condemned. The concern for public order, which dictated the rescript of Trajan, was also found in that of Hadrian.

After these preliminaries were set forth, the emperor laid out the governor's duty. If anyone came forward to accuse, the governor was to examine the accusation. In a case in which the accuser could prove

[8]Meliton, in Euseb., *Hist. Eccl.,* VI, 20, 10; Tertullian, *Apol.,* 5.

[9]Euseb., *Chron., ad olymp.,* 226.

[10]Today's critics are unanimous in recognizing the authenticity of the rescript to Minicius Fundanus (c. 124), inserted by St Justin following his first *Apology.*

that the people denounced as Christians "have done anything contrary to the laws," the magistrate must determine their punishment in accordance with the gravity of the offence, and might even pronounce the death sentence. Here, some vagueness appears in the ideas and expression. Was Hadrian responding to the demand of Granianus, wishing for a planned offence to be added to religion if the Christian were to incur punishment? Or, as Trajan would have it, was religion alone sufficient to constitute a crime? Hadrian did not speak clearly, as if he wished to leave the governors latitude according to circumstances to either follow the strict interpretation of the first rescript or adopt the broader interpretation to which several, following Granianus' example, seemed to have inclined. In any event, the concession was more or less an illusion, for it doubtless sufficed for the accuser to prove the Christian's refusal to worship the gods and to pay homage to the imperial image in order for the facts to be established and charges of legal impiety, perhaps of lèse-majesty, to be brought against the accused. But what dominated the emperor's intention was the need for "regular accusation." He indicated this again at the end of his letter, threatening the slanderer, i.e., one who accuses without proof, with severe penalties under the law in such a case.

The rescript's somewhat ambiguous character, coupled with the natural tolerance of the skeptical emperor, allowed Christians to interpret Hadrian's decision in the most favorable light, at least until illness and misfortune embittered his jaded soul during the last years of his reign. This was what the apologist Meliton would do a few years later. However, we find in this interpretation a clever tactic born from the pen of advocates searching for precedents useful to the cause of the Church, rather than an exact exposition of the facts. The writings of the apologists themselves, like the authentic accounts of martyrdom from Hadrian to Marcus Aurelius, reveal that on the contrary Christians were usually condemned without investigation, based only on the stating of their name, just as they show the absolution of those who, after sentencing and faced with the sword or the beasts, were weak enough to renounce their faith. The author of the beautiful *Epistle to Diognetus,* written under Hadrian or Antoninus, says of the faithful,

"One throws them to wild beasts in order to make them renounce their master," clearly showing that exposure to the beasts was not ordered to punish a crime independent of the quality of being "Christian" and provable separately from this. As at the time of Pliny, only religious "obstinacy" was punished by torture. "They behead us, they crucify us, they throw us to the beasts, they burn us, they put us in chains, they let us suffer every torment, because we do not wish to abandon our confession," writes St Justin.[11] Of this procedure, established by Trajan, the convert philosopher complains to Antoninus Pius in his *Apology*. He becomes indignant that Christians were punished based on their affiliation alone, while apostates were absolved without examination, and asks that this right ultimately replace common law.[12] If by chance Hadrian were inclined to do so, we note that his intentions, vaguely indicated, were never observed. Even under Hadrian's successor, the law of Trajan reigned supreme.

Still, in ways relatively favorable to Christians, this policy was not always followed. The church of Smyrna's letter regarding the martyrdom of St Polycarp,[13] which occurred in 155,[14] makes clearer than any speculation the situation of the faithful under the reign of Antoninus Pius. Twelve among them had been condemned to the beasts. A single Christian, weakening at the sight of the ferocious animals, consented to swear by the genius of the emperor and to offer sacrifice; he was let go, absolved. The other eleven underwent torture courageously, even a very young man, whom the proconsul vainly exhorted to repentance by saying: "Have pity on your age!" Until now, everything was correct and in conformity with Trajan's rescript: grace for the renegade, death for the obstinate Christian. However, soon popular passion, which Trajan and Hadrian after him had wished to contain, could not be controlled; the crowd entered violently upon the scene. "No more atheists!" they cried from every spectator's bench. "Let Polycarp be

[11]St Justin, *Dial. cum Tryph.*, 110.

[12]*Apol.*, I, 4, 11, 45.

[13]Funk, *Opera patrum apostolicorum*, vol. I, p. 282–308; Lightfoot, *St Ignatius and St Polycarp*, vol. III, p. 363–403.

[14]The date of 155, established by M. Waddington's calculation, is today almost universally accepted. See the new arguments provided by Lightfoot, vol. I, p. 616–715.

fetched!" This was a first irregularity; having tolerated it, the proconsul himself committed a second by permitting, or ordering, the search. Police soldiers arrested the old bishop of Smyrna, in a house where he had taken refuge, despite the *conquirendi non sunt* ["they are not to be sought out"] of Trajan. Taken away by the chief of police, who implored him en route to save himself by renouncing Christianity, Polycarp appeared before Quadratus, the proconsul. The latter questioned him, although nothing in the story that has come down to us indicates a formal accusation. He tried, in turn, to bring the martyr to apostasy: "Swear by the genius of Caesar. Swear, and I will let you go free: revile Christ." We know Polycarp's answer, in which he refused to insult God "who for eighty-six years had done him nothing but good." The proconsul insisted, threatening the martyr with fire and the beasts. Upon his persevering in his refusal, the proconsul then had a herald proclaim: "Polycarp has confessed to being a Christian." This was to precede sentencing, but the crowd left him no time to pronounce one. Contrary to the law, the crowd anticipated the sentence by executing it. Excited by the Jews, people poured into the stadium, built a pyre, and had Polycarp mount it. Thus ended a trial in which everything, it seems, was illegal: the tumultuous demands of the crowd, the search for the Christian, the absence of any regular accusation, and execution by the people. It shows how the barriers raised by the mighty emperors—if not to protect the Christians, then at least to prevent disturbance of the peace—easily gave way under the pressure of the riot.

Incidents analogous to that of Smyrna probably occurred elsewhere. Antoninus was thus required to renew the instructions of his predecessors. Along these lines, he wrote to the inhabitants of Larissa in Thessaly, Thessalonica in Macedonia, and the Athenians along with "all the Greeks," which probably meant the assembly of the province of Achaia. Meliton, who quotes these rescripts, summarizes them in a word: it was forbidden to make trouble on account of Christians.[15]

---

[15]Meliton, in Eusebius, *Hist. Eccl.,* IV, 26, 10. We should not confuse these missives of Antoninus, which are certainly historic, with the rescript to the council of Asia, much more favorable to the Christians, published by Eusebius, IV, 13, and generally viewed as being

This was a reminder, for Greece, of the warnings given to Asia by Hadrian.

Antoninus' policy with respect to Christianity appears to be a continuation of that of his two predecessors. Even while he repressed, to the extent of his power, the raucous hatred with which the Christians were pursued, we see him giving free rein to accusations properly charged against them. Most likely an accusation of this type, in the first year of his reign, led to the "glorious martyrdom" of Pope Telesphorus.[16] An episode at the end of this same reign, as reported in St Justin's *Second Apology*, makes clear how the trials of Christians were regularly carried out and disposed. One Ptolemaeus, accused by a pagan whose wife the accused had converted, was brought before the tribunal of the prefect of Rome, Q. Lollius Urbicus. The latter conducted no investigation, and the questioning consisted of these few words: "Are you a Christian?" "I am." The death sentence was pronounced immediately.

The apologists never ceased protesting this hasty procedure, which condemned based on the name alone in accordance with Trajan's rescript. This time, the protest was borne to the tribunal of the prefect by the spontaneous shout of a courageous spectator, who cried:

> How can you condemn a man who is guilty neither of adultery nor seduction, nor homicide nor theft nor rape, who is accused of no crime, and has done nothing but confess he is a Christian? Your judgment, O Urbicus, is worthy neither of our pious emperor, nor of the philosopher-son of Caesar, nor of the sacred senate.

By way of reply, Urbicus interrogated the speaker. "You too seem to be a Christian." "I am." "Let him be executed." Another Christian indignantly lifted his voice in turn, and was condemned to the same fate.

---

apocryphal. The authenticity of this rescript has been supported by von Harnack (*Texte und Untersuchungen*, XII, 4, 1895), but he was unable to remove the considerable objection that the new jurisprudence contained in the rescript at the council of Asia left no traces in the writings of the Christians, who would have failed to prevail over it, nor in the trials of the martyrs, where the opposite rules were constantly applied, and seems to be contradicted by the standard practice of the second century.

[16]Eusebius, *Hist. Eccl.*, IV, 10; V, 6.

In these last two cases there were no regular charges, but a type of *flagrante delictu* [in the act] most likely took its place.[17]

Other facts reported by St Justin, unfortunately without details, show that sometimes not even this summary procedure was followed. "By means of torture," he says, "they wrung from slaves, children, and weak women the revelation of imaginary crimes."[18] This occurred when an accuser, believing the slanderous rumors spread against the Christians, formally accused one of them not only of professing an unlawful religion but also of being tainted by some crime attributed to them by popular opinion. This brought to bear emergency proceedings, applicable only to Christians under common law. If proof of the stated grievances was not made, he could still be condemned for the abstract crime of religion. Besides, the trials whose details have come down to us never had any intent beyond the latter. The incidents to which St Justin alludes in the passage cited above must have been rare. Outrageous slander was more frequently spread by means of conversation, pamphlets, and speeches than formulated into precise charges referenced at the tribunals.

3. Christian Apologists

The time was past, however, when Christians allowed themselves to be condemned or slandered without raising their voices. In the second century Christianity no longer spoke merely the language of its origins, intelligible only to initiates: it now had at its service numerous writers with a Greek or Latin education, capable of placing its teachings within reach of every mind, answering objections, and discussing attacks. The second century was the age par excellence of the apologists. From Hadrian to Marcus Aurelius, advocacy in favor of Christianity multiplied. These pleas were sometimes addressed to the emperor, the senate, or the magistrates, sometimes to public opinion at large. Most of the time, their authors sought to make the new religion known, calculating that light was its best defense. They thus

[17]St Justin, *Apol.,* II, 1.
[18]St Justin, *Apol.,* II, 12.

explained, in general outline, the fundamental dogmas of Christianity, and then described the mores of its followers. Such was the plan of the *Apology*[19] presented by Aristides, a convert philosopher from Athens, to the Emperor Hadrian.[20] An anonymous letter, probably written around the same time to a personage called Diognetus who may have belonged to the imperial court, contains a portrait of the Christians and a protest against the ill treatment to which they were subjected in order to bring them to renounce their beliefs. Like his predecessor and model Aristides, the convert philosopher Justin addressed to Antoninus an apologetic treatise, of which the first part is an exposition of Christian dogma, presented as the reconciliation and fulfillment of all earlier philosophies, the divine fruit grafted onto reason by faith. The second part is a picture of the simple religion and innocent ways of the Christians, and the third a discussion of the summary trials unjustly applied to them, punishing them on account of their name alone without any investigation, and without criminal charges being brought against them. A second *Apology*, composed by Justin during the last years of the reign of Antoninus Pius, returned to this last point with great insistence and by advancing some recent examples.

Under the reign of Marcus Aurelius, the arguments of the apologists were further expanded. It no longer sufficed for these defenders of the Church to show Christianity to be a great and reasonable religion and the Christians to be unfairly slandered, nor to insist that it was unfair to put them, if not beyond the law, then at least beyond the reach of common law. They went directly to the most delicate point of controversy, to the most dangerous and tenacious prejudice. The originality of what we may call the second generation of apologists—the philosopher Athenagoras, the bishops Theophilus, Meliton, and Apollinaris—was to boldly bring their defensive action into the terrain of

[19]This Apology can be reconstituted by means of an Armenian fragment, published in 1878 by the Mekhitarist Fathers of Venice, a Syriac version discovered in 1889 in a Sinai convent by Mr Rendel Harris, and of a Greek text inserted into the legendary life of Barlaam and Joasaph. See Rendel Harris and Armitage Robinson, *The Apology of Aristides*, Cambridge, 1891.

[20]According to Eusebius, St Jerome, and the Armenian fragment; to the Emperor Antoninus, according to the Syrian version.

politics. Those who were at first banned, and who continued to be denounced as "enemies of the human race"—meaning adversaries of Roman civilization, the established order, the empire itself—were, on the contrary, its most peaceful and loyal servants. They did not worship the sovereign, but nevertheless respected him, obeyed him, loved him, and prayed for him.[21] They desired the firm establishment and perpetuity of the dynasty, gratefully enjoyed the *pax romana*, the splendor of the cities, the wisdom of the laws.[22] They were pleased by the fact that Christianity was born during the time of the empire, and that their destinies were linked providentially to one another.[23] They liked to highlight the contrast between the cruelties to which Christians had been subjected under mad emperors like Nero and Domitian, and the relative kindness they had obtained from good leaders such as Hadrian and Antoninus.[24] This burst of loyalty was not only found in the writings of the authors of *Apologies*;[25] rather, it seems that these sentiments were sincerely shared by the majority of Christians. The number of those who cursed Rome was relatively small, after the style of the redactors of the pseudo-Sibylline Oracles, a Judeo-Christian work of this epoch. The ideals of the majority were entirely different. Indeed, the Phrygian bishop Abercius, a contemporary of Marcus Aurelius, called Rome in the epitaph for his tomb the "royal city," giving his native Hieropolis the epithet "excellent," and himself the title of "citizen." He condemned anyone who profaned his grave to pay a thousand gold pieces to the Roman treasury and two thousand to the municipal bank.[26] Such expressions and patriotic sentiment were a

---

[21]Theophilus of Antioch, *Ad Autolycum*, I, 12.

[22]Athenagoras, *Legatio pro Christian.*, 17.

[23]Meliton of Sardis, quoted by Eusebius, *Hist. Eccl.*, IV, 26, 7, 8.

[24]Meliton, in Eusebius, Hist. Eccl., IV, 26, 9, 10, 11.

[25]With the exception of Tatian, who remained intransigent (*Orat. adv. Graecos*, 11; cf. 29, 30, 31, 35, and 42).

[26]Eusebius names an Abercius (*Hist. Eccl.*, V, 16) probably identical to Abercius, bishop of Hieropolis, in Phrygia, of whom we have a legendary *Vita*. An antique text is inserted into it. Ramsey has discovered the epitaph of the saint in Hieropolis, in two fragments of the original marble. See the photographic reproduction of this stela in *Nuovo Bullettino di archeologia cristiana*, 1805, pl. III–VI–VII. The Christian character of the epitaph of Abercius has been contested by Ficker (*Die heidnische Character der Abercius Inschrift* (1804), Harnack (*Texte und Untersuchungen*, vol. XII, 1895), Dietrich (*Die Grabschrift des Aberkios*,

striking feature of the declarations of Athenagoras, Theophilus, Apollinaris, and Meliton.

Despite the excellence of its reasoning, the apologists' campaign could not succeed. Opposed to it was the inattention, indifference, ingrained habits, and prejudices that at all times make the success of any movement in defense of religion so difficult. Furthermore, this campaign encountered obstacles inherent to the disposition of its contemporaries and the spirit of the age.

Before the emperors, the campaign had undoubtedly won its cause on certain points. The rescripts and the very practice of the tribunals show that neither the leaders of the state, nor the most enlightened of the magistrates, believed in the crimes with which popular imagination charged the Christians. But Hadrian's thoughtlessness, Antoninus' nonchalance, and the deep disdain of Marcus Aurelius prevented them from attaching to the campaign the importance merited by the Christians' sincere and thoughtful allegiance to the imperial regime. Either the principes did not believe in this allegiance, or they did not care; in any event, they treated it as a negligible thing and, free of personal prejudice toward the Christians, continued to allow them to be exposed to the intermittent action of laws that treated them as public enemies any time an accuser arose. As for the dogmatic aspect of the pleas offered in their name, Hadrian was undoubtedly too skeptical, Antoninus too devoted to the national religion, and Marcus Aurelius too attached to his own reasoning to pay any attention.

If the reasoning offered in favor of the Christians found no footing in the soul of principes superior in intelligence and morality to the mass of their contemporaries, we should not be surprised that the great

---

1896). There is little doubt if one compares the symbolic language with the texts, inscriptions, and paintings of the first Christian centuries. See Duchesne, *Mélanges de l'école française de Rome*, 1895, p. 155ff, and *Bulletin critique*, 1894, p. 177. In the same sense, De Rossi (*Inscript. christ.* Vol. II, p. xii–xxix), Marucchi (*Nuovo Bull. di arch. crist.*1895, p. 17–41), Wilpert (*Fractio panis*, 1895, p. 103–127), the Bollandists (*Analecta*, vol. xiii, 1894, p. 402; vol. xv, 1896, p. 331–334; vol. xvi, 1897, p. 74–77), Th. Zahn (*Eine altchristliche Grabinschrift und ihre jungste Ausleger*, in *Neue Kirchliche Zeitschrift*, 1895, p. 863–866), F. Cumont (*Les inscriptions chrétiennes d'Asie Mineure*, in *Mélanges de l'École française de Rome*, 1895, p. 200), H. Leclercq (art. *Abercius*, in the *Dictionnaire d'archéologie chrétienne et de liturgie*, 1903, p. 66–87).

majority of the people, even enlightened minds, would remain insensitive. The second century was simultaneously the era of philosophy and of superstition. Through jealousy or professional pride, the orators and philosophers then at the peak of favor showed themselves the declared enemies of a religion that disputed with them over the direction of the mind. From Crescens, the personal adversary of St Justin, to Celsus, the formidable polemical author, and the satirist Lucian, they all spoke, wrote, and declaimed against Christianity. In this matter, vulgar charlatans such as Alexander of Abonuteichos were their auxiliaries. Easily suggestible, the people naturally made the Christians responsible for every calamity which at that time, in a thousand forms (invasions, revolts, plagues, famines) began to ravage the empire. Simultaneously, the empire continued to lend credence to the odious rumors, oft denied, always resurrected, which had dogged Christians since the time of Nero. It is astonishing to see learned people occupying official positions sharing the prejudices of the vulgar on this point. Celsus possessed too penetrating a mind to believe in these views, and does not seem to recall them in his book, but Frontonius, friend of Antoninus and tutor of Marcus Aurelius, was unafraid, in his public address concerning the Christians, to speak of incests performed in the dark after their ritual banquets.[27] Against such a strong current, made even stronger by unsuspected tributaries, of what avail were the denials of an Athenagoras or a Justin?

4. The Persecution under Marcus Aurelius (161–180)

After half a century of apologetic efforts, the Christians had obtained no easing of their legal status. Although they had not ceased to grow in numbers as well as in the social rank of the converts, public opinion as a whole refused to rehabilitate them. Under Marcus Aurelius, even more so than under his predecessors, they suffered the harshness of the law and the people's injustice. In the provinces, several governors published police ordinances whose terms we do not know, but which certainly aggravated the Christians' situation.[28] The writings of the

[27]Minucius Felix, *Octavius,* 9.
[28]Meliton, in Eusebius, *Hist. Eccl.*, IV, 26, 5.

time, pagan as well as Christian, present them as hated by the crowds and treated cruelly by the magistrates. They even seem, in some places, to have contravened Trajan's rescript with animosity; while the latter forbade searching them, Celsus speaks of errant Christians pursued in order to bring them before the tribunals and have them condemned to death.[29] However, as a rule the religious trials whose records have survived show that the jurisprudence of Trajan and Hadrian was still in force. Marcus Aurelius did not modify it, either for good or ill, through any new disposition.[30] We find it applied in Rome, in the trial of St Justin and his companions. In that of the Christians of Lyon, we see the emperor-philosopher recalling its observation to a governor who had departed from it.

The affair of St Justin dates to 163, the second year of Marcus Aurelius' reign. The Christian doctor had been accused in the forum by his enemy, the philosopher Crescens.[31] The first word of the prefect Junius Rusticus, in questioning him, was not to accuse him of some crime under common law, nor to charge him with illicit association, although he gathered disciples in his house and several were prosecuted at the same time as he. "Submit yourself to the gods and obey the emperors," the magistrate told him simply. This statement reminded him that apostasy, by law, led to acquittal. The interrogation continued with Rusticus asking several questions, none of which dealt with any particular charge, and Justin replying by expounding on his beliefs and the defense of his faith. At the end the decisive question was asked: "Thus, you are a Christian?" "Yes, I am a Christian." The prefect addressed himself successively to the other accused, asking the same question of each and receiving the same answer. Once more he tried to weaken the resolution of Justin, then that of his companions. Only when all had answered, with a common voice: "Do quickly what you want, we are Christians and we do not sacrifice to idols," did he decide to pronounce the sentence. The latter reads as follows: "Let those who did not want

[29]Origen, *Contra Celsum,* VIII, 69.

[30]The rescript given by Modestin, and cited in the *Digest,* XLVIII, XIX, 30, does not seem to refer to the Christians. As to the letter of which Tertullian speaks (*Apol.* 5), and to which Orosius and Xiphilin allude, it is manifestly apocryphal.

[31]Tatian, *Adv. Grecos,* 19.

to sacrifice to the gods and obey the emperor's order be lashed and led away to undergo the death sentence, in conformity with the laws."[32]

At the end of the reign of Marcus Aurelius, the trial of the martyrs of Lyon shows the same jurisprudence applied not only by virtue of the previous rescripts, but in conformity with a new act of imperial power. On August 1, 177, as the annual feast drew near that reunited delegates of the three Gauls around the altar of Rome and Augustus, the population of Lyon had pursued and ill-treated the Christians. Many were arrested by soldiers, questioned by the municipal magistrates, and referred to the tribunal of the legate. Most confessed their faith courageously; a few, however, apostatized. This trial was probably the first of a religious nature conducted in Gaul; the governor showed as much inexperience as Pliny in Bithynia a short while ago. He ordered, or allowed, the search for other Christians, which was contrary to the rescript of Trajan. He then deviated in his direction of the affair: instead of limiting himself to recording the religious obstinacy of the accused, he tried to convict them of crimes under common law. Under the guidance of the soldiers and tormentors, slaves under torture charged their masters with the most heinous crimes such as "the banquets of Thyestes [i.e., cannibalism—*Ed.*], the incests of Oedipus, and other enormities of which one cannot speak or think, and which we cannot even believe were ever committed by humans."[33] This declaration, rejected energetically by the Christians, complicated the affair considerably. If the trial had dealt merely with the crime of religion, the outcome remained very simple: the apostates would have been sent away free, the confessors led away to be tortured. But the testimony extracted from the slaves laid upon one and all charges of crimes distinct from that of Christianity. Could the apostates still be viewed as innocent, and did they have to be sent away absolved? Such was the question the legate asked himself with some embarrassment, and which he submitted to the ruling of the emperor.

Without hesitation, Marcus Aurelius set his representative on the correct road. He responded with a rescript not unlike that of Trajan.

[32]*Acta S. Justini*, in Otto, *Corpus apologetarum christ. saec. secundi*, vol. III, 1879, p. 266–278.

[33]Letter of the Christians of Lyon and Vienne to those in Asia and in Phrygia, in Eusebius, *Hist. Eccl.* V. 1, 14.

"Let those who declare to be Christian," he informs him, "be condemned to death; but if any renounce, these must be absolved." This
statement rejected with a word the deposition of the witnesses for the
prosecution, repealing the entire procedure and ordering that trial start
over. The legate expected the new interrogation to be purely a matter
of form. In his mind, he only had to certify once more the obstinacy
of one group and the weakness of the other. To his great surprise, he
saw nearly every renegade admit to being Christian. The example and
exhortations of the confessors had converted them in prison.

There were thus more of the condemned than he thought. The
Roman citizens perished by the sword; the others, delivered to the
beasts, served in the amphitheater to the amusement of the people.
We know, thanks to the lively relationship between the Christians of
Lyon and Vienne with those of Asia and Phrygia, the grand and poi-
gnant episodes of this torture. However, we can see, by virtue of the
rescript of Marcus Aurelius, a confirmation of those of his predecessors. All committed the sole crime of religion; they died because they
had refused the mercy offered by the emperor to apostates.

If St Cecilia's martyrdom is, as I believe, contemporary to Marcus Aurelius, we find in that interrogation the rescript of 177 not only
recalled, but quoted. "Do you not know," the prefect of Rome asks the
accused noblewoman, "that our invincible masters have ordered that
those who will not deny being Christians shall be punished, while
those who deny will be absolved?"[34] The "invincible masters" were
Marcus Aurelius and his son Commodus, named Caesar in 166 and
invested with the power of a tribune in 177. Since the prefect cites these
two emperors, it is clearly not Trajan's rescript to which he alludes, but
a more recent and entirely contemporary order.

The death of Marcus Aurelius and the accession of his unworthy
successor did nothing to alter the situation of the Christians. The procedures followed against them remained the same. We find it at work
in one of the most precious documents remaining from Christian
antiquity, the *Acts of the Scillitan Martyrs* in Africa.[35] The proconsul

---

[34]De Rossi, *Roma sotterranea*, vol. III, xxxviii and 150.
[35]Ruinart, *Acta martyrum sincera*, p. 77–81; Aube, *Étude sur un nouveau texte des Actes*

begins the interrogation with these words: "You can obtain the emperor's mercy if you return to wisdom and sacrifice to the all-powerful gods." Next, addressing each of the accused in turn, he seeks to make him abandon his faith. One detail, which we have not seen before now, sheds light on the magistrate's desire to lead them to apostasy. "Perhaps," he says, "you are in need of a delay in order to deliberate?" In spite of the refusal of one of the accused, who appears to speak most frequently on behalf of the others, the proconsul insists: "Accept a delay of thirty days to reflect." Only when all reject this proposal, repeating with one voice, "I am a Christian, I will always worship the Lord my God, who has made heaven and earth, the sea and all therein," does he decide to pronounce the sentence. He condemns in them, as Pliny had done, the "obstinacy" that forms, in essence, the substance of the crime. This very word appears in the sentencing: "Considering that Speratus, Nartallus, Cittinus, Donata, Vestia, and Secunda have declared they live in the manner of Christians and, upon the offer being made to them to return to the Roman manner of living, have persisted in their obstinacy, we condemn them to perish by the sword."

These events date to 180, the first year of Commodus' reign. In the years that followed, numerous condemnations of Christians occurred both in Asia, under the cruel proconsulate of Arrius Antoninus,[36] and in Rome itself. The trial of Apollonius is famous.[37] The discovery of his authentic Acts[38] allows us today to complete the stories Eusebius and Jerome wrote on the subject. Denounced as a Christian, Apollonius was brought before the senate by the prefect of the praetorium Perennis. He made an apology for his religion in an elegant speech,

des martyrs Scillitains, 1881; *Analecta Bollandiana*, vol. viii, p. 6–8; Armitage Robinson, *The Passion of Perpetua with an Appendix on the Scillitan Martyrdom*, 1891, p. 106–110.

[36]Tertullian, *Ad Scapulam*, 5.

[37]Eusebius, *Hist. Eccl.*, V, 21, 2–4; St Jerome, *De viris Ill.*, art. *Apollonius*.

[38]Armenian version, published by the Mekhitarist Fathers of Venice in 1874; trans. by Conybeare, *The Apology and Acts of Apollonius and other monuments of Early Christianity*, 1894. See two memoranda of Harnack and of M. Mommsen, in the *Comptes rendus de l'Académie des Sciences de Berlin, section d'histoire et de philologie*, 27 July 1804; and *An Appendix of Hardy*, in *Christianity and Roman Government*, 1894, p. 200–208. A Greek version, according to the Greek MS 1219 of the *Bibliothèque nationale*, published by the Bollandists (*Analecta*, vol. xiv, 1894, p. 281–294). Cf. Harnack, *Theol. Literaturzeitung*, 1805, p. 590; Hilenfeld, *Zeitschrift f. Wiss. Theologie*, 1803, 180.

offering reasons for his refusal to sacrifice to the gods and swear by the good fortune of the emperor, and protesting that sentiments of political loyalty animated the believers. Three days later, he was interrogated by the prefect alone. He persisted in his refusal to apostatize. Then Perennis, citing the advice given by the senate during the first audience, condemned him to be beheaded. If Apollonius was himself a senator, as St Jerome maintains (and which we can believe, if we consider Christianity's great progress among the Roman aristocracy of that day[39]), this sentence may be easily explained. True, the Acts do not give him this title, but the first part is far from complete. It appears that Apollonius was an important person since Perennis believed, despite the omnipotence invested in him by the weak Commodus, that he had to take the advice of the high assembly concerning Apollonius. During the entire interrogation, he treated the accused with great courtesy and showed consideration for him even when the sentence was passed. The well-known details of this trial[40] show the accusation to concern religion alone, without the admixture of an accessory act, that Apollonius defended himself on this ground alone, and that no other motive existed for his condemnation.[41]

---

[39]Eusebius, *Hist. Eccl.*, V, 21, 6; cf. De Rossi, *Roma sott.* vol. i. p. 309–315ff., vol. ii, p. 366ff.; Bruzza, in *Bull. della comm. arch. com.* 1883, 137–143.

[40]The Acts do not speak of punishments that, according to Eusebius, would have been inflicted upon the accuser. For this detail, perhaps suspect, see Harnack in the memoir cited, and Fr Semerla, *Conf. d'archéologie chrét. de Rome*, January 14, 1894, in *Bull. di arch. crist.* 1894, p. 113.

[41]The theory of Edmond le Blant (*Note sur les bases juridiques des poursuites dirigées contre les martyrs*, reproduced in *Les Persécuteurs et les Martyrs*, 1893), according to which the Christians of the first two centuries were prosecuted not according to a particular law against them, but for crimes against common law, such as lèse-majesty, sacrilege, unlawful association, and magic, is rejected today; see its refutation by Duchesne, *Les Origines chrétiennes*, p. 116, and by Beaudoin, *Revue historique*, 1898, p. 159–167. Neumann accepts it partially when he maintains (*Der roemische Staat und die allgemeine Kirche*, vol. I, 1890, 7–25) that the refusal of the Christians to take part in the imperial cult fell under the twofold charge of sacrilege and lèse-majesty. This is the thesis Mommsen has assumed by making it more precise, and introducing a new element (*Der Religionsfrevel nach roemischen Recht*, in *Historische Zeitschrift*, vol. LXIV, 1890, p. 380–420; *Christianity in the Roman Empire*, in *The Expositor, vol.* VIII, 1890; *Roemisches Strafrecht*, 1899). His system may be summarized as follows: 1) the refusal of Christians to swear by the genius of Caesar and to render religious honors to the emperor raised against them the accusation of lèse-majesty; 2) even more often, they were pursued not by virtue of a regular accusation but through the exercise

We see that the legal situation of the Christians was still, at the close of the second century, just as Trajan had established it, while he himself sorted out a state of affairs that can be traced back to Nero. During the final years of the reign of Commodus, however, this situation became more relaxed. For the first time, the implacable rigidity of Roman justice softened under a new stimulus. Credit for this cannot be given to the arguments of the apologists, nor to any sudden awakening of the sentiment of fairness or humanity in the masters of the world. The influence exercised by Christian servants—and above all by a beloved woman[42]—on Commodus turned to the marked advantage of the Christians. Commodus was too indifferent to politics to resist; he pardoned numerous Christians with as much ease as he had condemned others previously. Thus confessors who worked in the mines of Sardinia were called back; the list had been requested from Pope Victor by the favorite Marcia. We find in this act a lucky whim of absolute power, not the beginnings of a better policy. Yet it ushered in a new age by showing that laws against Christianity had ceased to be inflexible, and that the imperial power, so often asked to address this question, could not remain inexorable.

of the right of police (*coercitio*), belonging to magistrates and left to their initiative. This thesis seems to be contradicted by the terms of Trajan's rescript (*conquirendi non sunt . . . si deferantur et arguantur . . .*) and by the numerous passages of the apologists, particularly Tertullian, that suppose a legislation directed against the Christians. Along these lines, see Guérin, *Étude sur le fondement juridique des persécutions,* in *Nouvelle Revue historique de droit français et étranger,* Sept.–Dec., 1895, p. 601–649 and 713–737; Callewaert, *Les premiers chrétiens furent-ils poursuivis par édits généraux ou par mesure de police?* in *Revue d'histoire ecclésiastique,* Louvain, vol. II, 1901; vol. III, 1902; a series of articles by the same author in *Revue des questions historiques,* July 1903, July 1904, April 1905, July 1907; and chapter III of my *Dix leçons sur le martyre,* 3rd. ed. p. 87–96.

[42]*Philosophumena,* IX, 11; Dio Cassius, lxxii, 1; St Irenaeus, *Haeres.,* IV, 30. Cf. De Rossi, *Inscr. christ.,* vol. I, n. 5, p. 9.

CHAPTER THREE

Church and State in the Third Century

1. Christian Propaganda—Septimius Severus (202–211)

In the third century, Christian society finally emerged from the shadows where its development had long lain hidden. The faithful were now too numerous to remain unnoticed. Their number accordingly required the establishment of a variety of services and material installations. The large communities at the time of Septimius Severus and Valerian necessarily led a more complicated existence than did the smaller groups of believers gathered around the apostles or their first disciples. To this period in the life of the Church corresponds a visible evolution of its relations with the Roman state.

Until the end of the Antonine dynasty the situation of the Christians remained as it had been established under the rescript of Trajan, itself interpretive of an earlier law. They were prosecuted not as a group but individually, by virtue of an accuser delivering one of them to the risks and perils of the tribunals. Except in unusual circumstances, the magistrates did not automatically rule against the worshippers of Christ. The persecution that hung over their heads had not yet become universal, since private individuals, rather than the state, put it into motion in the service of local or personal passions. In the third century conditions changed. The further development and constitution of the Church concerned the civil authorities. In what had previously seemed to them mere disobedience under the law, a punishable desertion of the state religion, they now perceived a public danger. From then on they took charge of the proceedings, which until that point had been left up to individual initiative. Persecution by edict began. However, because the persecution now became universal, it was less constant. Once war had been declared, it was a times interrupted by truces. By formally prohibiting the Church, the state would, in a certain fashion, recognize it and resolve to deal with it. The two powers—for we can already give them this name—would live under this regime during the entire third century.

The large number of believers at this time does not, in itself, proclaim the importance of the Christian population. Its significance is indicated perhaps even more by the intense life and continual movement of the faithful. The Christian East and West attracted and permeated each other; between them flowed an uninterrupted exchange of people and ideas. An inscription particular to the Gallo-Roman faithful might be Asiatic in symbolism and style;[1] a funeral stone in Phrygia recounted the impressions of a bishop of that country who had traveled all over the Christian world and visited Rome.[2] Letters and alms were sent from the eternal city to the most remote Christian communities, and travelers and pilgrims from every church flocked to Rome.[3] When a doctrinal controversy, such as the one concerning the date of Easter, caused a disturbance, councils gathered at once in Italy, Gaul, Greece, Africa, and many parts of Asia.[4] Having now taken root in every province—sparsely in some, but solidly ensconced in many others—the Christians no longer sought to conceal their numbers. If we are to judge by Tertullian, some took pleasure in exaggeration, evincing the faithful to be widespread in town and countryside, in the palace and the forum, like a flood that already covered the heights of the Roman world. If the African apologist is to be believed, their strength would have been so great that only patience and virtue could have prevented them from exacting revenge upon their enemies.[5] Such careless language is not entirely wrong. Even though members of the Church generally avoided parties, a word uttered by one of the lieutenants of Pescennius Niger reveals it was necessary to heed the sentiments that such-and-such a public event would inspire.[6] The conquests

[1]Edmond le Blant, *Inscriptions chrétiennes de la Gaule*, vol. I, n. 4, p. 8.

[2]*Nuovo Bullettino di archeologia cristiana*, 1895, pp. 17–41.

[3]Eusebius, *Hist. Eccl.*, IV, 23; cf. *Bullettino di archeologia cristiana*, 1864, p. 52; 1866, p. 9, 40, 87.

[4]Eusebius, *Hist. Eccl.*, V, 23, 24; St Jerome, *Chron. ad ann.* 196; *Libellus synodicus* (in Mansi, *Conc.* Vol. I, p. 275); cf. Héfélé, *Hist. des conciles*, vol. I, p. 80–83.

[5]Tertullian, *Ad nat.* I, 1, 8; *Apol.*, 37.

[6]Tertullian, *Ad Scapulam*, 3.

made by Christianity among the highest aristocracy were now known to all. Septimius Severus had to take this into account on the day a riot occurred, and he generously defended the Christians of the senatorial order against the people.[7]

The growth of the Christian population was to a certain degree the result of births. At least in the West, families in which Christianity was received early and transmitted by heredity did not comprise the majority of the faithful. For a long time to come, children of Christian parents would be honored as a result of their parentage.[8] "One is not born a Christian, one becomes one," Tertullian writes, doubtless with some exaggeration but not without a grain of truth.[9] The great progress of Christianity was due to an active, tireless propaganda, ever vigilant. It was practiced in every fashion, from philosophers like Justin and erudite catechists such as Origen, to artisans and servants whose zeal Celsus mocks bitterly.[10] Propaganda had its agents everywhere.

Their labors and success could not escape the politicians' attention. As guardians of the official religion, they saw ever greater numbers of people departing from it and, barely won over by the new faith, already vying to attract new adherents. It was difficult for a princeps inclined to tolerance, as Severus was during the first years of his reign, to observe these public conquests by Christianity without anxiety. They proved the doctrinal weakness of Roman paganism, which was incapable of defending itself against a living religion exerting influence on both reason and the heart at the same time. Despite being rejuvenated through contact with eastern cults, and by the artificial creation of seductive legends such as that of Apollonius of Tyana, the state religion seemed more vulnerable every day. One might well wonder whether the hour was at hand when desertion en masse would lead to a repetition throughout the empire of the spectacle that took place in a region of Bithynia under the reign of Trajan.[11] Apparently, reflections of this

[7] *Ibid.*, 4.

[8] It is carefully marked on the tombs. See Bayet, De titulis Atticae christianis, p. 136, and Edmond le Blant, *Les Actes des martyrs*, p. 237.

[9] Tertullian, *Apol.*, 18; cf. *De testimonio animae*, 1.

[10] Origen, *Contra Celsum*, III, 44, 55.

[11] Pliny, *Ep.*, x, 97.

nature led Septimius Severus, until then rather favorable toward the faithful, to decide in 202 to place an obstacle in the way of Christian propaganda by forbidding, under the most severe penalties, conversion from paganism to the Christian religion.[12]

He placed the same prohibition on Jewish propaganda, but the latter had ceased to be a formidable threat. The time when the Jews exercised real seduction on the Roman world lasted barely beyond the first century. Their political intrigues and open revolts, the destruction by Titus of their nationality, and the ruin of the temple broke the spell. Jaded third-century Romans no longer dreamed of embracing the Jewish observances so much in fashion at the time of Horace and Juvenal. After Severus' order Jewish propaganda, which had lost its fervor and success, was only sluggishly repressed. Not only did Judaism remain a *religio licita* (it even became an object of particular consideration on the part of Severus and his son, Caracalla),[13] but a blind eye seems to have been turned on the rare conversions it made. We also encounter at this time faint-hearted Christians who became Jewish to escape persecution.[14] Most likely the prohibition of Severus was directed only at the material act of circumcision,[15] which Antoninus had already forbidden the Jews to practice on strangers to their race.[16]

The edict or rescript relating to the Christians was carried out more strictly. Before this date, and during the first years of the reign of Septimius Severus, the former law had continued to be applied to believers. Although they were often hunted down during riots, besieged and captured in their secret meetings,[17] this was the doing of the people rather than of the magistrates. These officials did not persecute them officially, but only condemned the Christians brought before them who confessed their faith.[18] Torture was used, not to extract from

---

[12]*Judaeos fieri sub gravi poena vetuit, item etiam de cristianis sanxit.* Spartian, *Severus,* 17.

[13]*Digest,* L, II, 2, 3.

[14]Eusebius, *Hist. Eccl.,* VI, 12.

[15]Paul, *Sentent.* V, xxiii, 3, 4.

[16]*Digest,* XLVIII, viii, 1.

[17]Tertullian, *Ad nation.,* I, 7; *Apol.,* 7.

[18]*Perducimur ad potestates. Ad nat.* I, 1. *Christianus . . . interrogatus, confitetur; damnatur, gloriatur. Apol.,* 11.

them the confession of some crime, but in the hopes of making them recant.[19] Exile, death, and, for women, tortures even worse than death, punished the crime of obstinacy.[20] Such things still happened in Africa around 197 or 198, the likely date of the books *Ad nationes* and the *Apologeticus,* in which Tertullian provides these details. From a legal standpoint, this was the state of things under Trajan's rescript. Nothing indicates that Septimius Severus repealed it with his order of 202. The latter order does not concern Christians in general, whose legal situation had been fixed long ago, but rather new Christians—the converts. The establishment of a special offence concerning them necessarily implied a procedural change. For this category of faithful, the *conquirendi non sunt* ["they are not to be hunted out"] of Trajan was removed. Instead of waiting for an accuser to bring them before the court, the magistrates received the order to prosecute them directly—and, along with them no doubt, the accomplices of their conversion. In this manner they hoped to halt the evangelical propaganda.

A kind of discretionary power was given to the provincial governors, making them masters who could unleash a persecution at their pleasure. Thus in the third century we see them intervene in a much more personal way than their predecessors. Once the magistrates were satisfied to judge the Christians; now some hunted them. The writings of that time have preserved the legacy of legates and proconsuls who made themselves famous for their cruelty, and of others who applied the authority to prosecute that had been given them moderately, or not at all, and left a reputation for clemency.[21] A question now arose that seemed to receive no consideration during the preceding period, when magistrates were officially forbidden to seek out and prosecute Christians: did the latter have the right to escape danger by fleeing? The foolhardy, along with certain heretics, said no,[22] while the reasonable replied affirmatively.[23] As may be expected, many of the most famous victims of the persecution that came as a necessary consequence of

[19]*Apol.*, 9, 11.
[20]*Apol.*, 12, 31, 50.
[21]Tertullian, *Ad Scapulam,* 4.
[22]Tertullian, *De fuga in persecutione,* 3, 10, 12, 14.
[23]Clement of Alexandria, *Strom.*, IV, 4.

the act of 202 were Christian neophytes or catechumens. Among these were several of Origen's disciples, sacrificed at Alexandria,[24] and the celebrated martyrs of Carthage—Perpetua, Felicity, Revocatus, and their companions—who prepared themselves for baptism.[25]

Above all, Septimius Severus seems to have been preoccupied with preventing an increase in the number of Christians. Neither in his edict, as Spartian summarizes it,[26] nor in the persecutions to which this edict gave rise (the character of which is made known through such an authentic and detailed document as the *Acts of St Perpetua*) do we find anything that leads us to believe the emperor sought to achieve anything other than going after individuals in the Church. Nevertheless, his reign coincides with the hour when the Church became materially rooted in the soil as a landowner.

2. The Legal Status of the Churches

From the first moments of its existence, through the generosity and foresight of its children, the Church had received the resources necessary for the costs of worship, for the maintenance of the clergy, whose manual labor did not always suffice to nourish,[27] and for assistance to orphans, widows, and the poor. However, these resources were at first only securities. Even in the primitive Christianity of Jerusalem, we do not see believers offering buildings to the Church. The Book of Acts, on the contrary, records that they were sold in order to place the price paid at the feet of the apostles.[28] However, as the Christian population increased, the need arose to possess places of worship beyond borrowed rooms[29] and, above all, to acquire cemeteries where the deceased faithful could await the resurrection far from any con-

[24]Eusebius, *Hist. Eccl.,* VI, 1–4.

[25]Ruinart, *Acta sincera martyrum,* p. 85; Armitage Robinson, *The Passion of St Perpetua.*

[26]Spartian does not mention whether the order of Septimius Severus was an edict or a rescript. Even if it took the latter form, it certainly had a general application, as did the rescript of Trajan to Pliny, which established law for the entire empire.

[27]St Paul, *1 Cor.,* IX, 14; *2 Cor.,* XI, 8, 9; *1 Thess.* 11, 9; *2 Thess.,* III, 8, 9. See also the *Didache,* 13.

[28]*Act. Apost.* IV, 31, 35, 37; V, 1, 27.

[29]Cf. *Act. Apost.* XX, 7, 8. St Paul, XVI, 5; *Recognit. Pseudoclement,* X, 71.

tact with pagan graves. For a long time it had been possible to avoid such contact, thanks to the generosity of rich believers who opened their own family tombs to their deceased fellow believers. In Roman antiquity, where such family tombs often received freedmen and even slaves, sometimes forming the center of very large funerary domains,[30] such liberality was not at all unusual. We see how the growing number of Christians brought this practice to an end, however, by making such hospitality of the tomb costly and difficult, and also perceive its precarious character, ever at the mercy of accidents of succession, which might give a pagan heir a place consecrated by the burial of saints and martyrs. Thus, the Church sought ownership of cemeteries belonging to it alone, removed from any possibility of profanation and under its own administration. This process seems to have begun in Rome under the reign of Septimius Severus. As a result, most likely, of a donation by a noble Christian family,[31] the church of this town became owner of a common burial place, the first it had ever owned, for a document of the time calls it, with a certain emphasis, "the cemetery."[32]

Around the same time, a "worshipper of the Word" gave to "the holy church" of Caesarea of Mauretania "an area for burials," with "a *cella* [chapel] built at his expense" for services.[33] Another Christian of this same town enlarged this burial ground by joining to it a second plot "for all the brothers."[34] The church of Carthage also seems to have had burial grounds at this time.[35] In Rome, Pope Zephyrinus confided the administration "of the cemetery" to the first deacon, who was charged with the material affairs of the community.[36]

Here was a substitution of corporate ownership for individual ownership regarding possession of the premises required for church administration. In towns where the church, having many adherents, sensed the need for a stable patrimony, an evolution of this type had to

---

[30]See my *Histoire des Persécutions,* vol. II, 3rd ed. p. 471ff.; Appendix A: Domaines funéraires des particuliers et des collèges.

[31]De Rossi, *Roma sotterranea,* vol. II, p. 368ff.

[32]*Philosophumena,* IX, 11.

[33]*Corpus inscr. lat.,* vol. VIII, 9385. Cf. *Bull. di arch. crist.,* 1864, p. 58.

[34]*Corpus inscr. lat.,* vol. VIII, 9586. Cf. De Rossi, *Roma sotterranea,* vol. I, p. 100.

[35]Tertullian, *Ad Scapulam,* 3.

[36]*Philosophumena,* IX, 11.

take place. However, such matters did not proceed without difficulty. We have seen how Christians lived under perpetual threat of charges of illicit religion, and how conversions to Christianity, at the time of Septimius Severus, might even lead to official proceedings against the converts. How could Christians collectively enjoy some type of legal existence, even property rights?

This difficulty, although it appears almost insurmountable, was in practice fairly easy to circumvent. The legislation on funeral associations, which were viewed favorably under imperial policy, seems to have furnished the means. Unlike other fellowships that needed a special authorization to exist, societies formed with a view to guaranteeing funeral honors for their members could be formed without the intervention of public authority. This was true in Rome at the end of the first century and the start of the second, and for the provinces at the time of Septimius Severus, by virtue of a rescript of this emperor. Considered *collegia tenuiorum* [social colleges] or *collegia salutaria* [beneficial colleges], these associations had their own burial plots, gathering places, funds, dignitaries, and administrators. Since the dues paid by the poor, freedmen, and slaves who composed the majority would not always have sufficed to cover the costs of their funerals and the rather frequent meals and gatherings, they also recruited among the rich various benefactors (*patroni*) whose role more or less corresponded to that of honorary members in a modern mutual aid society. This organization, infinitely varied and replicated in thousands of models across the whole Roman empire, was perfectly suited to the concrete circumstances and economic organization of the Christian churches.

Like the funeral *collegia*, they ranked the assurance of the burial of their members first among their duties, and it was the accomplishment of this duty that made it indispensable for them to acquire the right of collective ownership. Like the funeral associations, they were composed for the most part of the lower class and the poor, and allowed slaves to attend their meetings. Like the colleges, they had benefactors, patrons among the rich Christians who bestowed upon their brethren their superfluous wealth. The inscriptions that relate the donation of a cemetery or chapel resemble those that mention the gift to one of the *collegia* of a funeral plot or a gathering place.[37] Further resembling the *collegia*, the churches had leaders chosen by election; in contrast to the colleges, however, those elections were altruistic and money played no role in them.[38] Like the colleges, the churches held meetings on certain anniversary days, but a devotional calendar, for them, replaced the *ordo coenarum*. Instead of celebrating with banquets the *natalitia* [birthdays] of the gods or their benefactors, they observed the *natalitia* of their martyrs with prayers and the offering of the holy sacrifice.[39] Like the colleges, they received dues from their members (*stips menstrua die*) one day each month; in contrast to the colleges, where this contribution was required on pain of revocation,[40] it was paid in the churches by those who could and wished to do so.[41] Like the colleges, the churches had a temporal administrator,[42] in the colleges called the agent or trustee,[43] who in Christian society was called the protodeacon.[44] There was a till (*arca*) into which dues and alms were poured but, unlike the colleges, anything not used for the burial of the poor was employed in works of charity instead of being spent on banquets and festivals.[45] Even the fees, whether in the form of money or in kind,

[37]Compare the two inscriptions of Caesarea of Mauretania, cited above, to *Orelli* 2417, 4003, and 4121.

[38]*Praesident probati quoque seniores, honorem istum non prelio, sed testimonio adepti; neque enim pretio ulla res Dei constat. Etiam si quod arcae genus est, non de honoraria summa, quasi redemptae religionis, congregatur.* Tertullian, *Apol.,* 39. The *summa honoraria*, sometimes recalled in the inscriptions, was the sum the city magistrates or officers of the collegia had to disburse as the price of their election.

[39]Compare the festal calendar of the college of Aesculapius and Hygie, of Sylvanus, of Diana, and Antinoe (Orelli, 2417; Orellienzen, 6085, 6080, 6086) with the *depositiones episcoporum* and the *depositiones martyrum* of the philocalian calendar. See also *Ep. Eccl., Smyrn. de martyrio Polycarpi*, 18, and Tertullian, *De corona*, 3.

[40]Orelli-Henzen, 6086.

[41]Modicam unusquisque stipem menstrua die, vel cum velit, et si modo velit et si modo possit, apponit. Tertullian, *Apol.,* 39.

[42]*Ministrator christianus.* Inscription cited by De Rossi, *Roma sotterranea*, vol. III, p. 526.

[43]Gaius, at the *Digest*, III, IV, 1, 1. These words are not found in the inscriptions: the *curator* or *procurator* who is sometimes named is perhaps the equivalent.

[44]*Philosophumena* , IX, 1; St Cyprian, *Ep.* 49, *ad Cornelium;* St Ambrose, *Off.,* II, 38; Prudentius, *Peri Stephanon*, II, 37–44.

[45]*Nam inde non epulis nec potaculis, nec ingratis voratinis dispensatur, sed egenis alendis humandisque, et pueris et parentibus destitutis, jamque domesticis senibus, item naufragis,* etc., Tertullian, *Apol.,* 39. Cf. Waltzing, *Les Corporations de l'ancienne Rome et la charité,*

which were distributed to guests according to rank at the meals of pagan associations,[46] were found at the gatherings of the faithful under the same name, but with a more noble cause: they provided salary for members of the clergy, or sometimes for the confessors of the faith.[47] Although in spirit everything was different, virtually everything in pagan and Christian communities was alike, based on external forms. Thus, the expressions used by Tertullian to describe the assemblies of the faithful[48] happen to be the very same ones used by the senate consul for the funeral associations[49] and by the jurists Gaius[50] and Ulpian[51] concerning the colleges.

Based on such striking analogies, we conclude that in order to follow the rules of Roman law the churches, at least where they wished to have a regular patrimony, adopted an organization identical to that of the *collegia tenuiorum* [social colleges]. The monthly basis for the contributions, as reported by Tertullian even before the third century, can hardly be explained except by the Christians' intent, from that point on, to comply with the regulations of these colleges, which demanded monthly payments, for ritual meetings took place in the churches every Sunday, and thus occurred weekly rather than monthly.[52] By this means the churches seem to have acquired legal standing. An epitaph from Heracleon in Pontus, addressed to the inevitable grave robbers, contains a threat of payment of a fine "to the brothers"—in other

---

in *Compte Rendu du 3e Congrès scientifique international des catholiques*, 1805, Sciences historiques.

[46]Orelli, 2417, 4075; *Atti della r. Accad. dei Lincei*, 1888, p. 270–281.

[47]St Paul, 1 *Tim.*, v, 17; Tertullian, *De jejunio*, 17; St Cyprian, *Ep.* 34, 64. Cf. De Rossi, *Bull. di archeologia cristiana*, 1806, p. 22.

[48]*Coimus . . . arcae genus est . . . modicum unusquisque stipem menstrua die apponit . . . egenis alendis humandisque.* Tertullian, *Apol.*, 39.

[49]*Qui stipem menstruam conferre volunt in funera in id collegium coeant neque sub specie hujus collegii nisi semel in mense coeant conferendi causa unde defuncti sepeliantur.* Senatus consultus reproduced from the funeral collegium of Diana and Antinoe, at Lanuvium. Orelli-Henzen, 6086.

[50]*Quibus autem permissus est corpus habere collegii, societatis, sive cujus que alterius eorum nomine, proprium est ad exemplum reipublicae habere arcam communem.* Gaius, in the *Digest*, III, IV, 1, 1.

[51]*Permittitur tenuioribus stipem menstruam conferre dum tamen semel in menso coeant conferendi causa.* Marcian, in the *Digest*, XLVII, XXII, 1.

[52]Pliny, *Ep.*, x, 97.

words, to the local Christian community.[53] For such a threat, if need arose, to have legal effect,[54] this community must be considered legitimate in its constitution.[55] There are numerous indications that lead us to think that the churches, in their legal relationship with the secular world, took the title of a society of brothers (*fratres, ecclesia fratrum*) that has just been cited.[56] Such a designation is most appropriate to the charitable ways of the Christians, and as vague as those of many pagan funeral colleges.[57] It is also possible that groups of the faithful were known by the name of "worshippers of the Word" (*cultores Verbi*),[58] analogous to the names borne by the many pagan colleges which were both religious and funeral: *cultores Jovis, Herculis, Mercurii, Silvani,* etc.[59]

Thus every detail of the Christians' external life, by evoking in things or words a detail of similar appearance borrowed from the life of the associations, seems to justify the proposed hypothesis. It explains, in the simplest fashion, how the churches were able to become owners of buildings no longer belonging "to such and such Christian, but to the Christian body."[60]

No matter how logical this system may appear, it has been criticized[61] and faulted for not being based on formal texts. The document in which Tertullian describes the organization of the Christian communities seemingly establishes only incidental links, having as its object

---

[53]De Rossi, *Roma sotterranea,* vol. I, p. 107.

[54]Daniel-Lacombe, *Le droit funéraire romain,* 1886, p. 191.

[55]We note that in the famous epitaph of the Phrygian bishop Abercius who, as a contemporary of Marcus Aurelius lived at a time when church property was not yet established, the *mulcta sepulcralis* imposed upon grave robbers is attributed to the municipal bank and the Roman treasury.

[56]De Rossi, *Roma sotterranea,* vol. I, p. 107.

[57]Cf. Gatti, in *Bull. della comm. arch. com. di Roma,* 1890, p. 145–147.

[58]*Corpus inscript. lat.,* vol. VIII, 9585. Cf. Eusebius, *Hist. Eccl.,* VII, 13.

[59]See Boissier, *Les Cultores Deorum,* in *Revue archéologique,* vol. xxiii, 1872, p. 81.

[60]Lactantius, *De mort. pers.,* 48; Eusebius, *Hist. Eccl.,* X, 5—see De Rossi, *Roma sotterranea,* vol. I, p. 101–108; vol. II. p. vi–ix, 371; vol. III, p. 473, 507–514; *Bull. di arch. crist.* 1864, p. 27, 59–63, 94; 1805, p. 89, 97, 98: 1866, p. 11, 22; 1870, p. 36.

[61]See Duchesne, *Les Origines chrétiennes (leçons d'histoire ecclésiastique professées à l'École supérieure de théologie de Paris,* 1878–1881, p. 386–396; and *Compte rendu du 3e Congres historique international des catholiques,* Bruxelles, 1805, *Sciences historiques,* p. 488; *Histoire ancienne de l'Église,* vol. I, 1906, 381–387.

less to show how they resembled the colleges than to indicate how they differed from them.[62] It has also be suggested that the Roman authorities could not, without an excess of naiveté or indulgence, have taken the churches for funeral colleges. The latter were ordinarily composed of a small number of associates,[63] while the church always formed one body which sometimes contained thousands of members.[64] Moreover, the religious character of the Christian communities was too evident[65] for confusion to be possible, even to the most uninformed eye. It would therefore be erroneous to identify the churches as true funeral colleges, fulfilling every condition demanded of them under the law and entering into this category of associations as completely and exactly as the countless pagan societies whose the inscriptions have preserved the model. Yet alongside the clearly defined colleges—these were of two types: professional associations bearing a special authorization from the emperor and senate, and funeral colleges authorized wholesale by law—there in fact existed numerous societies belonging to neither of these types. As a consequence they enjoyed no civil standing, yet were tolerated as long as they did not degenerate into unlawful factions. The goal of the Christian apologists, and Tertullian in particular, was to demonstrate that their co-religionists did not form illicit factions, and thus deserved toleration.[66] This tolerance was often accorded not

[62]Cf. Waltzing, *Les Corporations de l'ancienne Rome et la charité*, in the *Compte Rendu*, cited, p. 175.

[63]Numerous domestic collegia, composed of members and servants of a single family. (De Rossi, *I collegii funeratici famigliari privati e le loro denominazioni*, in *Comm. Philol. In hon. T. Mommsen*, 1877, p. 704). A donation made to the funeral college of Esculapius and Hygie, on condition that it would not be more than sixty members (Orelli, 2417).

[64]We note that "the Roman colleges that bore a professional name, but which were above all societies of friends, religious and funerary" (Waltzing, *l.c.,* p. 166), sometimes consisted of several hundred members; see Wilmanns, *Exampla inscript.*, Vol. II, Index, p. 637, *s.v. centuriae in collegiis*.

[65]*Corpus sumus de conscientia religionis, et disciplinae unitate, et spei foedere*, says Tertullian, *Apol.*, 39.

[66]*Inter licitas factiones sectam istam deputari oportebat, a qua nihil tale committitur quale de illicitis factionibus timeri solet . . . Eaden jam nunc ego ipse negotia christianae factionis, ut qui mala refutaverim, bona ostendam . . . Cum probi, cum boni coeunt, cum pii, cum casti congregantur, non est factio dicenda, sed curia . . . At e contrario ille nomen factionis accomodandum est qui in odium bonorum et proborum conspirant*, etc. *Apol.* 38, 39, 40. One of the phrases quoted (*non est factio dicenda, sed curia*) has always been translated: "It is not a faction; it is a senate." It may have another meaning. In proconsular Africa few inscriptions

only to individuals but also to Christian groups, who took advantage of it to acquire goods and peacefully possess gathering places and cemeteries. To attain this goal, it was unnecessary for them to enter into one of the legally defined types, since many societies often had silent permission to exist and to develop at the margins of the law. These included the brotherhoods devoted to the cults of the oriental gods. In all probability, this also applied to Christian churches during times of appeasement, when the authorities neither sought to dissolve them nor believed they were obligated to persecute them.

The reader must choose between the two systems. If the first one cannot be fully demonstrated, the second is open to serious objection. The collective property of the churches seems to have been established without objection between the end of the second century and the middle of the third. One of these dates is very close to the time when we observe that the church of Rome has a cemetery for the first time, while the second is at that key time when the imperial power begin to worry about buildings belonging to "the Christian body." If during this half-century the Church had enjoyed uninterrupted tolerance, we would conclude that the Roman state had allowed her to acquire goods and administer them freely. Under the reign of Septimius Severus, who persecuted the Church nevertheless, it is possible that the recent formation of the ecclesiastical patrimony escaped the magistrates' notice. But under successive regimes, when the Church was often tolerated and also sometimes persecuted violently, we note that none of these changes altered its status as owner. Until 257, the Church's most professed enemies allowed her to enjoy her properties, meddling neither in their use nor in their administration. Before mid-century, no act of receivership nor of confiscation occurred to the Church's detriment. Its believers might be forced to renounce the faith, or be condemned to exile or death, but no one touched its properties. This respect for

---

are found that refer to *collegia*, properly speaking, but the epigraphal texts alluding to societies that bear the name of *curia* (no connection with the municipal senate) are numerous. These *curiae* greatly resemble corporations and *collegia tenuiorum*, and seem to be a form particular to Africa (Toutain, *Les Cités romaines de la Tunisie*, 1896, p. 285). It is possible that Tertullian wishes to say here that the assembly of the Christians, composed of honest people, is not a "faction," but a *curie* or regular "association."

the ecclesiastic patrimony during the time of greatest intolerance for the members of the church seems difficult to explain, apart from the hypothesis that distinguishes between the Christian body, identified with the funeral colleges to the point of enjoying legal protection like them, and Christian individuals who were subject to intermittent persecution as insubordinate to the state religion.

3. Alternating Persecution and Tolerance (211–250)

Under the reign of Caracalla (211–217), the persecution begun by Severus continued, at least in Africa where the legates of Numidia, Mauretania, and especially the governor of the proconsular province, treated the Christians cruelly. "They burn us alive on account of the name of the true God," writes Tertullian, "which one does neither to true public enemies nor to those committing crimes of lèse-majesty."[67] The latter word makes it clear that disciples of the gospel were not being persecuted as guilty of lèse-majesty, but only of the crime of religion. Yet, at this very moment, the apologist does not complain about the violation of the Christians' grave *areae*, nor about the destruction and confiscation of their places of worship. Caracalla's extension of "citizenship" to every provincial does not seem to have influenced the status of the believers, except in one respect: appeals to the emperor against the judgment of the governors, which we saw lodged by St Paul in the first century, and in the second by some who were subject to Pliny in Bithynia, were no longer received. As soon as everyone became a citizen, this privilege of citizenship disappeared. However, it seems to have been so rarely used by Christians up to then that we cannot say their condition was aggravated considerably by its disappearance.

The coarse soldier Septimius Severus was succeeded by a greedy and bloodthirsty maniac. Caracalla, in turn, had as his successor a fool who transported the worst orgies of the East from Syria to Rome. Elagabalus (218–222) was not Roman enough to persecute the Church in the name of the national religion. Totally preoccupied with abasing the latter in favor of the cult of Baal of Emesa, he tolerated or simply

[67]Tertullian, *Ad Scapulam,* 4.

forgot the Christians. Upon his own ascent, his cousin Alexander
Severus (222–235) purified the throne soiled by this shameful sovereign. But he was scarcely more Roman than Elagabalus. An instinctive
sympathy inclined him towards Jewish and Christian monotheism.
Christians were numerous in his palace. His mother, Mammea, had
attended Origen's school for a time. He himself professed a naïve eclec-
ticism in religion, which made him place the image of Christ in his
household shrine next to those of Abraham, Orpheus, Apollonius of
Tyana, and the best of the Caesars. The Church had no fear of persecution from such a princeps, and thus plucked up her courage to plead
before him. The association of tavern owners disputed with Christians
over a plot of land, formerly part of the public domain, where the latter
wanted to establish a place of worship. Alexander resolved the dispute
by a rescript. "It is better," he declared, "that God be worshipped in any
manner in this place, than to give it to the tavern owners."[68] This decision had serious consequences. It established the right of the Church
not only to possess land, but to sue like any other corporation. The
decision even conceded a detached portion of the public domain, in
preference to a rival corporation. Above all, it granted the Church for
the first time a right in seeming contradiction to previous legislation:
that "of worshiping God in its own way." Never had the Church come
closer to being recognized officially, not only as a legitimate corporation or *de facto* association, but as a religious society. "*Christianos esse
passus est* [Christians were allowed to exist]," writes Alexander's biographer.[69] We might be tempted to believe that the entirety of imperial
policy towards the Christians was disavowed by this princeps, and that
the era of the persecutions had closed forever.

Unfortunately the son of Mammea, although he may have shared
in advance the feelings of a Constantine, lacked his prestige and
strength. His reign was bloodied by riots he was powerless to put down.
Ulpian, Alexander's prefect of the praetorium, to whom is attributed
a collection of every edict and rescript concerning the Christians,[70]

[68]Lamprides, *Alex.*, 40.
[69]Lamprides, *Alex.*, 22.
[70]Lactantius, *Div. Inst.*, v, 2.

perished in one such riot; during another Pope Callistus was martyred.[71] Alexander himself died as the victim of a soldiers' revolt. He
had as his successor Maximinus Thrax, whose hatred of his predecessor made him a persecutor. With a shrewdness proper to barbarians, he banned the leaders and theologians of the Church,[72] thinking
that the best way to destroy the Christians would be to remove the
repositories of hierarchical authority and the most active agents of her
propaganda. The proceedings directed against the bishops reveal that
the organization of the Church was by now well known. It has been
conjectured that the bishops, by virtue of their role as administrators of regularly established associations, may have had their names
inscribed in the registers of the urban prefecture at Rome, and of the
governors in the provinces.[73] In accordance with Maximinus' orders,
Pope Pontian and Hippolytus, one of the most famous doctors of the
Roman church, were deported to Sardinia. Pontian, not wishing to
leave the church without a leader, at once proffered his resignation
and was replaced by Anterus, who died, likely as a martyr, after one
month in the episcopacy. Pontian survived him by a few months and
died in exile, the victim of harsh treatment.[74] Directed against leaders and influential people in the Church, the persecutions affected
many simple believers in various locales. It was especially cruel in
Cappadocia, where violent earthquakes had agitated the pagans. Origen, who was in this province at the time, says that many churches
there were destroyed by fire.[75] This detail reveals that Christian communities possessed places of worship distinct from private homes,
and known to all. They were built, perhaps, thanks to the peace of
Alexander Severus.

The Church regained its tranquility under the Gordians, especially Philip (244–249). The latter appears to have been a Christian;
we know the story of a penance imposed on him by Babylas, bishop

[71]De Rossi, *Bull. di archeol. crist.*, 1806, p. 93.

[72]Eusebius, *Hist. Eccles.*, VI, 28; Orosius, VII, 19.

[73]De Rossi, *Roma sotterranea*, vol, II, p. vi–ix. Cf. Tertullian, *De fuga*, 13.

[74]Liberian catalogue and notices of Pontian and Anterus, in Duchesne, *Le Liber Pontificalis*, vol. I, p. 4, 5, 145, 147.

[75]Origen, *Comment. Series in Matth.*, 28.

of Antioch.[76] Philip and his wife corresponded with Origen.[77] During his public life he undoubtedly gave no sign of his intimate beliefs; celebrating Rome's millennium, he conducted himself as a pagan princeps.[78] But his policy towards the Church was marked by a visible kindness. He permitted Pope Fabian to solemnly return the relics of his predecessor Pontian from Sardinia to Rome, surrounded on the ship by all his clergy.[79] His contemporary Dionysius, bishop of Alexandria, speaks of "the most merciful empire of Philip."[80] In his book *Contra Celsum*, probably written during Philip's reign, Origen states "that the magistrates have ceased making war against the Christians, that in a world that hates them the latter enjoy a marvelous peace, that Providence expands the frontiers of their religion every day, and has finally given them freedom."[81]

As inferior as they seem when measured against the intellectual and—with the exception of Alexander—the moral qualities of their famous second-century predecessors, the sovereigns who succeeded one another at the beginning of the third century better served the cause of progress. A break in the narrow exclusivity of the Roman spirit was opened by them and daily enlarged. Septimius Severus extended freedom of association, until then restricted to Rome alone, to the provinces.[82] Caracalla lowered the wall that separated citizen from subject.[83] Alexander Severus tried to give labor an awareness of its strength by pushing the professions to organize themselves into industrial corporations.[84] Under his reign and Philip's, and even that of Elagabalus, the state religion was put in check first by tolerance, then by the express permission granted to the Christians "to worship God

---

[76]Eusebius, *Hist. Eccl.*, VI, 34; *Chron. ad olymp.* 256; St John Chrysostom, *de S. Babyla*, 6.

[77]Eusebius, *Hist. Eccl.*, VI, 36; St Jerome, *De viris ill.*, 51.

[78]Aurelius Victor, *De Caesaribus*, 28; Eutropius, *Brev.*, IX, 3; Eusebius, *Chron. ad olymp.* 257; Cohen, *Médailles impériales*, vol. IV, p. 146–147, n. 34 and 39.

[79]*Liber Pontificalis*, Pontianus; ed. Duchesne, vol. I, p. 115.

[80]Cited by Eusebius, *Hist. Eccl.*, VI, 41, 9.

[81]Origen, *Contra Celsum*, III, 15; VII, 26; VIII, 15, 44.

[82]*Digest*, XLVII, XXII, 1.

[83]*Digest*, I, v, 17.

[84]Lamprides, *Alex.*, 22, 33.

in their way." As we have mentioned, the ancient world did not long survive the Antonines. After them a new society formed confusedly under the reign of principes haphazardly recruited in Africa, Asia, and Arabia; underneath the purple, they remained orientals or barbarians. But the Roman spirit would not let itself be defeated without resistance or renewal. It had too many secular roots to fall with one blow. It suddenly revived, under Philip's successor, with all its strengths and defects—more domineering, more traditional, and more obstinate than ever. Trajan Decius represented Rome's revenge against the East, the old mores against the spirit of the new, the state religion against religious liberty. The Christians would become the first victims of this revenge, summed up in an immense effort to destroy them.

4. The Edict of Decius (250)

The text of the edict rendered against the Christians by Decius has not survived, but a number of reliable documents allow us to divine its terms by showing how it was carried out. Here, for the first time, was an edict of universal prohibition, composed in such a manner that no Christian could escape it. The same net would catch one and all at the same time. Not only was the principle laid out, but every detail of the proceedings was set. The degree of initiative until then left to the magistrates, who were masters of applying the law more or less completely according to the demands of local opinion, or even according to their temperament, no longer existed. The emperor's will alone drove the mechanism, imprinting on this engine everywhere the same movement, at the same time. On a fixed day,[85] across the empire, those whose religion seemed doubtful were ordered to declare their faith. Not only in Rome, Carthage, Alexandria, or Ephesus, in the large towns, provincial capitals, or district county-seats, but even in the market-towns and smaller towns[86] the test took place.

---

[85]St Cyprian, De lapsis, 2, 3.
[86]St Dionysius of Alexandria, in Eusebius, Hist. Eccl., VI, 42, 1. The papyri published by Krebs (1893) and Wessely (1891) are certificates of sacrifice, delivered in two Egyptian villages. See Nuovo Bull. di archeol. crist. 1895, p. 68–73 and pl. VIII; cf. Theol. Literaturzeitung, vol. XIX (1894), p. 37 and 102.

A local commission, composed of magistrates and notables, presided.[87] The suspects were told to appear in the temple. When his name was called[88] each one must offer a sacrifice,[89] or at least burn incense on the altar and pour a libation.[90] He must then pronounce a blasphemous formula in which Christ was denied.[91] Then a meal, where wine consecrated to idols was served with the flesh of the sacrificial victims, united those who had sacrificed in a sort of pagan communion.[92] A certificate of these various acts was to be delivered by the commission. The piece consisted of two parts. The first was a request, addressed to "those attending the sacrifices" of that town or village[93] from one who wished to certify his compliance. After indicating his name, age, place of birth, and proof of identity,[94] he declared to the authorities that he had always sacrificed and that "recently, in their presence, in conformity with the prescriptions of the edict, he has offered incense, poured a libation, and has partaken of the sacrifice," which he asked them to certify.[95] The commission, or one of its members, placed his stamp at the bottom of the request along with the date.[96]

Two original certificates, from different localities, have been found. The names vary, but the redaction is identical, allowing us to believe that a single model was used for the whole empire. People suspected of being Christians, and who had been weak enough to sacrifice, did

[87]St Cyprian, *Ep.* 43.

[88]St Dionysius of Alexandria, in Eusebius, *Hist. Eccl.,* VI, 42, 11.

[89]St Cyprian, *De lapsis,* 6.

[90]St Cyprian, *Ep.* 52.

[91]St Cyprian, *De lapsis,* 8. Analogous formulas required of the apostates in the second century: Pliny, *Ep.* X, 97; *Epist. Eccl. Smyrn. De martyr. Polycarpi,* 9.

[92]St Cyprian, *De lapsis,,* 8. 9, 10, 15, 24, 25.

[93]*Tois epi tōn thusiōn herēmenois kōmēs.* . . . A papyrus from the village of Alexander, following the same formula as that of the village of Philadelphia. *Nuovo Bull. di arch. crist.,* 1895, p. 60, 70.

[94]In the Alexander papyrus, the petitioner, Aurelius Diogenes, son of Satabus, seventy-two years of age, is shown as having a scar on his right eyebrow. *Ibid.*

[95]*Kai aei thuōn tois theois dietelesa, kai nun epi parousin humein kata ta prostetagmena ethusa kai tōn hiereirōn egeusamēn, kai axiō humas hyposēmiōsastai.* Papyrus of Alexander. In the papyrus of Philadelphia, the formula is in the plural, signed by a scribe in the name of the illiterate petitioners.

[96]This last part is missing in the Philadelphia papyrus. In that of Alexander it is mutilated but readable, and is in a different handwriting than the request. See *Nuovo Bull. di arch. crist.,* 1895, pl. VII.

not fail to equip themselves with this certificate in order to remain immune from lawsuits. At that time a traffic even developed—indeed, more than one—for obtaining false certificates for a certain price without having to obey the law.[97] As for Christians too resolute to resort to this subterfuge, which they saw as partial apostasy, they sometimes passed unnoticed, or were forgotten by the persecutors. Otherwise they had but one alternative: to escape prison by fleeing, or to allow themselves to be arrested. The detention was often long, and several died in solitary confinement.[98] Decius, never bloodthirsty by nature, did not seek to make martyrs, but rather to defeat the Christians. Any means looked good to him, from the most cruel tortures to the most vile seductions. For those whose recantation was most desirable, the trial, conducted with calculated leisure, sometimes lasted several months.[99] Only when every effort to defeat the Christian had failed was the sentence pronounced: deportation or exile, more often death. The property of the condemned, and even that of the fugitives, was confiscated and put up for sale.[100] The apostates were numerous, especially among the rich and the great.[101] But in every class of society there were also numerous martyrs.

Never before had Christianity undergone such an ordeal, or run such a great risk. The persecution was short; it began in the year 250 and was virtually over by May 251, even before the death of Decius. However, it left deep wounds that were slow to heal. The large number of apostates, and those who carried the certificate or *libellatici*; their efforts to re-enter the Church; the authority usurped by confessors of the faith, to the detriment of the bishops; the conflict that arose between supporters of severity and those favoring indulgence; the Novatian schism, which arose as a result; and the mingling of personal ambitions with disciplinary and doctrinal struggles all prolonged the

---

[97]St Cyprian, *Ep.* 31, 52, 68; *De Lapsis*, 27; *Ad Fortunatum*, 11.

[98]Letter of St Cornelius, in Eusebius, *Hist. Eccl.*, VI, 43; Liberian catalogue, in Duchesne, *Le Liber Pontificalis*, vol. I, p. 4.

[99]St Cyprian, *Ep.* 8, 16, 33, 35, 53; Eusebius, *Hist. Eccl.*, VI, 39.

[100]St Cyprian, *Ep.* 13, 18, 69; *De lapsis*, 3; St Dionysius of Alexandria, in Eusebius, *Hist. Eccl.*, VII, 22, 11.

[101]Letter from the clergy of Rome, in St Cyprian, *Ep.* 2; *St Dionysius of Alexandria*, in Eusebius, *Hist. Eccl.*, VI.

turmoil. The brief persecutions of Gallus and Aemilianus followed, during which Popes Cornelius and Lucius were successively exiled. The Church found brief respite during the early years of Valerian, who showed himself favorable to the Christians; the passing dissent between the African episcopate and the see of Rome caused only a superficial agitation. But soon Valerian yielded to contrary influences and the persecutions began again, assuming a new form that revealed an unsuspected aspect of the relationships between Church and state.

5. The Edicts of Valerian (257 and 258)

Decius believed that he would be able to suppress Christianity with a single blow, by forcing the Christians to apostatize. He attacked only the religion. With the help of cruel means in the service of false beliefs, he had pursued an unquestionably lofty goal: the restoration of religious unity by means of the return of the dissidents to the national cult. Pagan obstinacy, superior in his case to political acumen, prevented him from perceiving the true state of this cult, already half destroyed, and surviving thanks in large part to the foreign superstitions that surrounded it, with their parasitic roots, and lent it an appearance of life. Valerian had less lofty aims. What drew his attention, awakening his distrust and perhaps his cupidity, was less the matter of religion than of religious society. Dispersing this society by destroying its hierarchy, bringing down its foundations, forbidding its gathering, and seizing its genuine or presumed wealth by confiscating and sequestering its buildings—such were the tactics of the new persecution. Valerian did not try to reach every Christian, as Decius had aspired to do, but his more certain blows struck the head of the Church—its leadership— and at the same time its base, the temporal domain of the Christian community.

For the first time, the Church was treated as an unlawful association. Such was the main object of the edict of 257. We do not have its text, but it can easily be reconstructed by means of authentic records such as St Cyprian's first interrogation and that of Dionysius of Alexandria.[102] Its orders did not bring Christians to trial indiscriminately, but rather the principal members of the clergy. "The emperors have deigned to write me concerning not only the bishops, but also the priests," the proconsul of Africa tells Cyprian. The clergy were put on notice to sacrifice to the gods. The nature of the sentence to be pronounced if they should disobey shows that the religious question—the first, or rather the only one, at the time of Decius—had now moved to a second plane. The punishment was exile: Cyprian would be sent to Curubis, Dionysius to Kufra. The edict's severity was reserved for those rebels who persisted in reviving the dissolved association. They were treated like criminals in conformity with the laws passed against abettors of illicit colleges.[103]

"The emperors," says the proconsul of Africa to Cyprian, "have forbidden the holding of assemblies and entering the cemeteries. Anyone who will not observe this beneficial precept incurs the death penalty." The same declaration was made to Dionysius by the prefect of Egypt. Capital punishment had two degrees, death and forced labor.[104] In Africa, many clergymen and laypeople were condemned to forced labor in the mines, not for refusing to apostatize, but for illicit gatherings.[105] The state had seized Christian cemeteries and places of worship, and controlled their entrances. If anyone entered nevertheless, it was done stealthily through secret passages,[106] at the risk of being caught in the vicinity of the catacomb of Callistus, like Tarsicius the acolyte,[107] or being buried alive, like the faithful who prayed together in a crypt on the *via Salaria,* which was stopped up immediately by soldiers with stones and sand.[108]

---

[102]*Acta proconsularia S. Cypriani,* in Ruinart, *Acta sincera,* p. 216; St Dionysius of Alexandria, in Eusebius, *Hist. Eccl.,* IV, 11.

[103]Ulpian, Marcian in the *Digest,* XLVII, 2; XLVIII, 1, 3.

[104]Callistratus, in the *Digest,* XLVIII, XIX, 28.

[105]St Cyprian, *Ep.* 77, 78, 79.

[106]De Rossi, *Roma sotterranea,* vol. II, p. 258, 259, and 2nd part, p. 45–48.

[107]*Ibid.,* vol. II, p. 7–10; *Inscr. christ. urbis Romae,* vol. II, p. 109, n. 62.

[108]*Acta SS.,* October, vol. X, p. 483, 487; Gregory of Tours, *De gloria martyrum,* I, 38; De Rossi, *Inscr. christ. urbis Romae,* vol. II, p. 84, n. 30; p. 87, n. 31; p. 100, n. 17; p. lo3, n. 34, p. 121, n. 9; p. 135, n. 9.

We may surmise that the edict of 257 did not produce the effect intended by its author; a second edict, promulgated the following year, supplemented it and made it worse. On the one hand, the relatively mild punishment of exile probably had not frightened the bishops; even when exiled they continued their work, like Cyprian who, from Curubis, sent encouragements and help to the Christian convicts, and even more Dionysius, who took advantage of his forced stay in Libya to preach the gospel there.[109] It was necessary to reduce these troublesome voices to silence. On the other hand, the measures directed against the Christian community remained ineffective so long as the latter retained their powerful protectors among the nobles, equestrians, rich and high-ranking women, and even the opulent and influential servants of the palace called the Caesareans. One might confiscate the cemeteries held under the corporate title of the Church and close her places of assembly; however, the Church's friends among the hereditary aristocracy and the wealthy remained, as before, lords who provided her refuge in their funerary holdings. Indeed, several cemeteries were accessible even after the edict of 237 because they remained privately held. Valerian addressed a new edict to the senate, accompanied by a model letter sent by the imperial chancery to various governors. It said that any bishop, priest, or deacon who refused to renounce his faith would be put to death immediately. Any noble or equestrian confessing Christianity would be stripped of his rank, divested of his possessions, and beheaded. Women of that same rank would be sent into exile; Christians of the house of Caesar would see their fortune confiscated and, after being integrated into the lowest rank of the slaves, they would be condemned to work the soil.[110]

The executions were not long in coming. On August 6, 258, Pope Sixtus II, surprised with his clergy in a chamber at the cemetery of Pretextatus, was beheaded on that very spot while sitting in the bishop's chair; several of his deacons perished with him.[111] In Spain, Bishop Fructuosus was put to death along with his two deacons and in Carthage, Cyprian.

[109]St Dionysius of Alexandria, in Eusebius, *Hist. Eccl.,* VII, 11.
[110]St Cyprian, *Ep.* 80.
[111]Ibid., cf. De Rossi, *Roma sotterranea,* vol. I, p. 87–97.

The words of the propraetor of Tarraconaise to Fructuosus reveal an intention to curtly suppress and cut off any exchange with the leader of Christian society. "You are a bishop?" "I am." "You were," said the governor, while sending him to be tortured.[112] The terms of the sentence pronounced against Cyprian offer even more telling insight into the imperial thinking. He was not condemned merely on account of his Christianity—that is to say, for religious dissent—but above all as a sacrilegious conspirator, the instigator of an unlawful association. In the middle of the third century, these three crimes merged with that of lèse-majesty, and the same penalties were applied.[113] Previously, according to Tertullian, Christians had incurred charges of sacrilege and lèse-majesty,[114] but what was punished under this name was the refusal to worship the gods and offer sacrifices for the well-being of the emperors,[115] which was, upon closer examination, a religious offence. No martyr's trial before the third century reveals charges on any other grounds.

Now, under the clearly defined terms of another order, these legal qualifications were applied to Christian leaders. "Very close to the charge of sacrilege is that of lèse-majesty," writes the jurist Ulpian, "and the latter crime refers to any attack against the Roman people and against public security. Anyone who, through action, ruse, or counsel, has assembled armed folk in Rome, united them against the Republic, occupied public places or temples or has organized assemblies and gatherings, and pushed people to revolt is guilty of this crime."[116] These words comprise the substance of the proconsul's discourse to Cyprian. "You have long lived in sacrilege," the magistrate tells him. "You have gathered around you many accomplices in your guilty conspiracy; you have been the enemy of the gods of Rome and of its sacred laws. Our pious and most sacred emperors Valerian and Gallienus, and Valerian the most noble Caesar,[117] have been unable to compel you to

---

[112]*Acta SS. Fructuosi, episcopi, Augurii et Eulogii, diaconorum,* in Ruinart, p. 221.

[113]Ulpian, in the *Digest,* XLVII, XXII, 2; XLVIII, IV, 1.

[114]Tertullian, *Apol.* 10.

[115]*Ibid.,* cf. 15, 31, 35.

[116]Ulpian, in the *Digest,* XLVIII, IV, 1.

[117]In 253, Valerian was associated with his son Gallienus under the title Augustus; in 255 he made Caesar his grandchild, Valerian.

return to the practice of their worship. This is why, as the instigator of great crimes, the standard bearer of the rebellion, you will serve as an example to your associates in crime." With this recital the sentence was imposed, read by the proconsul from a tablet: "We command that Thascius Cyprian be put to death by the sword."[118]

In some respects, the persecution of Valerian thus displays a novel character and bears witness to concerns of which documents relating to the earlier persecutions bear no trace. Another aspect is yet to be discovered. For the first time, the question of money plays a role in the harshness exerted against the Christians. Under Decius, the property of believers condemned to death or banishment was confiscated, yet confiscation, even when it made things worse for them under common law,[119] was only an accessory and did not occupy first place in the calculations of the persecutors. Things were different under Valerian. To alleviate the stress on the public treasury, which at that time was very great, the emperor was prepared to seize the Christians' property. Even before the official inauguration of the persecution, we see him fussing about the wealth of faithful coming from Greece to Rome, called to the attention of the police through the abundance of their alms.[120] Confiscation moves from accessory to the rank of principal punishment in the edict of 258. It stipulates that senators, nobles, and equestrians who profess Christianity will first be deprived of their wealth; then, if they persist in being Christians, they will incur beheading. The same holds for the Caesarians. Not only those who might confess the faith in the future, but those who confessed it during one of the preceding persecutions, would lose their fortune retroactively, to be acquired by the state treasury. In his haste to acquire the Christians' riches, the emperor, in defiance of all precedent and logic, confiscated first and reserved punishment for later. We understand why he was less eager to appropriate the Church's collective patrimony. A remnant of respect for religious burial, so powerful

---

[118]*Acta proconsularia S. Cypriani,* 2, in Ruinart, p. 218.

[119]The *relegatio* or banishment did not ordinarily lead to a total loss of one's goods, except for the Christians; a total loss was the consequence of capital punishment alone. See *Digest,* XLVI, xxii, 1, 4.

[120]Acts of the Greek martyrs, published by De Rossi, *Roma sotterranea,* vol. III, 202, 205.

in Rome, prevented him from awarding Christian funerary grounds to the tax collectors; he was content with impounding them. Other corporate properties, such as buildings devoted to worship, were seized and some perhaps sold for the benefit of the treasury.[121] Even more so than buildings, the personal wealth of the Christian community seems to have been fair game. The story of St Lawrence is too typical to have been entirely invented. This protodeacon, an administrative trustee of the Roman church, was summoned before the prefect after the martyrdom of St Sixtus and ordered to deliver the treasuries entrusted to his care. He agreed, and on the appointed day presented to the magistrate a group of poor people[122] recruited from among the fifteen hundred indigents fed daily by the church of Rome.[123] This clearly shows that the monthly contributions and alms poured into the ecclesiastical coffers did not remain there, but were dispersed immediately among the poor. St Cyprian expresses this idea more simply at the same time when he writes that the Church did not retain any savings; everything she received went to the orphans and widows.[124] Valerian was mistaken in believing that the wealth of the Christian assemblies would offer fruitful prey. He found real estate such as cemeteries, oratories, and chapels difficult to sell, while the liquid reserves on which he was counting did not exist. But in the absence of church wealth, which frustrated the persecutor's hopes, that of rich Christians, who were a special target of one of his edicts, perhaps satisfied his greed.[125]

6. The Peace of Gallienus (260–268)

The reign of Valerian ended in catastrophe, which the Christians saw as providential punishment. Imprisoned by the Persians, the persecuting

---

[121]Further down one will see the distinction between cemeteries and other "religious places" of the Christians, made by the edict of restitution of Gallienus. Eusebius, *Hist. Eccl.*, VII, 13.

[122]St Ambrose, *Off.*, I, 41; ii, 28; Prudentius, *Peri Steph.*, II.

[123]St Cornelius, in Eusebius, *Hist. Eccl.*, IV, 43, 11; cf. De Rossi, *De origine, historia, indicibus scrinii et bibliothecae sedis apostolicae*, p. xii, xxiv.

[124]St Cyprian, *De opere et eleemosynis*, 15.

[125]*Huic persecutioni quotidie instant praefecti in Urbe, ut qui sibi oblati fuerint in eos animadvertantur, et bona eorum fisco vindicentur.* St Cyprian, *Ep.* 80.

princeps died in captivity, virtually a slave, after serving as his victors' toy. Gallienus succeeded him in 260. Probably following the advice of the Empress Salonina, whose sympathy for the Christians had perhaps extended as far as embracing their faith, the new emperor put an end to the persecution. He did this in an unusual way. Until then, several persecutions had actually ceased without the law being changed. The Romans let the Christians live and the emergency laws against them became obsolete, but Christianity remained an unlawful religion, still punishable in theory. Gallienus seems to have wished to erase this original blot. A general edict returned to the bishops and their clergy—"the magistrates of the Word," according to Eusebius' expression[126]—their freedom of ministry. Then rescripts regulating the proceedings were sent to several bishops. One of these rescripts has been preserved. Addressed to Dionysius of Alexandria and his eastern colleagues, it transfers to them the "religious places" seized by the treasury.[127] Other rescripts lifted the impoundment established on the cemeteries and allowed the bishops to regain use of them.[128] The significance of these acts was apparent to all observers. The leaders and ministers of the Church who had been suppressed by Valerian received from his son a type of investiture as an official title. The various categories of Church properties sequestered or confiscated by Valerian were returned to the representatives of the Church. No longer implicitly, nor by virtue of a legal maxim like that of Alexander Severus, but rather formally, by means of an edict and several rescripts, the Church was awarded the right to exist and own property. Certain indications lead us to believe that individual Christians whose wealth had been awarded to the tax collectors were themselves compensated.[129] Already, we see in broad outline the edict of pacification taking shape, which Constantine would sign into law fifty years later.

Unfortunately, Gallienus lacked the strength to impose his will and create a legacy for his work. History reveals that the edict was executed in the greater part of the empire, East as well as West, and that the

---

[126]*Tois tou Logou proestōsi,* Eusebius, *Hist. Eccl.,* VII, 13.
[127]*Ibid.*
[128]*Ibid.*
[129]St Paulinus of Nola, *Nat.,* XVI, 259, 263, 270–272.

Christians regained possession of their religious places. At that very hour, however, governmental unity slipped from the weak hands that held it. In the era of the "thirty tyrants," Gallienus was sovereign only in Italy and Africa. In the West, a large confederation uniting Gaul, Spain, and Britain was formed under the scepter of valiant warriors; the Danubian provinces were given a master; and Egypt became the prize of the ambitious Macrinius. In the Far East, the flourishing royalty of Palmyra prospered under Odenath and Zenobia. The fate of the Christians was bandied about among these principes, although only one, Macrinius, seems to have persecuted them. Under his ephemeral successor, Aemilianus, an episode of the civil war that desolated Alexandria further reveals the influence they had acquired and the services they were able to render at a time when all authority seemed to have been obliterated.[130] If the Christians' present situation was rarely aggravated by the anarchy into which the empire had fallen, the power of Gallienus' reforms nevertheless perished almost entirely. The religious peace he believed he had established continued to be at the mercy of events.

7. The End of the Third Century

Apart from a short and local persecution under Claudius Gothicus (269),[131] the faithful were undisturbed until the end of Aurelian's reign. This emperor seems to have known their organization quite well. "One would think you were gathered in a church of the Christians, and not in the temple of all the gods," he writes impatiently to the senators who, during Italy's extreme peril, hesitated to open the Sibylline books.[132] He was even familiar with the nuances of theological language, to the point of settling a question of property using a rule of church discipline. In 272, the faithful of Antioch disputed over a church building with the heresiarch Paul of Samosata. "The disputed building," Aurelian said, "will belong to those who are in communion with the bishops of Italy

[130]Eusebius, *Hist. Eccl.*, VII, 32.
[131]Doubts hardly founded of Goerres on the historic reality of the main martyrs of this persecution; *Jahrbuch fuer protest. Theologie*, 1891, n. 1.
[132]Vopiscus, *Aurelianus* 10.

and the bishop of Rome."[133] By awarding it to the orthodox faction, he again recognized the catholics' collective existence and right to common property. This was the policy of Alexander Severus coupled with a new element introduced by Gallienus: namely, the recognition of the bishops as legitimate leaders, almost official personages.

What pushed Aurelian, two years later, to abandon this policy? History does not say, and we are reduced to conjecture. Possibly Aurelian, by suddenly turning against the Christians, yielded to a movement of religious fanaticism. His own religion was very personal. Politically, he supported the official cult of Rome; in the depth of his heart, he believed in a god from the East. As the son of a priestess of Mithras, he worshiped the Sun, proclaiming it "the most certain of the gods." He made him "the lord of the Roman Empire," built a magnificent temple for him in Rome, and instituted in his honor a second college of great pontifices.[134] The Sun whom Aurelius exalted in this manner was less the Greco-Roman Apollo than the Mithras served by his mother in a grotto of Pannonia, or the Baal praised at Emesa and Palmyra. Even better, he was all of these, a divine composite who summed up the long labors of pagan syncretism, and whose cult Julian would attempt to resuscitate in opposition to that of Christ. The tone with which Aurelian spoke of his god on several occasions reveals a living, fervent, fanatical devotion; we are not surprised that this devotion became intolerant and led to persecution. In any event, an edict was issued in 274 against the Christians ("a bloody edict," says Lactantius,[135] who unfortunately does not provide a summary of its contents). A persecution followed that claimed its victims and would probably have become quite violent, had not the death of Aurelian, which occurred a few months later, brought it to an end.

From the elevation of Tacitus to the imperial throne to the establishment of the tetrarchy by Diocletian, the situation of the Christians was relatively peaceful. However, martyrs were reported in Rome and

[133]Eusebius, *Hist. Eccl.*, VII, 30, 19.
[134]Vopiscus, *Aurelianus* 5, 11, 25, 31, 35; Aurelius Victor, *De Caesaribus*; Zosimus, I, 60; Eckhel, *Doctr. Numm.* Vol. VII, p. 483; Marquardt, *Roem. Staatsverw.*, vol. III, p. 82, 236; *Bull. della comm. arch. com.*, 1887, p. 225.
[135]Lactantius, *De mort. pers.*, 6.

in the provinces. It is interesting to investigate the laws under which they were condemned. The edict of Aurelian had not yet been formally repealed, but it almost immediately fell into disuse. It had sufficed, nevertheless, to destroy every effect of the legal recognition the Church enjoyed under Gallienus, and to revive, in theory, the previous law outlawing the Christians. Specific local severities could be based upon this law, where its memory had been preserved. However, such remembrances did not last long, and the closing years of the third century saw religious tranquility scarcely disturbed.

Even in the West, where Christians were less numerous and perhaps for this reason suffered greater violence, the Church breathed freely. In the East, where the faith had put down roots in every province long ago, to the point that in some the faithful already formed a majority, every obstacle seemed to have been lifted and security forever ensured. When Diocletian transported his court to Nicomedia, believers there were numerous, and many appeared highly advanced in the favor of the sovereign. Many Christians managed municipal magistracies or even administered provinces.[136] As under Gallienus, the clergy was treated with great respect by the representatives of public authority.[137] Peace seemed so solidly established that the churches began to suffer the ills of prosperity. Here, morals became lax,[138] while elsewhere ambitious men quarreled over ecclesiastical rank.[139] Economic security asserted itself everywhere by means of external signs, as spacious basilicas in many towns replaced the dark churches and narrow chapels of former times.[140] In Rome, however, the popes had the foresight to continue maintaining places of worship far from the worldly and tumultuous inner city, applying their zeal and freedom above all to enlarging the catacombs.[141] They appear to have understood that this freedom would be brief and peace would remain fragile.

[136]Eusebius, *Hist. Eccl.,* VIII, 1, 6, 9, 11; council of Illiberis, canons 3, 4, 55; *Passio S. Philippi,* 7, 10 (in Ruinart, p. 447, 450).

[137]Eusebius, *Hist. Eccl.,* VIII, 1.

[138]Council of Illiberis, canons 5, 6, 8, 9, 10, 13, 18, 19, 20, 21, 45, 53, 57, 59, 73, 79.

[139]Eusebius, *Hist. Eccl.,* VIII, 1.

[140]*Ibid.*

[141]De Rossi, *Roma sotterranea,* vol. I, p. 203; vol. III, p. 45, 46, 49, 61–64, 71–73, 122, 123, 125, 187, 188.

However, the third century did not come to an end without favorable modifications to the relationship between Church and state. During the first half of the century, by making itself accepted either as a legally authorized funeral college or at least as a de facto association, the Church succeeded in establishing the endowment necessary for worship, burial, and the other economic and spiritual needs of an organized society. All legal fiction had become superfluous since the imperial decision around 225 that treated the church of Rome as a recognized corporation, even a legal religion, by granting it land with permission to worship God therein. It took the cruel edict of Decius to make the Christian religion illegal again, but even then the Church's status as a land-holding corporation was not undermined in the least. Its position was still so strong at mid-century that Valerian seized upon it as the main goal of a new persecution, wearing himself out in a vain effort to dissolve the Christian association. The failure of his attempt led to a second recognition of the Church, more formal than the first, by Gallienus. Again, such recognition was abrogated by Aurelian's edict of persecution. The Church then fell once again into the legal position it had had during the previous century, often enjoying a precarious peace which individual charges, or even new general persecutions, could shatter at any moment. At the very least the experiment had been tried: it had been demonstrated that imperial authority could coexist with the Church, and the right to worship a god other than the official divinities could be granted without endangering the state. On two occasions, ancient Roman religious law had been placed in check. However difficult the trials that still lay ahead for Christian society, the foundations for lasting peace were now laid.

CHAPTER FOUR

The Last Persecution—
The Edict of Milan

1. From the Establishment of the Tetrarchy to the Abdication of Diocletian (292–305)

Religious peace would probably have been maintained had Diocletian remained sole emperor. What we know of his character and intimate circle allows us to make this supposition. But an accurate sense of the times soon led him to select colleagues.

Attentive to the lessons of the recent era of the thirty tyrants, Diocletian understood that a hierarchical and regular division of the empire was the only means of preventing it from fracturing anew. If one insisted on maintaining an apparent unity, one ran the risk of seeing the empire sooner or later fall apart, be it due to ambitious revolutionaries, the needs of local defense, or even by virtue of the nationalistic instinct already stirring in the hearts of various populations subject to Rome's hegemony. Truth be told, in a Roman world pressed on all sides by barbarians, Rome was nothing more than an historical center. Actual authority would be exercised from now on by moving toward the frontiers and becoming as multifarious as they were. This is what Diocletian started doing as early as 285, having Maximian Hercules join him in the capacity of Caesar, then of Augustus, and charging him with the defense of the West while he himself retained the East. In 292[1] he brought this far-sighted idea to completion, and believed he would perfect the system by establishing a tetrarchy that divided the office even further, subordinating in the West, under the title of Caesar,

---

[1] *Or.* 293; see the note of Goyau, *Chronologie de l'Empire romain*, 1891, p. 346, n. 6. For the dates and nature of the connections between Diocletian and Maximian Hercules, we should take into account the new views expressed by Otto Seeck, *Die Ehrebung des Maximian zum Augustus* (in *Commentationes Woelfinianae*, Leipzig, 1897).

Constantius Chlorus to Maximian Hercules, and in the East, Maximian Galerius to Diocletian. As the first of the Augusti, Diocletian retained Asia under his direct control, along with its natural dependencies; Egypt, which was like an extension; and Thrace, which insured his communications with Europe. The second Augustus gathered under his scepter Italy, Africa, and probably Spain. The latter's auxiliary, Constantius Chlorus, received Gaul and Britain; Galerius, sovereign of the Danubian provinces, moved into Diocletian's orbit.

Galerius instigated the resumption of the hostilities against the Church. We then see the influence easily acquired by a vulgar yet energetic and tenacious mind over a more refined nature. The portrait of Galerius drawn by pagan as well as Christian authors—Aurelius Victor as well as Lactantius—depicts a crude soldier, a good general, a barbarian in origin and manners, joining, like many of his ilk, great cunning to a violent temper, and knowing how to handle men without having learned it. By natural instinct as much as by family tradition, he hated the Christians. He did not try right away to convince Diocletian to persecute them. However, he moved toward this goal with a calculated step. Under the pretext of promoting military discipline, he obtained from his colleague, over whom his recent victories gave him influence, the authorization to reestablish, for all army officers, the obligation to participate in the sacrifices. Many Christians strenuously objected to this measure and were stripped of their rank. A general purge followed. It reached even soldiers who could be deprived of their rights as veterans. Some of the more energetic refusals were punished by torture. But according to Eusebius there was little bloodshed, even in the provinces directly under the authority of Galerius.[2] If hagiographic accounts may be believed, there were a small number of executions in the provinces of Maximian Hercules.[3] The lands governed by Constantius Chlorus probably saw none.[4] Diocletian, in Asia, was content

[2]Eusebius, *Hist. Eccl.,* VIII, 1, 4, 18; *Chron.* (see Migne, *Patr. Graec.,* vol. XIII, col. 305, note 1). *Acta S. Julii,* in Ruinart, p. 616; *Acta SS. Marciani et Nicandri, ibid.,* p. 618.

[3]*Acta S. Marcelli centurionis,* in Ruinart, p. 312. Prudentius, *Peri Stephanon,* I (if the martyrdom of Emeterius and Chelidonius belongs to this phase of the persecution).

[4]If, as we suppose, Spain and Mauritania, to which the pieces cited in the preceding note refer, belonged to the domain of Hercules, as Lactantius maintains it, *De mortibus pers.,* 8.

to ban officers and soldiers who professed Christianity from the army and the Palatine militias, but he refrained from violence.[5]

The first step, meanwhile, had been taken; it would then be easy to further direct the still-hesitant will of the emperor. If Lactantius is well informed, Galerius directed every effort toward this goal: insinuations, lies, gatherings of officials calculated to advance his plans. Constantine, then at the court, would later tell of the decisive blow struck by the oracle of Apollo at Miletus, which denounced the Christians in ambiguous terms that were sufficiently clear. In consenting to the persecution, Diocletian wished there to be no bloodshed. He had the cathedral of Nicomedia razed and, on February 24, 303, posted in this town an edict ordering 1) the suspension of Christian assemblies; 2) destruction of the churches; 3) destruction of sacred books; 4) the recantation of every Christian on penalty, for those of higher rank, of being demoted and excluded from civic life; for those of more humble means, of being reduced to slavery; and for slaves, of never gaining their freedom.[6]

Galerius had probably expected more, but he was relying on some incident to incline Diocletian toward further severities. In an act of righteous indignation, a Christian tore to pieces a copy of the edict posted at the forum; this act implicated only its author, for they found no accomplices. Fire broke out in the imperial palace on two different occasions. Galerius blamed the Christians; Lactantius formally accuses Galerian of the act.[7] At the very least, the latter cleverly took advantage of the fire to compromise his enemies. He feigned terror, departing in haste, while Diocletian, believing that he had been betrayed, sent his Christian servants to be tortured. A segment of the population of Nicomedia became suspect. The bishop, clergy, and their families and servants perished in the torments; numerous believers were imprisoned. Blood flowed profusely in spite of Diocletian's earlier resolutions. He was compelled to mercilessly punish as arsonists those he

---

[5]Lactantius, *De mort. pers.*, 10.

[6]Lactantius, *De mort. pers.*, 10, 11, 12, 13; Eusebius, *De vita Const.*, II, 50, 51; *Hist. Eccl.*, VIII, 2. IX, 10; Rufinus, *Hist. Eccl.*, VIII, 2.

[7]Lactantius, *De mort. pers.*, 14. Eusebius attributes the fire to chance (*Hist. Eccl.*, VII, 6). Constantine, who was there, cites lightning (*Oratio ad sanctorum coetum*, 25, 2).

had first wished to turn from Christianity by means of an edict in which no death penalty was included.[8]

However, the local persecution in Nicomedia did not affect the provinces; everywhere else the edict was strictly enforced. In some places it was executed with reluctance, so much had the residents grown accustomed to religious tolerance. A month or two sometimes elapsed before the governors decided to apply it—not only in the West, where Maximian Hercules and Constantius learned of it only through a message from Diocletian,[9] but also in the East.[10] The destruction of the churches was not carried out in the same way everywhere. Here, walls were actually knocked down;[11] there, it was enough to burn the doors and pulpits, then leave them standing like abandoned buildings.[12] But the search for books seemed to have been actively pursued everywhere. Most Christians put to death in this first phase of the persecution perished because they refused to hand over the books and furniture owned by the churches.[13] We can ascertain the ferocity of these proceedings by studying various episodes in the history of the African church, especially the minutes of the searches made at Cirta, an authentic document that sheds great light on the conditions of the Christian communities at the beginning of the fourth century.[14] Those who submitted were branded with the name of traitor; many resisted at risk of their lives; some used ruses or, with the cooperation of Roman authorities, got out of trouble by delivering insignificant papers.[15] As it has come down to us, the edict does not mention confiscating buildings owned by the Christian communities; the latter penalty seems to have been a consequence of the prohibition of assemblies and the order

[8]Lactantius, *De mort. pers.*, 13–15; Eusebius, *Hist. Eccl.*, VIII, 5–6.

[9]*Ibid.*, 15.

[10]Eusebius, *Hist. Eccl.*, VIII, 2; *De mart. Palest.*, Prooemium; Theodoret, *Hist. Eccl.*, V, 38.

[11]Even in Gaul, under Constans; Lactantius, *De mort. pers.*, 15.

[12]*Gesta proconsularia quibus absolutus est Felix* (following the *Works* of St Augustine, ed. Gaume, vol. IX, col. 1088).

[13]*Acta S. Felicis, episcopi et martyris*, in Ruinart, p. 376.

[14]*Gesta apud Zenophilum consularem* (following the *Works* of St Augustine, ed. Gaume, vol. IX, col. 1100–1107).

[15]Saint Augustine, *Contra Cresconium*, III, 30; *Breviculus coll. cum Donat.*, III, 25.

to destroy places of worship. Thus in Rome we see church properties placed in the hands of the tax collectors.[16] To save the most venerated tombs in the cemeteries from possible desecration, several tunnels were filled with dirt. This worked so well that the believers had great difficulty locating the most renowned sanctuaries in the catacombs, after peace came to the Church.[17]

Documents from this era show that the parts of the edict concerning the destruction of buildings, books, and liturgical furniture were executed promptly; the articles concerning persons seemed to have largely remained threats. Those who would remain Christians, the edict stated, would be demoted or reduced to slavery; no action, however, had yet been taken to oblige the Christians to recant. Only by degrees do we arrive at the torture of individuals. For this to occur, it was necessary for Diocletian's political suspicions to be awakened. Tentative revolts that recently broke out in Syria and Roman Armenia served as the pretext. The church leaders were presented to the emperor as accomplices of the rebels. In the course of 303 he promulgated a second edict, ordering the jailing not of every Christian, but of bishops, priests, deacons, readers, and exorcists. Then came a third, ordering that members of the clergy thus incarcerated would be set free if they consented to sacrifice to the idols, or punished by death if they refused.[18] The bloody persecution now began in earnest.

The amnesty that Diocletian declared on the occasion of the twentieth anniversary of his accession seems to have been suspended the persecution for a time.[19] However, it soon resumed. The historian Eusebius' account of Asia, and various hagiographic documents from the Western countries,[20] allow us to assess its character. It varied according to the temperament of the magistrates, who were at times merciless and at other times content with a semblance of obedience,

---

[16]*Liber Pontificalis*, Silvester, ed. Duchesne, vol. I, p. cl and 182.

[17]De Rossi, *Roma sotterranea*, vol. I, p. 213; vol. II., p. 106, 259, 379; and 2nd part; p. 52–58; *Inscript. christ. urbis Romae*, vol. II, p. 30, 66, 90, 104, 105, 108.

[18]Eusebius, *Hist. Eccl.*, VIII, 6.

[19]Eusebius, *De mart. Pal.*, 2, 4.

[20]Eusebius, *De mart. Pal.*, 1–5; *Hist. Eccl.*, VIII, 7; *Passio S. Vincentii*, in Ruinart, p. 390; *Passio S. Philippi, episcopi Heracleae, ibid.*, p. 443.

even allowing those who had refused any voluntary act of pagan worship to pass as obedient.[21] Other documents show the persecution, after having reached the clergy, extending to the faithful, although the new edicts were not directed against this group. We must remember that the first edict, which forbade assemblies, remained in force; where Christians persisted in holding gatherings, they were punishable on this ground. The rather puzzling *Acts of the African Martyrs* record the trial of numerous faithful of both sexes, prosecuted at the same time as a priest for having celebrated the *dominicum,* that is, assisting at the Sunday office.[22]

A fourth edict, rendered at the beginning of 304, marks a new step forward. Here is how Eusebius summarizes its dispositions: "At the beginning of the second year, the fervor of the attacks against us having increased, imperial letters were sent through which it was ordered, in general terms, that everyone, in every country and town, publicly offer sacrifices and libations to the idols."[23] This time the persecution was general. If the first edict of 303 seemed to be inspired by the dispositions of Valerian, the fourth practically copied those of Decius. The documentation of its execution are numerous, since in addition to the historians' accounts we have Acts of the martyrs for virtually every province in the East and West.[24] However, we know less about the procedures themselves than we do about those during the time of Decius,[25] and we do not see as clearly the mechanism by which the Christians were obliged to sacrifice. Perhaps a larger share was left to the initiative of the magistrates. In certain places all food products were consecrated to the idols before being sold,[26] while elsewhere, when buying or selling, one had to offer incense to the statues of the gods placed near the entry to the markets.[27] The same obligation was imposed upon those

[21]Eusebius, *De mart. Pal.,* 1, 3, 4; *Hist. Eccl.,* VIII, 3.

[22]*Acta SS. Saturnini, Dativi, et aliorum plurimorum martyrum in Africa,* in Ruinart, p. 410.

[23]Eusebius, *De mart. Pal.,* 3.

[24]I have analyzed the most important of these Acts in the *Persécution de Dioclétien,* vol. I, p. 276–440.

[25]See above, p.

[26]*Passio S. Theodoti,* in Ruinart, p. 357.

[27]*Acta S. Sebastiani,* 65, in *Acta SS.,* January, vol. II, p. 275.

who wished to draw water from the public fountains.[28] The refusal to submit to these practices exposed many Christians. Those identified in this way were directly invited to sacrifice and to eat the sacrificial meats. In Numidia "the days of incensing"[29]—times when Governor Florus compelled anyone suspected of Christianity to enter the temples and offer sacrifices, or at least to burn incense before the gods[30]—were long infamous. But it appears that a uniform rule was not imposed on every province, town, and village, as under Decius, which permitted a softening of the edict in certain places, particularly in the districts under Constantius. On the whole, however, the persecution was universal and, according to the words of a fourth-century African, "made of some martyrs, of others confessors, of others renegades, saving only those who had managed to hide themselves."[31]

One characteristic of the persecution, which is attested not only by hagiographic documents but also by the accounts of witnesses such as Eusebius, was the atrocity of the tortures, which sometimes achieved the most extreme limits of cruelty.[32] Another was the large number of martyrs put to death together: in some places, ten, twenty, sixty, or even one hundred were executed on the same day.[33] There were real massacres, such as the one in which the entire population of Phrygia, whose inhabitants had embraced Christianity, perished.[34] We also note more frequently than in the past a refusal to allow burial by parents or friends of the condemned, out of an avowed fear that the cult of their relics would encourage the surviving Christians.[35] Finally, what

---

[28]*Ibid.*

[29]*Qui sunt passi sub preside Floro in civitate Milevitana in diebus turificationis. Bull. di arch. crist.,* 1876, pl. III, n. 2.

[30]*Sub persecutore Floro cristiani cogebantur ad templa . . . immundis fumabant arae nidoribus, ubicunque thus ponere nitebantur.* S. Optatus, *De schism. Donat.,* III, 8. *Scis quantum me quesivit Florus ut thurificarem. Actes du Concile de Cirta,* in S. Augustin, *Contra Cresconium,* III, 30.

[31]*Quae alios fecit martyres, alios confessores, nonnullos funesta prostravit in morte, latentes dimisit illaesos.* S. Optatus, *De schism. Donat.,* I, 13.

[32]Besides the numerous Acts of the Martyrs, see Eusebius, *Hist. Eccl.,* VIII, 8, 9, 12; *De martyr. Pal.,* 4.

[33]Eusebius, *Hist. Eccl.,* VIII, 9.

[34]*Ibid.,* 11; Lactantius, *Div. Inst.,* V, 11.

[35]Eusebius, *Hist. Eccl.,* VIII, 6, 7; *De martyr. Pal.,* 4, 9, 11; *Acta SS. Claudii, Asterii, etc.,* 4,

we frequently find—and which is nothing more than the putting into practice of the first edict of 303—is a loss of the privileges of rank for the accused Christians, or even the loss of the privileges of free people. Not only were members of the nobility tortured like those of baser origins, and punished with shameful ordeals,[36] but believers who had a right to trial under common law were deprived of this exception as a result of their religion. As a consequence, the tribunals declared them unable to plead in civil court, retaining their case in the criminal courts and punishing them as Christians.[37]

2. From the Abdication of Diocletian to the Illness of Galerius (305–311)

The persecution had lasted for two years when a portentous political event occurred: the tetrarchy fell apart. Whether as a result of threatening demands by Galerius, as Lactantius relates,[38] or for another reason,[39] Diocletian abdicated at Nicomedia. Maximian Hercules had to follow suit at Milan (305). However, the political system, deemed necessary for the defense of the empire, was preserved by the elevation of the Caesars to the rank of Augustus and the creation of two new Caesars. Galerius now assumed control of the eastern part of the empire, in Europe as well as in Asia; Constantius Chlorus remained sovereign over the entire West, adding Spain to Britain and to Gaul. Flavius Severus and Maximin Daia were named Caesars, the first receiving Italy and Africa and the other Egypt and Syria. Contrary to expectations, these two principes, the second of whom was Galerius' nephew, had been favored over Maxentius, son of Maximian Hercules, and Constantine,

5; *Acta S. Vincentii*, 10; *Passio S. Irenei*; *Passio S. Philippi*, 15; *Acta S. Tarachi, Probi, Andronici*, 11 (Ruinart, p. 281, 395, 435, 453, 490); Prudentius, *Peri Stephanon*, V, 381–383.

[36]Numerous Acts of martyrs; and, concerning his saintly relative Sotera, St Ambrose, *De exhortatione virginitatis*, 12; *De virginibus*, III, 6).

[37]St Basil, *Oratio* V (in Ruinart, p. 573). Cf. Lactantius, *De mort. pers.*, 15.

[38]Lactantius, *De mort. pers.*, 18.

[39]Lactantius' views on the subject are discussed by Coen (*l'Abdicazione di Diocletiano*; see *Revue critique*, 1879, 1) Morosi (*Intorno al motivo dell' abdicazione de l'imperatore Diocleziano*; see *Archivio storico italiano*, vol. v, 1880), Schiller (*Geschichte der roem. Kaiserzeit*, vol. II, p. 163), and appreciated favorably as to their general exactitude by R. Pichon (*Lactance*, 1901, p. 362–365).

son of Constantius Chlorus, whose parentage seemed to destine them for second place in the reorganized tetrarchy.

The Church felt the effects of these changes almost immediately. Having become subordinate to the tolerant Constantius, whose estate had scarcely known persecution,[40] Flavius Severus suspended its harshness in the provinces that had just been assigned to him. "The countries situated beyond Illyria," Eusebius writes, "which is to say, all of Italy, Sicily, Gaul, and the Westerns lands, Spain, Mauretania, and Africa, after having suffered the fury of war during the first two years of the persecution, promptly obtained the benefactions of peace through divine grace."[41]

We might hope that the eastern Christians would be no less fortunate. Upon arriving in his estate, Caesar Maximin Daia seems to have advised the magistrates to use clemency rather than violence to bring the dissidents back to the worship of the gods.[42] The church of Alexandria believed the truce would last: it promulgated admirable canons, written by Bishop Peter, resolving the fate of those who had weakened to some degree during the persecution.[43] Almost immediately, however, the persecution started up again in the half of the empire governed by Galerius and Maximin. "Then," Eusebius continues, "we saw the Roman world divided into two parts. The brethren living in one part enjoyed peace. Those who inhabited the other were forced into countless battles."[44] In the first few months of 306 a new edict was published in the East, "commanding the governors to compel the inhabitants of their towns to publicly sacrifice to the gods. Heralds circulated in the streets and summoned the heads of families to the temples. Tribunes of soldiers took roll call for the record. Everything was engulfed in an inexpressible storm."[45] Eusebius adds that Maximin was the author of this new declaration of war.[46] However, it was not

[40]Lactantius, *De mort. pers.*, 15; Eusebius, *De vita Constantini*, I, 16, 17; letter of the Donatist bishops to Constantine, in Optatus, *De schism. Donat.*, I, 22.

[41]Eusebius, *De martyr. Pal.*, 13.

[42]Eusebius, *Hist. Eccl.*, IX, 9, 13.

[43]Routh, *Reliquiae sacrae*, vol. IV, p. 23.

[44]Eusebius, *De martyr. Pal.*, 13.

[45]*Ibid.*, 4.

[46]*Ibid.*

limited to the Caesar's provinces, and other documents reveal at this same time a similar edict published in the districts under Galerius.[47] It is evident that the resumption of the persecution had been devised jointly by the two colleagues.

Its violence was extreme; there is mention of refinements of cruelty unheard of until then.[48] We note one special feature in particular: the magistrates for whom contemporary accounts offer us insight no longer persecuted merely for reasons of state, or out of fanaticism. Their moral level had sunk to that of the emperors. Chosen by the vulgar Galerius or the licentious Maximin, they often appeared to be upstarts from the lower class. We see them profiting from their office in order to serve their greed or satisfy the most vile passions. Hence the great number of Christian women who preferred martyrdom to the shameful propositions of their judges, or who committed suicide to escape the brutality of the governors and soldiers, which was not seen in the preceding persecutions.[49]

Meanwhile, the tetrarchy broke up again. After the abdication of Diocletian, Constantine had remained at the court of Galerius, treated simultaneously as a princeps and a hostage. Constantius Chlorus, feeling his health decline on the eve of his departure for Britain, called for him. Galerius had to authorize him to leave. Constantine, who feared being recalled or pursued, lent his departure the appearance of an escape, driving away or mutilating the horses on every relay, so they say, in order that they would not be able to overtake him. He arrived in Gaul at the moment his father was to embark; he followed him to Britain, where some time later he drew his last breath. Six young children survived Constantius' marriage to the daughter-in-law of Maximian. Only Constantine, who was born from a previous marriage, was able to succeed him. Acclaimed by the legions, he hastened to notify the emperors of his accession. In all probability this improvised election upset the plans of Galerius, who nonetheless accepted the fait accompli. Constantine had

---

[47]*Acta S. Acacii*, 1, in *Acta SS.*, *May*, vol. I, p. 702; *Acta S. Adriani*, 1, in Surius, *Vitae SS.*, vol. IX, p. 88; St Gregory of Nyssa, *De magno martyre Theodoro*, 3 (in Ruinart, p. 531).

[48]Eusebius, *Hist. Eccl.*, VIII, 10; Lactantius, *De mort. pers.*, 21.

[49]Eusebius, *De mart. Pal.*, 5; *Hist. Eccl.*, VIII, 12, 14; Lactantius, *De mort. pers.*, 38; St Ambrose, *De virginibus*, III, 7; *Ep.* 37; Saint John Chrysostom, *Homil.*, XI, LI.

content himself with the title of Caesar rather than of that of Augustus, which his troops had conferred upon him. He became sovereign of the districts where his father had reigned, i.e., the three great western countries of the empire. This example awakened the ambition of another disgraced prince. Maxentius, son of Maximian Hercules, lived as a private citizen in the vicinity of Rome. He took advantage of the unpopularity of Severus, who was detested by the Romans because he scorned the privileges of the eternal city. On October 28, 306, Maxentius was proclaimed emperor by the people in unison with the Praetorians. At this news the elder Hercules, who had abdicated grudgingly, hastened out of retirement to resume the title of Augustus. Thus, the Roman world presently had six emperors: Maximian Hercules and Maxentius in Rome, Severus in Italy, Constantine in Gaul, Galerius and Maximin in the East. Diocletian's achievement was shattered.

The fragmentation continued in the following years. In 307 first Severus, then Galerius, tried to retake Italy; Severus perished in the attempt. In 308 Galerius, Maximin, Constantine, and a new colleague, Licinius, all bore the title of Augustus. Maxentius held Rome, while Hercules, who had separated from him, wandered about Gaul as a conspirator, and the tyrant Alexander was master of Africa. In 310, Hercules killed himself. Sick, almost desperate, Diocletian from his refuge in Salone saw the people pulling his statues down along with those of his former companion. All of these events, however, shook the western provinces in particular. The East did not cease to be governed by Maximin and Galerius. The situation of the Christians also scarcely changed. It remained peaceful in the West and had even improved since Maxentius, struck by the large numbers of people who professed Christianity in Rome, demonstrated feelings that were almost Christian.[50] The Church took advantage of these circumstances to reorganize. Lacking her old cemeteries, which were still in the hands of the Roman treasury, the Church opened new ones. At the same time parishes were reformed "on account of the large number of pagans who prepare themselves for baptism."[51] Two popes, first Marcellus, then

---

[50]Eusebius, *Hist. Eccl.*, VIII, 14.
[51]*Liber Pontificalis*, Marcellus; ed. Duchesne, vol. I, p. 164.

Eusebius, were exiled successively by Maxentius following a disturbance excited by a matter of discipline by the dissidents, and ended
by a clumsy intervention of civil authority.[52] Nothing in these events,
however, resembled an act of persecution.

Only the western provinces of Moesia and Pannonia, which composed the lesser grant of Licinius, still saw martyrs. The most famous
was Quirinus, the bishop of Siscia, whose death seems to have occurred
in 309.[53] Licinius, a pawn of Galerius, pursued his policy of hostility
toward Christians. This policy continued to distress the East. Unfortunately, in this part of the empire, the internal dissensions within the
Church, which are mentioned by Eusebius,[54] played into the hands
of her enemies. Since he resided in the districts ruled by Maximian,
the historian provides us with an abundance of detail, especially with
regard to Syria and Egypt. Neither wisdom nor age were respected
by the persecutors. Alongside young men and girls who were piti-
lessly tortured and put to death, we see a learned man like Pamphilius,
founder of the Christian library of Caesarea and the compiler of critical editions of the Bible, sent to torture.[55] In Egypt, the long trial of
bishop Phileas, who related to the leading families of the province,
and of Philoromus,[56] a high-ranking official of Alexandria, ended with
a death sentence. Christian women continued to be condemned to
prostitution.[57] In 308, a new edict (the sixth since 303) appeared in
Maximin's territory, ordering the inhabitants to sacrifice to the idols
according to a forced roll call and, to ensure that no one escaped, to
sprinkle foodstuffs offered for sale with lustral water and force bath-
ers to burn incense at the feet of the gods before entering the bath
houses.[58] The tortures multiplied, as did the refusals to allow burial;
at Caesarea, the environs surrounding the city become a mass grave

[52]De Rossi, *Roma sotterranea*, vol. II, p. 204–208; *Inscr. crist. urbis Romae*, vol. II, p.
60, 62, 102, 104, 138.

[53]*Passio S. Quirini*, in Ruinart, p. 155; Prudentius, *Peri Stephanon*, VII. De Rossi, *Roma
sotterranea*, vol. II, p. 180– 181 and pl. V, VII; *Bull. di arch. crist.*, 1894, p. 53, 147–150.

[54]Eusebius, *De mart. Pal.*, 13.

[55]*Ibid.*, 7, 8, 9, 10, 11.

[56]*Acta SS. Phileae et Philoromi*, in Ruinart, p. 548.

[57]Eusebius, *De martyr. Pal.*, 8.

[58]Eusebius, *Ibid.*, 9 (2–3).

where dogs and birds of prey gathered.[59] However, the feature most characteristic of this phase of the persecution was the condemnation to forced labor. From 308 to 310, in the quarries of the Thebaid, the mines of Cilicia, Palestine, and Cyprus, we see the arrival of long lines of shackled Christians, near all of them limping and blind. Sometimes they were allowed to gather to pray, forming something like small churches in the places of their forced labor. Then they were violently dispersed, transferred from one mine to another, and the convicts who were too weak to be transported were beheaded.[60]

3. The Edict of Galerius and the Persecution of Maximin (311–312)

In 311, an unexpected event suspended the suffering of the Christians in the East. For several months Galerius was ill with a horrible disease, and seemingly devoured alive by worms. Neither the advice of the oracles nor the remedies of the physicians relieved his ills. He had the strange idea of turning towards the God of the Christians and essentially making a deal with him. The result was an edict for which Lactantius reproduces the original Latin, and Eusebius a Greek translation.[61] Galerius begins by recalling the fruitless efforts of the emperors to restore religious unity. Among the Christians, he says, some obeyed out of fear, others were punished, and most abstained from honoring the gods, all the while following their own cult. Galerius declares "that they may again be Christians and hold their assemblies, provided they do nothing contrary to proper order." Instructions regulating these points in detail were to be sent to the magistrates. In conclusion, Galerius asks Christians to pray to their God for his safety, for that of the state, and for themselves.

The edict, headed with the names of Galerius, Constantine, and Licinius, was promulgated in the districts of these three emperors. Lactantius read it on April 10, 311, posted on the walls of Nicomedia. No promulgation occurred in Italy, where Maxentius reigned, nor in Africa, which that very year had fallen under his dominion, but in

---

[59]*Ibid.*, 9 (8–12).
[60]*Ibid.*, 7, 8, 11, 13.
[61]Lactantius, *De mort. pers.*, 34; Eusebius, *Hist. Eccl.*, VIII, 17.

these countries Christians were no longer persecuted. What is more surprising is that the edict was never published officially in the districts of Maximin, that is, in Cilicia, Syria, and Egypt. Yet Maximin was part of the tetrarchy, and thus his name should have appeared in any official document signed by his colleagues. For reasons we do not know, this was not the case. However, Maximin could not refuse the new policy inaugurated by Galerius and ratified by Constantine and Licinius. He supported it reluctantly. He merely gave his prefect of the praetorium a verbal order to halt the persecution and send instructions to this effect to the governors of the various provinces, who were charged in turn with communicating them to the magistrates of the cities. Eusebius has preserved for us the circular written by the prefect. It enjoins public employees to cease proceedings against the Christians and to toler- ate the practice of their worship, "for long experience has proved that there is no way to deter them from their stubbornness."[62] This piece contains nothing resembling the expressions of the edict, allowing the Christians "to exist" and "hold their assemblies," that is to say, grant- ing them not only individual tolerance but also legal recognition as a church or corporation.

At first, this difference escaped notice; in the districts of Maximin, as in those of Galerius, there was unmitigated joy. Eusebius, an eye- witness, reports confessors leaving prison or returning from exile, churches raised from their ruins, and the pagans themselves shocked by this sudden reversal.[63] Yet at this very moment Maximin's power increased. Galerius had just died; his European districts became the share of Licinius, and those, much more extensive, that he possessed in Asia increased the privilege of Maximin, who thereby became master of the entire East. Before the end of 311, this hateful prince had with- drawn the concessions he had at first seemed to offer the Christians. He began by forbidding them "under any pretext" to hold gatherings in the cemeteries.[64] Then he organized an outpouring of public opinion against them, which based on the means used—petitions, pamphlets,

[62]Eusebius, *Hist. Eccl.*, IX, 1.
[63]*Id., ibid.*; Lactantius, *De mort. pers.*, 35.
[64]Eusebius. *Hist. Eccl.*, IX, 2.

conferences, posters, schools—reveal in Maximin and his advisors an entirely "modern" ability to stir up the mind of the crowds.

Maximin traveled through his domain during the final months of 311. In each town he visited, deputies appeared as if obeying a spoken order.[65] They asked him to banish Christian worship again, or at least forbid its followers to continue living in that province or town. Maximin acquiesced to the request. The petition, with the decree prohibiting Christians from staying, was engraved on marble or bronze to brief the forum, with the text of the imperial rescript, probably the same for every town, in the form of a sermon or encyclical. These things took place in Nicomedia, Tyre, and "in a great number of cities."[66] Recently, the petition "of the faithful people of the Lycians and Pamphilia," accompanied by certain still-legible lines of the imperial response, has been discovered on a marble in the ruins of Aricanda.[67]

At the end of 311, posters of another nature were affixed by order of Maximin in the towns of his districts. This was the report of false depositions received by the military commander of Damascus against the morals of the Christians. Long-forgotten slander took on new life and began to gain popular credulity.[68]

Prepared in this way, the persecution promptly became bloody. The Christians, hunted in many place, fled. A great number of bishops and priests were judged and condemned to death. Among them were notable personages like Peter of Alexandria; Methodius, bishop of Pataria, who authored a refutation of Porphyry and a Christian imitation of Plato's *Symposium*; and the exegete and apologist Lucian.[69]

Even as he was bringing down the Christian clergy's top leaders, Maximin in a fashion borrowed arms from his victims by attempting to organize the fluid hierarchy of pagan priests on the model of this clergy, with the goal of opposing an idolatrous church, regularly

[65]*Id., Ibid.;* Lactantius, *De mort. pers.,* 33.

[66]*Id., Ibid.,* IX, 7, 9.

[67]Mommsen, *Suppl.* to vol. III of *Corpus inscr. lat.,* n. 12132, p. 2056; Duchesne, *Bulletin critique,* April 15, 1893, p. 157; Reinach, *Revue archéologique,* December 1893, p. 55; De Rossi, *Bull. di arch. crist.,* 1894, p. 54; Preuschen, *Analecta,* 1893, p. 87.

[68]Eusebius, *Hist. Eccl.,* IX, 5.

[69]Lactantius, *De mort. pers.,* 36; Eusebius, *Hist. Eccl.,* VIII, 13; IX, 6; St. Jerome, *De viris ill.,* 83.

constituted, to the Christian Church whose solidity he had experienced.[70] Understanding that the official religion, even in a rejuvenated framework, had long failed to touch the soul, he attempted at the same time to awaken superstition alongside it. Hence, in Antioch, he solemnly inaugurated a new cult of Jupiter with priests, fortunetellers, and initiates, and in whose name an oracle spoke, whose first utterance was to ask for the banishment of the Christians.[71]

A still more direct blow had to delivered: Maximin and his advisors attacked the very person of Christ, by falsifying the gospels. The so-called *Acts of Pilate*, a blasphemous parody of the gospel, were abundantly spread among the people.[72] Thousands of copies were carried in bales to the provinces. The magistrates received the order to make them known in the towns and villages. They were propagated by means of conferences and public lectures. Their text was placarded on the walls. The study of this sacrilegious lampoon became obligatory in the schools. The instructors had to make their pupils learn about it and make it the subject of written homework or oral presentations.[73]

Thus the war against Christianity was carried to every land with a skill not found in the preceding centuries, and which Julian himself would not possess to this extent a few years from now. But events were stronger than the persecutor's will. The charity demonstrated by the Christians during a terrible famine, which was followed immediately by a contagion, restored public opinion.[74] The severity lessened. Soon the attention of Maximin was diverted by a disastrous expedition in Armenia.[75] At last the intervention of Constantine, who became the avowed champion of Christianity, compelled his colleague in the East to extend peace to the Church.[76]

---

[70]Lactantius, *De mort. pers.*, 36, 37; Eusebius, *Hist. Eccl.*, VIII, 14, IX, 1.

[71]Eusebius, *Hist. Eccl.*, IX, 23, 11.

[72]These Acts were probably composed several years earlier, for an allusion is made to the Passion of SS. Tarachus, Probus, Andronicus (Ruinart, p. 485) and perhaps that of St Theodotos (*ibid.*, 365), martyred in 304. Eusebius (*Hist. Eccl.*, I, 9) goes to the trouble of highlighting errors of chronology.

[73]Eusebius, *Hist. Eccl.*, IX, 1; cf. Lucian, *Apol.* In Routh, *Reliqiae sacrae*, vol. IV, p. 6.

[74]Eusebius, *Hist. Eccl.*, IX, 8; cf. Lactantius, *De mort. pers.*, 37.

[75]Eusebius, *Hist. Eccl.*, IX, 8.

[76]*Ibid.*, 9.

4. The Edict of Milan (313)

Under the pretext of avenging the death of Maximin Hercules, but in reality out of jealousy over the success and prestige of Constantine, Maxentius declared war on him at the close of 311. We know the events that changed in a few short months the face of the Roman world: a crossing of the Alps, the cities of Italy falling one after the other into the control of the master of Gaul, his victorious march on the *via Flaminia*, the decisive clash of two armies on the banks of the Tiber, Maxentius engulfed in the stream, and Constantine entering Rome on October 29, 312, to the acclamation of the people and the senate.[77] The political triumph of Christianity dates from the battle at the Milvian Bridge. In the war in which these two sovereigns were engaged, religion was not that important. When he undertook to supplant Constantine, Maxentius was rather favorable to the Church. Individually, Christians might have suffered from his tyranny and vices:[78] Christians, taken as a group, only had to trust his public deeds. War had already been declared when Maxentius authorized Pope Miltiades to claim from the prefect of the city church properties confiscated since 304[79] and allowed him to bring the remains of his predecessor back from Sicily in order to bury them at the cemetery of Callistus.[80] Even though he imitated his father's religious tolerance, Constantine, who found fewer ruins around him to repair, in all likelihood had not yet given as many pledges to the Christians. However, his victory over Maxentius was viewed at once by them as the very victory of their religion. This can be explained by this single fact: the conversion of Constantine had occurred during the very course of the expedition and had suddenly changed its character.

Having left Gaul a pagan, Constantine arrived in Rome hoisting the banner of Christ on his standards. Eusebius describes the inner drama

---

[77]Lactantius, *De mort. pers.*, 44; Eusebius, *Hist. Eccl.*, IX, 9; *De vita Constantini*, I, 38, 39; *Paneg. Vet.* 6, 7; Aurelius Victor, *De Caesaribus*, 40; *Epitome*; Zosimus, II, 15.

[78]Eusebius, *Hist. Eccl.*, VIII, 14; *De vita Constant.*, I, 33, 34.

[79]St. Augustine, *Brev. Coll. cum Donat.*, III, 34.

[80]De Rossi, *Roma sotterranea*, Vol. II, p. 209. Pope Eusebius was buried in a room on the second floor, removed from the papal vault, which had not yet been cleared of the sand used to obstruct access for the purpose of defilement.

that brought about this extraordinary change and the marvelous event that confirmed it, which was attested by the emperor's oath and even more, perhaps, by the sudden transformation of his military insignia.[81] We might believe that the idolatrous world of Rome would have accepted with difficulty a victory for which Constantine said he was indebted to the God of the gospel. But Maxentius had made himself so unpopular that his fortunate rival was accepted with equal favor by pagans and Christians alike. He cleverly concentrated at once on reassuring the first while giving numerous pledges of his favor to the latter. Above all, he proved attentive to keeping an equal balance between the two cults. At the same time he indicated his desire to reestablish religious tranquility everywhere.

One of his first acts, then, was to write an almost threatening letter to the persecutor Maximin.[82] The latter had to submit, although he did so unwillingly. A message sent by him to the prefect of the praetorium, in nearly the same terms as the one he had addressed the preceding year to this magistrate concerning the Edict of Galerius, recommended no further violence to the Christians, but rather trying to win them over to paganism through persuasion and clemency.[83] The rescript contained neither a disavowal of the past nor a formal promise for the future. Constantine was satisfied with it temporarily. He prepared a decisive act, destined to establish freedom of conscience on immovable foundations throughout the Roman Empire. This was the Edict of Milan, promulgated at the start of 313 in concert with Licinius, then his faithful ally.

The Edict of Milan is divided into two parts. One established principles for the future, the other set reparations for the past. In part one, the emperors first declared that "freedom of religion cannot be forced, and everyone should be allowed to obey, in matters divine, the movement of his conscience." Next, they applied this principle to the Christians, the only ones among the Roman subjects whose religious conscience had been violated in the past. After having stated that the

---

[81]Eusebius, *De vita Const.*, I, 27, 28, 31.
[82]Lactantius, *De mort. pers.*, 37.
[83]Eusebius, *Hist. Eccl.*, IX, 9 (13).

restrictions that accompanied Galerius' edict of tolerance were suppressed, the emperors add: "We simply desire that each of those who are willing to follow the Christian religion can do so today without fear of being hindered in any way. We give these Christians absolute freedom to follow their religion." Then, perhaps sensing that there was already reason to reassure the pagans against any fear of reaction or reprisal, the emperors recalled that the principle set forth would benefit not only Christians, but everyone: "What we grant to them, we grant also to others, who will enjoy the freedom of choosing and following the cult they prefer, in keeping with the tranquility of our time, so that no one suffers injury to his honor or religion."

What followed was a resolution of questions in detail. It was not enough to assure the Christians of freedom of conscience along with others; justice demanded that the battered Church receive assistance in rising from its ruins, and that she be given the means to practice her worship. The emperors thus decreed the reconstitution of the suppressed ecclesiastical patrimony. This patrimony primarily included the buildings required for religious gatherings. They must be returned to "the Christian body," "without payment or any claim of recompense, without delay and without dispute." The emperors were charged with compensating, if necessary, third parties who had received or acquired them from the tax offices. The Christians, furthermore, "not only possessed places of assembly but also other properties that belonged to their corporation, i.e., to the churches, not to individuals." The emperors ordered that

> by virtue of the same law, without any excuse or discussion, these properties are to be returned to their corporation or their communities in conformity with the rule set forth above, i.e., in expectation of compensation from the imperial treasury to those who make restitution without receiving payment.

Truth be told, these dispositions were not new. Their equivalent appeared in the rescripts Gallienus addressed fifty years earlier to the bishops. They were essentially present in the edict promulgated in 311 by Galerius. That very year, Maxentius had anticipated his conqueror's intentions for the city of Rome by restoring the *loca ecclesiastica* to Pope Miltiades. Now, however, such measures of reparation were the application of a principle, not mere political expediency. They solemnly consecrated freedom of conscience and established equality before the law for every cult throughout the Roman world. These features made the Edict of Milan the beginning of a new order. Its declarations of principle were coupled with sufficient power to enforce them. Its dispositions emanated neither from a weakened princeps like Gallienus, nor a dying Galerius, nor an embattled Maxentius, but from a sovereign in whose victory even the pagans recognized something divine,[84] and which had made him unchallenged ruler of the West and thus heard by the whole empire. This is what characterizes the imperious and pious tone of the words ending the edict:

> In all things you will lend your support to the body of the Christians, so that our order may be swiftly carried out, for it is favorable to public order. Let this be done, as has been said above, so that the divine favor that we have experienced in such great matters may always grant us success, and at the same time insure the happiness of all![85]

Constantine did not have to look for ways to compel Maximin to carry out the edict. At the same time the edict was being promulgated in the West, the tyrant of Asia invaded the districts of Licinius, who had remained at Milan near his powerful colleague, whose sister he had just married. Licinius rushed up to Thrace and defeated Maxentius, compelling him to recross the Bosphorus and follow him into Bithynia. Maximin fled away to Tarsus. There, desirous of regaining the favor of the Christians, he in turn published an edict of religious pacification. His ponderings were filled with ambiguity, but his disposition more or less replicated the Edict of Milan. It declared that "those who wish to follow the Christian sect may do so freely," and "each may

---

[84]*Instinctu divinitatis.* See the inscription on the Arch of Triumph dedicated by the senate to Constantine in 315; *Corp. inscr. lat.,* vol. VI, l039; cf. *Bull. di arch. crist.,* 1903, p. 40, 57–60, 80.

[85]For the complete text of the edict, see Lactantius, *De mort. pers.,* 48 and Eusebius, *Hist. Eccl.,* X, 5.

practice the religion he prefers." The faithful received permission to restore "the houses of the Lord," a remarkable expression from the pen of a pagan. All holdings seized by the treasury, or which towns have occupied to their detriment,[86] were to be "returned to their former legal status and to the property of the Christians." This was a recognition of the Church and her ongoing right of ownership. But this late change of heart did little to serve Maximin's interests. Learning of the arrival of Licinius, who had come by forced march over the Taurus, he either died suddenly or poisoned himself. He did not even receive credit for reestablishing religious freedom in Asia; it was the Edict of Milan, displayed by Licinius as soon as he arrived at Nicomedia, which would become law for East and West. History would have preserved no record of the edict from Tarsus, had Eusebius not made a copy of it.[87]

[86]In this last case, it is a matter of benefits granted by Maximin to the cities as a reward for their eagerness in requiring the expulsion of the Christians. In the rescript to the city of Tyre and what remains of the rescript to the city of Aricanda, we see Maximin's invitation asking what they might want.

[87]Lactantius, *De mort. pers.*, 46–50; Eusebius, *Hist. Eccl.*, IX, 10.

CHAPTER FIVE

The Religious Policy of Constantine and His Sons

1. From the Edict of Milan to the Death of Licinius (313–324)

Proclaiming freedom of conscience in the wake of a violent religious crisis and promising equal treatment to diverse religions is relatively easy, but it is not so easy to reconcile these new principles with the facts on the ground and acclimate them to public mores. The invitation to accept such principles is not extended to society in the abstract, but to a living organism with centuries-old secular habits, ingrained prejudices, traditions, and passions. There will be resistance among the followers of that religion, which up until then enjoyed sole dominance and long-standing support from the state. Among the adherents of the sect that has just received its freedom after recent persecution, an impatience to dominate in their turn will almost inevitably appear, especially when they feel assured of the sovereign's favor. The princeps himself, unless he is a skeptic, will have personal preferences that make neutrality difficult.

The work of religious pacification inaugurated by the Edict of Milan developed amidst such obstacles, and was often thwarted by them. The very constitution of the imperial power created a contradictory situation for Maxentius' conqueror. Constantine had become a Christian in terms of feelings and beliefs—a very imperfect one, undoubtedly, but sincere. As emperor, he maintained a forced allegiance to paganism. He was by right a member of every priestly college and the sovereign pontifex. This rank accorded him not only the presidency of the Vestal pontifices, for which it was easy to find a substitute,[1] but also

---

[1] *Promagister* of the college of pontifices: *Corp. inscr. lat.*, 1 vol. VI, 1128, 1700, 2158; vol. X, 1125.

conferred upon him virtually absolute power to direct and supervise the Roman religion and the foreign cults that depended on it in terms of both rites and personnel. Constantine could not have repudiated the supreme pontificate without diminishing the prestige of his sovereignty in the eyes of the majority of his subjects. Moreover, it would have been impossible to abolish it without endangering the religious freedom he had just proclaimed, nor could he leave the office in the hands of another individual without investing him with formidable power and almost certainly creating a rival for himself. Thus a pagan historian remarks that Constantine, "even after he turned away from the right track in terms of religion," took care to retain the title and the honors of *Pontifex maximus*.[2] This title appears in inscriptions and on coinage at various stages of his reign.

Tertullian seems to sense the contradiction of an emperor remaining official chief of a pagan cult after abandoning it, when he writes: "It is impossible to be at the same time Caesar and a Christian."[3] A more flexible genius, however, would try to achieve what the African's intractable logic showed him from afar to be impossible. For more than half a century, Constantine and his successors would practice this very dualism.

In order to appreciate how the problem was resolved by the first Christian emperor, we must recall that he did not reign alone from 313 to 324. His colleague Licinius, who at first fully agreed with his religious policy, moved away from it little by little to the point of becoming the declared champion of paganism in the East. This situation naturally imposed a greater reserve upon Constantine during the ten years prior to 324. Once Licinius had been defeated and killed, and the pagan reaction of which he had been the leader defeated along with him, East and West had only had one master, who was then free to manifest his feelings with full independence. Constantine's conduct towards pagans and Christians should therefore be examined separately for each of these periods.

---

[2]Zosimus, IV, 36.
[3]Tertullian, *Apol.*, 21.

During the first period four legislative acts, signed by him from Rome, Aquilea, and Sardica, refer to the regulation of the pagan religion. First, in 319, there was a rescript and an edict against the abuse of the art of divination. These were intended to prohibit entry into private residences by haruspices [those who practiced divination by inspecting the entrails of animals] and priests whose occupation was foretelling the future. The haruspex was allowed to practice only in the temples, according to the sacred rites.[4] The two rescripts of 321 completed the emperor's thinking. In one, he threatened severe punishments for those whose magical illusions were directed against life or modesty, exempting from this threat innocuous practices whose sole aim was to heal the sick or to preserve the harvest.[5] The other rescript declared, in conformity with ancient custom, that the haruspices must be consulted when lightning struck the palace or another public building; their answers, however, must be transmitted directly to the emperor.[6] Nothing in these various ordinances undermined the free practice of idolatry, but rather consecrated it in formal terms by recognizing the official practice of the haruspex while clearly punishing any secret maneuvers. We may compare them with similar ordinances enacted by the pagan principes. If Constantine's rescripts struck an indirect blow against paganism, it was by forbidding it to conspire in mystery and shadow, but rather obliging it to live in broad daylight and communicate its oracles to the sovereign. These measures, such as they were, addressed only abuses, giving the partisans of the ancient cult no legitimate cause for complaint; they seem to emanate from the pontifex no less than from the emperor.

Other measures of Constantine during this same period were in accord with the spirit of the Edict of Milan, for their object was to put Christians on an equal footing with the pagans, in conformity with the edict's recognition of the same rights for the various cults to which the empire's subjects belonged. Such were the laws and rescripts of 313, 319, and 320, declaring Christian priests exempt from all municipal

---

[4] *Theodosian Code*, IX, XVI, 1, 2.
[5] *Ibid.*, 3.
[6] *Ibid.*, 4.

expenses.[7] This equitable measure (pagan priests already enjoyed this exemption)[8] was unfortunately all but destroyed, to the detriment of the Christians, by another law of 320 limiting admittance to holy orders to "people of modest means," out of fear that the entry of too many of the wealthy into the ranks of the clergy might depopulate and impoverish the curiae.[9] The permission received in 321 to leave one's estate to the Christian churches[10] merely made those institutions equal to the temples, which were authorized from time immemorial to receive bequests and legacies.[11] When Christian basilicas were raised at the imperial treasury's expense in Rome, Italy, Africa, and Asia, when their dedication was celebrated with splendor, and the income from their lands assigned to them,[12] Constantine was only giving the Christian religion a splendor equivalent to that enjoyed by the pagans. Zosimus was unfair in reproaching Constantine for having exhausted the state's finances on these useless constructions.[13] The law of 312, which ordered judges, corporations, and their staffs not to work on Sundays,[14] was not, in itself, a special favor to the Christians; it simply made their public holidays equivalent in rank to the pagan feasts, during which all indispensable work was to be halted.[15] As for the law of 323, which prohibited forcing Christians to make a show of paganism, there is no need for comment;[16] it reveals the extent to which legislative vigilance was still needed to assure them the freedom of conscience promised to all.

However, we note a curious nuance. The emperor forbade forcing "the clergy and other members of the catholic sect" to sacrifice, still speaking in the neutral tone of the legislator. He then threatened

[7] Eusebius, *Hist. Eccl.*, X; *Theodosian Code*, XVI, II, 1, 2, 7.

[8] Cicero, *Acad.*, II, 38, 121. Titus Livius, IV, 54; Plutarch, *Numa*, 14; Dionysius of Halicarnassus, IV, 62, 74; Aulus Gellius, X, 15; *Corp. inscr. lat.*, vol. IX, 4200–4208; *Lex coloniae Genetivae*, 66, in *Ephem epigr.*, vol. III, p. 101.

[9] *Theodosian Code*, XVI, 3; cf. *ibid.*, 6.

[10] *Ibid.*, 4.

[11] *Digest*, XXXIII, I, 20; II, 16; XXXV, II, 1.

[12] Eusebius, *Hist. Eccl.*, X, 2, 1; *Liber Pontificalis*, Silvester, *passim*.

[13] Zosimus, II, 32.

[14] *Justinian Code*, III, XII, 2.

[15] Cicero, *De leg.* II, 12, 29. Cf. *Dict. des ant. grecques et rom.*, vol. II, p. 174, art. *Dies*.

[16] *Theodosian Code*, XVI, II, 5.

severe penalties against "those that would require the rites of a foreign superstition from the servants of the most holy law." This was now the language of a Christian. Up to this point, we have not been able to judge Constantine's personal feelings. Except for a few expressions, the series of laws and ordinances we have recounted could have emanated from a sovereign indifferent in religious matters, and concerned only with giving equal status to every cult. The law of 323 did not diverge from this goal, but revealed the intimate preferences of the princeps through an abrupt change in the official style. Much earlier events had already brought them to light. The panegyrists who related Constantine's entry into Rome after the battle of the Milvian bridge spoke of the performances he witnessed, but mentioned neither sacrifices nor even a visit to the Capitol.[17] In 313 he neglected to celebrate the secular games, which were fully pagan.[18] When a statue was erected for him in Rome, he wanted the lance placed in his hand to have the form of a cross, and the inscription on the pedestal to attribute his victory to "this salutary sign."[19] In the laws where he can do so without harming freedom of conscience, he was visibly inspired by the Christian spirit. This spirit probably left its mark on quite a few legislative acts designed to soften conditions for slaves and prisoners, to prevent the murder or abandonment of newborns, and to suppress immorality.[20] It seems especially evident in certain laws,[21] such as the one that in 315 forbade marking the condemned in the face "made in the likeness of the divine beauty."[22] In 316, Constantine allowed slaves to be freed in the churches, in the presence of the priests;[23] in 321, he recognized the enfranchisement thus conferred in a most solemn manner, transmitting the right

---

[17]Tillemont, *Hist. Des Empereurs,* vol. IV, p. 140.

[18]Zosimus II, 7.

[19]Eusebius, *Hist. Eccl.,* IV, 9, 10, 11; *De vita Const.,* I, 40.

[20]*Theodosian Code,* II, XXV, 1; III, V, 3; IX, IX, 1; X, 1; XXIV, 1; *Justinian Code,* I, XIII, 1, 2; V. XXVII, 1, 5.

[21]The abolition of torture by the cross (Aurelius Victor, *De Caesaribus,* 41; Sozomen, *Hist. Eccl.,* I, 8; St. Augustine, *Sermo* LXXXVIII, 9) did not occur beginning with this era, as is often said, but in the last years of Constantine; Pio Franchi de'Cavalieri, in *Nuovo bull. di archeologia cristiana,* 1907, p. 64–113.

[22]*Theodosian Code,* IX, XI, 2.

[23]*Justinian Code,* I, XIII, 1.

of Roman citizenship and even giving the clergy the power to make slaves into citizens, regardless of the method used.[24] Starting in 320, he had abolished laws enacted by Augustus against celibacy.[25]

Of the two great religious matters that agitated the Church in the fourth century, that of the Donatists arose before the death of Licinius. Even more than the proofs we have already set forth, it reveals the ardor of the Christian sentiments that animated Constantine in this first period of his reign.

As early as 313, when the party that had attacked the validity of Cecilian's ordination as bishop of Carthage brought its perverse cause before the emperor, Constantine postponed its consideration at a synod convened in Rome. "It will not escape you," he writes to Pope Miltiades, "that I hold the religious and legitimate catholic Church in such respect, that I would not see you endure schisms and divisions among you."[26] The following year, grappling with an an outrageous charge by the Donatists against Felix of Aptunga, who consecrated Cecilian, he made an inquiry in Africa (a strange reversal of situations) that demonstrated, through the testimony of magistrates who were present at the time of the persecution that, far from ever obeying them, Felix had remained firm in his faith. The proconsul of Africa's sentence then discharged his memory of the crime "of having burned the divine books."[27] When the obstinacy of the Donatists obliged the emperor in 314 to convene a council at Arles, the letters written on this occasion left no doubt about the religion he professed. In one, addressed to the vicar of Africa, he complained of the Donatists who "do not want to consider the interest of their salvation, nor, what is still more serious, the respect due to almighty God," and "give occasion to revile those who still freed their sense of the very holy observance of this religion."[28] He added these words, which prove the sincerity of

---

[24]*Ibid.*, 2.

[25]*Theodosian Code*, VIII, xvi, 1.

[26]Eusebius, *Hist. Eccl.*, X, 5, 20.

[27]*Gesta proconsularia quibus absolutus est Felix* (following vol. IX of the *Oeuvres* de saint Augustin, ed. Gaume, p. 1038).

[28]Letter to Ablavius, *ibid.*, p. 1090.

his belief along with the coarse element of personal interest that still mingled with it:

> Certain that you, also, are a worshipper of the supreme God, I confess to you in solemnity that I believe I am allowed neither to tolerate nor to neglect these scandals that may anger the divinity, not only toward humankind, but against myself, since by an act of his good heavenly pleasure he entrusted to me to govern the entire world; moved against me, God could make another decision. Thus I would not be completely and fully at ease, nor promise myself complete happiness through the kindness of almighty God, unless I should see all men joined in fraternal love, rendering to Holy God the regular worship of the catholic religion.[29]

His letter of that same year to Chrest, bishop of Syracuse, contained the same complaints against headstrong people who "forget their own salvation and the veneration due to the holy faith and, tearing each other to pieces by a shameful and detestable division, give occasion for mockery to those whose sentiments are far removed from holy religion."[30] The Donatists' appeal of the council's decisions inspired him to write another letter, addressed to the bishops seated there, which showed more fervently than ever the expression of his Christian convictions. "They ask my judgment," he cries out, "I, who await the judgment of Christ! . . . Yet I say this in truth, the judgment of the priests must be received as if God were seated in person on their tribunal to judge. For it is not permitted them to think and judge anything other than what they have learned through the teaching of Christ!"[31] We know the adventures that followed: the Donatists protesting against the episcopal rulings and persisting in their clamor for civil judges; Constantine consenting, out of weariness or weakness, to remand the matter; Cecilian's innocence solemnly proclaimed by imperial letter in 316; the princeps then turning against the Donatists, confiscating

---

[29] *Ibid.*

[30] Eusebius, *Hist. Eccl.,* X, 5, 22.

[31] Letter to the bishops (following vol. ix of the *Oeuvres* of St Augustine, ed. Gaume, p. 1096).

their churches, and banishing their leaders. When the banished were recalled in 320, Constantine announced this grace in touching terms to the catholic bishops:

> I have known you to be priests and servants of the living God, in that I have not heard you requesting any punishment against the impious, villainous, sacrilegious, profane, or irreligious men who are ungrateful toward their God and the enemies of the Church, but rather see you imploring mercy for them. This is truly knowing God and obeying his commandment; it is true knowledge, for one who spares the enemies of the Church on earth piles punishments upon their heads for all eternity.[32]

Regardless of whether these various pieces were written by Constantine's own hand, or dictated at his command, so that at times we recognize the style of a secretary, it is possible to find in them the sovereign's intimate thought. A princeps as active, personal, and impulsive as Constantine would not allow a subordinate to attribute sentiments to him without his approval. If he believed it useful to give his ideas an impersonal form, he knew how to do so, as witnessed by the Edict of Milan, which addressed followers of both cults and purposely left its expression vague so as to be accepted by all. When addressing Christians, however, he spoke as a Christian. He no longer invoked an abstract divinity, as in the edict, but the living God and Christ himself; he was worried about the good repute of the Church, which he did not wish to expose to the mockeries of the pagans. The "dossier of Donatism," whose initial parts were written in the days following the defeat of Maxentius, provides evidence that by this date Constantine's conversion to Christianity was already an accomplished fact.[33]

Notably, during this first period, Constantine did not indiscreetly hasten to interfere with ecclesiastical matters and to assume the role of "bishop from outside," as he would define himself later on.

---

[32]Letter to the bishops of Numidia (*Oeuvres* of St Augustine, ed. Gaume, vol. IX, p. 1103).

[33]See Duchesne, *Le Dossier du Donatisme*, in *Mélanges d'archéologie et d'histoire de l'École française de Rome*, 1890, p. 589–650. See the observations of Boissier, Acad. des Inscriptions, Nov. 28, 1890.

Undoubtedly, we are somewhat surprised to see this recent convert, who was not even a catechumen yet, convening councils and rendering decisions in matters already judged by them. However, his words and actions show that he was tired of the war forced upon him in some fashion by the Donatists who, after asking to be judged by the bishops, rejected the conciliar decisions and requested civil judges. The austere measures finally taken against them were merely the consequence of their determination to push the ecclesiastical courts to compel the imperial power to deliver a verdict. These measures were nothing less than the first breach opened unconsciously in the Edict of Milan, which allowed everyone to worship God at will. But the breach, as we have seen, was at least partially closed again by the prompt recall of the banished.

2. From the Death of Licinius to the Death of Constantine (324–337)

The battle of Chrysopolis, which ended Licinius' reign, took place in September 323. His death, of which Constantine was probably not innocent, occurred in March of the following year. Falling between these dates are two acts by Constantine of great importance to the history of his religious policies and personal ideas. The first was an edict of reparation, addressed to the bishops of Palestine, through which he restores to Licinius' victims their rank and property. The second was a proclamation to his new subjects in the East, in which he told the history of his life in his own way.

The edict's preamble energetically proclaimed the truth of Christian beliefs. Constantine joined to this an affirmation of his own providential mission. Never had a conqueror come across in this fashion.

> By sending me from the British ocean, from the place where the sun plunges into the waters, God has dissipated before me the clouds that covered the earth so that mankind, instructed by my efforts, was called to observe the sacred law, and the blessed faith grew under the leadership of a powerful master.[34]

---

[34]Eusebius, *De vita Const.,* II, 30.

Thus Constantine enters the East "full of faith in the grace that this holy ministry has entrusted to him." Then follow various articles of the Edict recalling the exiles and the condemned; discharging from the obligations of the curiae (feared at that time as the equivalent of a penalty) those enrolled through a hatred of their religion; restoring Christian officers and soldiers to their ranks, or to the right of an honorable discharge; restoring confiscated property to Christian owners or the martyrs' heirs; naming the church in the place where the martyrs suffered as their successor, if they left no heirs; and, finally, returning to the corporate patrimony of each church the real estate awarded to the treasury.[35] These details show how violent had been the pagan reaction attempted by Licinius. It is interesting to compare the edict of 323, intended to erase all traces of this reaction, with that of Milan. It enters into more details, provides for more cases. We sense that the hand that wrote it had become entirely free.

In his proclamation to the easterners,[36] Constantine, with an even more extraordinary liberty, describes Diocletian's persecution and his own victories, and outlines the program of his policy. Regarding the persecutions, we are listening to a true witness, since he spent the greater part of that time at the court of Nicomedia. When he recalls the atrocity of the edicts, the courage of the martyrs, and how nature itself was disturbed by their suffering, he sounds like Eusebius. When he sets forth the punishment of the persecutors, we seem to be reading Lactantius, but from the movement of the thought, the sound of the language, at once pious and domineering, and the triumphant tone of the words, we recognize Constantine alone. It is not the text that most clearly bears his mark of authenticity.[37] It is both a song of victory and a hymn of gratitude to God that Constantine, at the head of his armies, has borne the "sign" everywhere.

---

[35] *Ibid.*, 30–41.

[36] *Ibid.*, II, 48–60.

[37] The authenticity of the edict and the proclamation of 323 has been contested by Crivellucci (*Della fede storica di Eusebio nella vita di Constantino*) and Schultze (*Zeitschrift fuer Kirchengeschichte*, 1894, n. 4). See, in the opposite sense, the observations of Boissier (*La Fin du Paganisme*, vol. I, p. 17) and Seeck (*Zeitschr. Fuer Kirchengesch.*, 1897, n. 3).

But the newfound success that made the Christian princeps sole master of the empire did not make him abandon religious tolerance. In two places in his proclamation, he renewed his commitment to tolerance in formal terms. In the first, Constantine addresses God himself.

> I would that your people live in peace and concord, for the common advantage of mankind. Let those still involved in the error of paganism joyfully rejoice in the same peace and rest as the faithful. This resumption of good mutual relations will do much to bring people back on the right track. Let no one, therefore, harm another. Let each one follow the opinion he prefers. Let those who think well be persuaded that only those whom you yourself have called to observe your sacred laws will live in justice and purity. As for those who refuse, let them retain the temples of deception as long as they wish. We, for our part, maintain the splendid dwelling of truth, which you gave to us at the time of our (spiritual) birth. And we wish others to live happily, as a result of the union and concord of all.[38]

The second passage, which serves as the conclusion to the entire text, reveals the depth of Constantine's thought.

> Let no one pick a quarrel with another because of his opinions. Rather, let each make use of what he knows to aid his neighbor or, if that is not possible, to leave him in peace. For it is one thing to voluntarily accept combat for an immortal belief; it is another to impose it through violence and tortures. I spoke at greater length than the purposes of my clemency required, because I wished to conceal nothing of my faith, and also because several assure me that the rites and ceremonies of error, and every power of darkness, will be abolished altogether. Certainly, this would have been my counsel to everyone, but stubborn error is still too deeply rooted in the souls of some, to their misfortune.[39]

[38]Eusebius, *De vita Const.*, II, 53.
[39]*Ibid.*, II, 60.

On the day after the victory over Licinius, Constantine thus recalled the principles proclaimed after Maxentius' defeat. The language, however, is different, and the tone of the edict and of his proclamation to the East bears little resemblance to that of the Edict of Milan. On the one hand, this is because in 313 Constantine had Licinius, who remained a pagan, as his colleague and even collaborator; on the other hand, he felt too little strengthened by his recent victory to let his most intimate feelings show through an official act. As other texts more or less contemporary to the Edict of Milan have shown, he was very attached to Christianity. Yet if he allowed himself be seen in this light, in all frankness, by the Christians, he would not yet have dared or wanted to address himself in the same style to every inhabitant of the empire. Now, he spoke the same language in an edict as he did in a letter to a bishop or council. The official neutrality had disappeared even from his discourse to the pagans. He told them his greatest desire would be to see all his subjects embrace Christianity. If he respected the conscience of unbelievers, it was by deploring their "obstinacy." He authorized them to keep their rituals and ceremonies, but labeled them as "rites and ceremonies of error," the work of "the power of darkness." He left them the right to visit their temples, but contrasted these "temples of deception" to the "splendid dwelling of truth."

In another piece difficult to date, but which in all probability is linked to this same period, Constantine's expressions concerning pagan worship are harsher still, almost insulting, but the same promise of freedom is found there. It was a speech to "the assembly of saints,"[40] a type of conference or declamation of the sort that Constantine, as Eusebius reports, sometimes recited.[41] The harsher language is explained by the fact that the speech was destined, as the title indicates, for a Christian audience, probably an ecclesiastical one. The liberal conclusion that emerged from it thus has all the more value. Even when speaking of the old cult with spiteful passion, Constantine was committed to letting it live.

---

[40] *Oratio Constantini ad sanctorum coelum;* Migne, *Patr. Gr.,* vol. XX, col. 1233–1315. The authenticity of this speech has been contested.

[41] Eusebius, *De vita Const.,* IV, 17, 29.

We must now find out how these principles were applied. Constantine himself recalled that the pagans experienced great fear after the fall of Licinius. Since they had made common cause with him in the East, they expected reprisals. Measures contrary to their religion would have seemed natural to them, almost legitimate. Constantine confined himself to only the most basic. In the West, where his authority had never been threatened, and where at most there were reports of some local discontent[42] among the pagans, he did not need to make any changes. In the East, he eradicated the officially pagan character that Licinius had bestowed upon the entire administration, dismissing the officials. Where he did not establish Christian magistrates, he ordered the pagans he left in office to abstain from public sacrifice.[43] At the same time he reinstated the orders of 319 and 321 on divination, which had been repealed by his rival.[44] The only measure directly affecting pagan worship was a law cited by Eusebius: Constantine forbade the erection of new idols in the East.[45] Probably this law was purely circumstantial, inspired by the political necessities of the moment, and destined not to survive.

An examination of the public acts of Constantine during the last period of his reign shows no fundamental change in the system of tolerance adopted in 313. The changes were mostly in form. Constantine expressed his contempt for the old cult with less vehemence, and his attachment to the new. Officially, however, he remained the leader of paganism. Inscriptions from 328 assign him the title of sovereign pontifex.[46] A law posterior to Constantine, but making allusion to the events of 333, reveals that during this period in Rome one could not demolish a funerary monument, even when threatened with ruin, without previously having presented a request to the college of pontifices.[47] Laws of 335 and 337 confirmed the privileges of the perpetual flamines and the municipal priests.[48] Constantine made no distinction

[42] *Theodosian Code*, XVI, 5.
[43] Eusebius, *De vita Const.*, II, 41.
[44] *Ibid.*, 45.
[45] *Ibid.*
[46] Eckhel, *Doctr. numm.*, vol. VIII, p. 76; Orelli, *Inscr.*, 1080.
[47] *Theodosian Code*, IX, XVII. 2.
[48] *Ibid.*, XII, I, 21; V, 2.

between pagans and Christians in the distribution of magistracies and favors.[49] In the East, where he preferred to stay, the Christians probably formed the majority of those around him; in Rome, however, the inscriptions show many nobles invested under his reign with consulates or prefectures while remaining members of the sacerdotal college of fifteen, pontifices, augurs, or initiates of Hecate and Mithras.[50]

We must therefore set aside—or apply only to certain facts—the commonly held views of Christian writers who speak of Constantine as if he had declared war on the temples and forbidden sacrifices.[51] He prohibited secret sacrifices and those mixed with divination, and probably also sacrifices offered by the magistrates in the name of the state, but he did not touch the freedom of cults. He sometimes abused his power by removing statues and art objects from buildings consecrated to the gods in order to adorn Constantinople, which in 329 became the second capital of the empire,[52] but these blameworthy whims of the absolute sovereign do not constitute religious persecution. If he destroyed some temples in Egypt, Phoenicia, and Cilicia, it was because these degenerate sanctuaries sheltered scenes of revolting immorality.[53] In support of his conduct, he could invoke the example of pagan governments[54] and his rights and duties as sovereign pontifex. The demolition or closure of other temples during this period was most often at the initiative of the towns themselves. Under Diocletian, we saw this happen to an entire Christian city in Phrygia;[55] it is not surprising to encounter something similar in the East at the time of Constantine.[56] In an indirect manner, the emperor encouraged movements of mass conversion, which sometimes took place in villages and

[49]St Gregory of Nazianzus, *Oratio* VI, 98.

[50]*Corpus inscr. lat.*, vol. VI, 1675, 1690–1694; vol. X, 5061. Cf. Tillemont, *Hist.des Empereurs*, vol. IV, p. 183, 218.

[51]Eusebius, *De vita Constant.*, II, 45; IV, 23, 25; Socrates, I, 18; Sozomen, I, 8; Theodoret, I, 1; III, 21; Orosius, VII, 28; St. Jerome, *Chron. olymp.* 278.

[52]Eusebius, *De laud. Const.*, 8; Socrates, *Hist. Eccl.*, I, 16, 17; Sozomen, II, 5; Zosimus, II, 32.

[53]Eusebius, *De vita Const.*, III, 55, 57; *Praep. Evang.*, IV, 16; Socrates, *Hist. Eccl.*, I, 18; Sozomen, I, 8; V, 10.

[54]Titus Livius, *Hist.*, XXXIX, 8–10; Josephus, *Ant. Jud.*, XVIII, 3.

[55]Eusebius, *Hist. Eccl.*, VIII, 10.

[56]Sozomen, *Hist. Eccl.*, II, 5; V, 4.

market towns; he granted them honorific names, the title of "city," and the right to be called Constantia or Constantine.[57]

During the fourteen years he reigned alone, Constantine thus maintained religious tolerance. He showed kindness to people without regard for religious affiliation. But he took no pains to conceal his preference for the Christian religion, nor his growing aversion toward paganism. He followed the Edict of Milan to the letter, if not always in spirit. Little by little, he came to grant paganism only what was strictly necessary, parsimoniously meting out the air it needed to breathe. A law of 326[58] commanded the provincial governors to complete public buildings begun by their predecessors before undertaking new ones, with the exception of temples, which could be left unfinished.[59] Around 327, responding to the inhabitants of Spello, who asked him for permission to build a family temple which would become the center and occasion for a new institution of provincial games, Constantine laid down the formal condition that the temple be no more than a simple commemorative building, and would "not be sullied by the fraud of any contagious superstition,"[60] that is to say, by any act of paganism. Constantine's contempt for the gods even led him to forget the reserve imposed upon a sovereign. A scoffer by nature,[61] in 326 he not only refused to be part of a solemn procession in Rome, led by the equestrian order to offer sacrifice at the Capitol, but also mocked it publicly.[62]

Unfortunately, the time would come when his zeal for the Church would reveal itself to be as indiscreet as his hatred of paganism appears in this circumstance. With some indisputable excesses, which he quickly repressed, Constantine proved himself useful to the orthodox cause against the Donatists, so much so that, in the otherwise serious and important question of Arianism, he gradually spoiled what had

---

[57]Eusebius, *De vita Const.,* IV, 38, 39; Sozomen, V, 3.

[58]*Theodosian Code,* XV, I, 3.

[59]At least as it appears to me, this is the meaning of this often controversial law. See *Revue des questions historiques,* October 1891, p. 362.

[60]Orelli-Hensen, 5580.

[61]Aurelius Victor, *Epitome,* 41.

[62]*Id., Ibid.;* Zosimus, II, 20.

at first been beneficial about his intervention. The latter intervention began fortunately, proceeding from sentiments he had lately expressed in the matter of the Donatists. Probably without fully understanding the doctrinal importance of the new debate, Constantine was moved to find a division of minds there where he should have encountered only unity of faith and simplicity of belief. In a letter of 323, in which he tries to reconcile Arius with the bishop of Alexandria, there is a cry of anguish: "Give me back my quiet days and nights without anxiety.... How can my mind be at rest so long as the people of God, the people of my brothers in the service of God, is divided by a deep and unjust dissent?"[63] When the Council of Nicaea opened at his convocation, he addressed a welcoming speech to the bishops. He proclaimed himself "their brother in the service of God," and confessed that "the divisions of the Church seemed more terrible and dreadful to him than any war."[64] After the council's decision, he raged against Arius and his books,[65] then sent an enthusiastic and joyful letter[66] to the churches, particularly the one at Alexandria. Then, taking leave of the bishops, he recommended the avoidance of disputes "which are subject to laughter by those who always slander the divine law. It is of these," he adds, "that we must think, for we can gain them if everything done between us remains irreproachable."[67] With touching solicitude, Constantine watched over the faith that became his own as one would watch over a precious and fragile treasure. He wished to see it as mistress of the empire, and he suffered impatiently anything that compromised its good name, or delayed its conquests. But soon the sincere and naïve good will that allowed him to call himself "the bishop from outside"[68] would result in strange and ill-advised abuses. Receptive to the self-interested flatteries of Eusebius of Nicomedia, he began to lean towards Arianism, or at least to favor the troublemakers at the risk of compromising the work of Nicaea. Intoxicated by absolute power, he

[63]Socrates, *Hist. Eccl.*, I, 7.
[64]Eusebius, *De vita Constant.*, III, 12; Sozomen, *Hist. Eccl.*, I, 17.
[65]Socrates, *Hist. Eccl.*, I, 30; Sozomen, I, 30.
[66]Socrates, I, 9.
[67]Eusebius, *De vita Constant.*, III, 20.
[68]*Ibid.*, 21.

believed that everything was permitted and decided to be a religious dictator; he enjoined Athanasius to receive Arius and threatened him with deposition from the episcopal throne. Even then, however, his conscience and instinct for government reawakened. Not only did he never carry out his threat, but later, writing to the council of Tyre, which had deliberated under shrewd and fierce pressure from Athanasius' enemies, he uttered for the last time the lament of a believer scandalized to see discord where there should be union.

> I do not understand anything of what you have decided in your assembly in the midst of so many troubles and storms. I fear that the truth may disappear amidst such violence.... You will not deny that I am God's faithful servant, for it is thanks to the worship I render to him that peace reigns on earth, and that his name is blessed even by barbarians who were previously ignorant of the truth. These barbarians would serve well as our models, for they observe the law of God because they fear our power, while we, who profess rather than observe the holy faith of the Church, always do the things that inspire hatred and discord, and which tend to ruin mankind.[69]

Thus Constantine, in a sincere tone of suffering, was still speaking a year before his death, and a few months before the belated baptism that ushered him at last into the bosom of the Church that he had served and tyrannized in turn, but always passionately loved. A very remarkable sense of catholicity, which in some measure compensated for and corrected his errors, made him hate even the shadow of discord in the Church. Unity seemed to him to be its divine character. If he forgot religious tolerance from time to time, it was occasioned by Christians he considered rebels against this unity. Respecting the existence of pagan worship, which he sometimes reviled, and which hindered some of his actions, but whose essential liberties he at least guaranteed, he reserved his severity for heretics and those he considered such. He prosecuted them less to carry out the decisions of the councils than to satisfy himself and to fulfill the mission in which he believed himself

[69]Socrates, I, 31; Sozomen, II, 18.

invested. Hence, in addition to many detailed measures, a general law of 311 was issued forbidding sects of every denomination, banning their books, banishing their leaders, confiscating their churches, and forbidding their assemblies.[70] How could Constantine reconcile such legislation with the freedom of religion he solemnly promised on several occasions? It would easy to label it a contradiction or failure to keep his word on the part of an absolute and capricious princeps who, in the last years of his reign, allowed no obstruction of his will. We believe, however, that the explanation is simpler. When we closely examine Constantine's words and deeds, we recognize that religious freedom, according to his thinking, was concerned only with paganism, on the one hand, and the catholic Church on the other. Weighed side by side, the terms of the edicts of 313 and of 323 leave little doubt on this subject. What Constantine wanted to establish was not religious freedom, as we moderns understand it, but a sort of *modus vivendi* between two powers long at war: paganism, taken as a whole, and the catholic Church—to his eyes, the only legitimate form of Christianity. The various heretical denominations remained outside these promises and could not invoke official tolerance, but depended upon the imperial good pleasure. Constantine was forbidden to close a temple, but believed he was entirely right in confiscating and destroying a chapel belonging to the Valentinians, Marcionites, Kataphrygians, or even the Novatians, without violating his commitments.

3. Constans and Constantius (337–361)

What was to become of the religious policy inaugurated by Constantine? And how would relations between paganism and Christianity be continued by his successors?

Three years after the death of the first Christian emperor, the answers were no longer in doubt. A system rather simple in appearance, quite uncertain and contradictory in practice, yet nevertheless accepted by all—and thanks to which it was able to preserve the balance between two rival cults for a quarter century—now received an

---

[70]Eusebius, *De vita Const.*, III, 61, 65. Sozomen, *Hist. Eccl.*, II, 33.

initial attack. "Let superstition cease," states a law of 241 signed by the two Augusti, Constantius and Constans, "and let the foolishness of sacrifices be abolished; for whoever dares to celebrate the sacrifices, contrary to the order of our divine father, will be punished."[71] We note the care with which the two emperors invoked the standard intentions of Constantine in support of these severe measures. They even went so far as to claim a formal act on his part. No trace of such an act is preserved in the codes. The authentic texts from Constantine that survive all proclaim a different policy, as we have seen. Must we believe that in the last years of his reign Constantine repudiated it to the point of banishing the pagan cult, despite so many promises to tolerate it?[72] In his sons' allusion to a law made by the great emperor, should we see the altered, enlarged, and generalized memories of those laws he actually issued against divination and secret sacrifices, or the transitory measures he took in the East after the defeat of Licinius?[73] The answer will probably always remain uncertain, but the hypothesis we have outlined is not infeasible. Constantine's children seemed to have been willing to ascribe their own intentions to him. Thus, in pursuit of the praiseworthy goal of preparing the return of the exiled Athanasius, Constantine the Younger alleged without proof, and against all probability, a resolution that only death would have prevented his father from accomplishing.[74]

The law of Constantius and Constans could not fail to please certain Christians. Even in the West, where paganism still had many roots, it awakened premature hopes. The welcome it was given by eager minds seems to prove that it inaugurated a new policy and marked a decisive step along a path that Constantine had barely trodden. In his intriguing book, written between 343 and 350, Firmicus Maternus lauds the

[71]*Theodosian Code*, XVI, x, 2.

[72]In this sense, see Tillemont, *Hist. des Empereurs*, vol. IV, p. 202; Chastel, *Hist. de la destruction du paganisme en Orient*, p. 74; Schultze, *Geschichte des Untergangs des griechich-roemischen Heidenthums*, vol. I, p. 59.

[73]In this sense, La Bastie, *Mém. sur le souverain pontificat des empereurs romains*, in *Mém. de l'Acad. des Inscriptions*, vol. XV, 1743, p. 100; Beugnot, *Hist. de la destr. du paganisme en Occident*, vol. I, p. 100; A. de Broglie, *L'Église et l'Empire romain au IVe siècle*, vol. I, p. 462ff.

[74]St Athanasius, *Apol.*

two emperors as destroyers of the temples and the gods. "Your laws," he tells them, "have almost entirely defeated the devil and dissipated the fatal contagion by extinguishing idolatry."[75] He exhorted them to pursue their work and to overthrow through violence what remained of the old cult. It is hard to imagine such a text addressed to Constantine. It seems strangely out of place, even in the empire he passed on to his sons, and its tumultuous cry does not agree with the sound of the facts. A year after the law that inspired these strains from Firmicus Maternus, Constantius addressed another to the prefect of Rome. Knowing the attachments of the westerners over whom he reigned, especially the Romans' ties to paganism, he attempted to calm their uneasiness. He writes, "Superstition must be overthrown from top to bottom," and then adds, "However, we desire that the temples located in the vicinity of the city be preserved intact and without defilement, because several of them are attached to the origins of the games, races, and combats that from all antiquity are the joy of the Roman people."[76] The Romans scarcely felt the need of such reassurance: in the very year during which this law was promulgated, they had a pagan prefect who was a member of the college of augurs and very devoted to Hercules.[77] The consul of the following year freely adorned himself with the titles of augur, quindecemvir, and pontifex.[78]

We can continue the comparison between the laws designed to destroy idolatry and the facts, which show it to be in full vigor. Constans, having become sole master of the empire through the death of his brother, promulgated in 353 a new law injurious to the pagans (whom it treats as "lost") and terrible in its punishment: the death penalty for idol-worshippers. The temples were to be closed and the sacrifices forbidden.[79] Orfitus, prefect of Rome this same year, and who through an exceptional favor would remain in charge for the next five years, nevertheless retained the titles pontifex of the Sun and pontifex of Vesta in

[75]Firmicus Maternus, *De errore prof. relig.,* 21.

[76]*Theodosian Code,* XVI, x, 3.

[77]Wilmanns, *Exempla inscr. lat.* 1230 a b c; *Bull. della comm. archeol. com. di Roma,* 1889, p. 42.

[78]Wilmanns, 1228.

[79]*Theodosian Code,* XVI, x, 4.

the inscriptions.[80] The Roman calendar of 354 cited all the pagan feasts as still being observed, not only those consisting of games or spectacles, but also those involving pilgrimages, processions, and sacrifices.[81] A third law, from 356, once again decreed the death penalty against anyone convicted of having participated in sacrifices or worshipping idols.[82] In the year following its promulgation Constans visited Rome, admired the beauty of the temples, and confirmed the privileges of the Vestals and the customary subsidies to the pagan cult. Then, fulfilling the office of sovereign pontifex to the letter, he named members of the Roman aristocracy to the various priesthoods considered hereditary in their families.[83] The only indication he gave of his personal beliefs was to remove the statue of Victory from the curia on the day he took his seat there.[84] A few years later a pagan senator, describing his voyage to Rome, uttered this unexpected praise of the author of the laws of 341, 353, and 356: "He preserved the ancient cult for the empire, though he himself followed another religion."[85]

Does this imply that these laws remained unenforced everywhere? Probably not, but they were applied especially where public opinion made it possible. As we have seen, they had little effect in the West. In the East, the power of paganism varied according to province and town—extensive in one place, all but destroyed elsewhere. Places inhabited by fanatical idolaters were close to other locales where Christians already formed the majority or nearly the totality of the inhabitants. In such places, neither the closing of temples nor the outlawing of sacrifices presented problems; popular initiative sometimes even preceded the law. These favorable environments saw the construction of churches using the remains of pagan sanctuaries during this period.[86] There was also the less edifying spectacle of courtiers "stuffed with remnants

[80]*Corp. inscr. lat.*, vol. VI, 1737–1742.

[81]*Ibid.*, vol. I, p. 234ff.

[82]*Theodosian Code*, XVI, x, 6.

[83]Symmachus, *Ep.* X, 3; cf. Ammianus Marcellinus, XVI, 20. In the same year, 357, we see a most famous personage presiding over the Mithraic initiations at Rome. *Corp. inscr. lat.* Vol. VI, 749.

[84]St Ambrose, *Ep.* 18.

[85]Symmachus, *Ep.* X, 3.

[86]Sozomen, *Hist. Eccl.*, III, 37.

of temples," according to the testimony of Ammianus Marcellinus.[87] Yet even where such abuses were committed, at least one part of the laws forbidding idolatry was never exercised: we cannot cite a single case where the death penalty was inflicted on a pagan practicing his religion. The uncle of one of the classmates of the famous rhetor Libanius "lived more in company of the gods than with men," according to Libanius' expression; he never ceased to worship them, "in spite of the law that pronounced the death penalty against their worshippers."[88] In the cities where paganism was dominant, however, the law was not carried out against the temples any more than it was carried out elsewhere against individuals. Alexandria, under Constans, was full of pagan sanctuaries where the cult had undergone no interruption.[89] Many other cities, even in the East, kept up their temples and their feasts.[90]

Constans prosecuted paganism in other ways, attacking it indirectly through various laws against the divinatory arts. These laws belonged to the end of his reign, from 353 to 358. They employed purposely vague language, subjecting anyone who consulted with magicians, Chaldeans, diviners, augurs, or haruspices to severe penalties.[91] We cannot accept that Constans wanted to proscribe the official haruspex, recognized by Constantine, or still less to destroy the college of augurs, composed of the greatest figures in Rome, and which the inscriptions show to be still in operation until the close of the century.[92] He was evidently against private augurs and haruspices who worked in the shadows, with neither supervision nor sanction, and were no different from common diviners. But it was hard for this unreserved disapproval, which seemed to surround anyone engaged in divining the future, to be extended to the highest representatives of pagan divination. These laws were probably invoked at the numerous trials concerning sorcery

[87] Ammianus Marcellinus, XXII, 4. On the gifts made to Arian churches at the expense of the temples, see St Hilary, *Ad Constant. Imp.*

[88] Libanius, ed. Reiske, vol. II, p. 11.

[89] Libanius, *Pro templis*, ed. Reiske, vol. II, p. 181; Themistius, *Oratio* IV; *Vetus orbis descriptio*, ed. Godefroy, p. 17. See, however, Sozomen, IV, 10.

[90] Eunapius, *Vitae sophist., Prohaeresius; Vetus orbis descr.*, p. 15.

[91] *Theodosian Code*, IX, XVI, 4, 5, 6.

[92] *Corp. inscr. lat.*, vol. VI, 503, 504, 511, 1778.

and lèse-majesty that bloodied the end of Constans' reign. An example of one of these trials demonstrates once more the illusory character of the penalties imposed against another crime, that of sacrifice. The philosopher Demetrius Chytras was accused of having consulted an oracle in 359 concerning the fate of the emperor. In his defense, he declared that he had offered sacrifices several times, as he had been doing since childhood, but only to appease the gods and not in order to know the future. This explanation led to his acquittal.[93]

Such was Constans' policy with regard to paganism. Repudiating the tolerance promised by Constantine, its results did not make up for abandoning those commitments. Powerless and irritating, this policy did not undermine paganism where it was strong, precipitating its decline only where it fell of its own accord, and sowing in the pagan mind the seeds of anger that sprouted under Julian. Thus, on the whole, Constans' policy slowed more than it hastened the old cult's inevitable downfall.

Constans' conduct towards the Christians managed to discredit the cause he wished to serve with such impetuosity. The divisions between children of the one Church, which so often frightened Constantine, and in which he perceived the greatest obstacle to the conversion of the idolaters, soured under his successor's reign as a result of his personal actions. The time came when it could no longer be discerned whether he was at war against the idol worshippers or the Christians who remained faithful to the definitions of Nicaea. His soldiers never committed excesses inside a temple equal to those that bloodied the basilicas of Alexandria and Constantinople, for the purpose of driving out the orthodox pastors and installing interlopers. If at times we seem to see scenes borrowed from the worst eras of the persecution, the catholic Christians, not the idolaters, were its victims. Athanasius had to flee Alexandria in the face of Constans' assassins, just as his predecessors Dionysius and Peter had previously fled the executioners of Decius and Maximinus. Unanimous in passively resisting the laws that threatened the old cult, the pagans were strengthened in their convictions by the sight of the internal struggles of their conquerors. They

---

[93] Ammianus Marcellinus, XIX, 12.

sensed that Arianism, sustained by the imperial power, worked in their favor. We are told that in 356 troops of pagans enlisted by Constans' officers invaded a church in Alexandria where an orthodox population was assembled. They committed every of desecration while shouting: "Constans has become a Hellenist, and the Arians have recognized our mysteries."[94] They were sadly mistaken about the facts, for 356 was the same year that Constans rendered one of his laws against idolatry. But it was a matter of judging the situation with the sure instinct of the crowd and, but for a simple confusion of names, announcing the future avenger who, while silently assisting in Christendom's agony, waited impatiently for the hour of Hellenism's restoration.

---

[94]*Hellēn gegone Kōnstantios, kai hoi Arianoi ta hēmōn epe gnōskon.* Athanasius, *Ad solit.*

CHAPTER SIX
The Pagan Reaction—Julian (355-363)

1. The Religion of Julian

Julian's meteoric career may be summarized in a few words: the violent death of his parents; his studious and half-captive youth; his unexpected elevation to the rank of Caesar; his brilliant victories in Gaul and Germany; the military riot that proclaimed him Augustus; his break with Constantius; his taking possession of the empire; his unfortunate war against the Persians; his death near Ctesiphon. In this life cut short by so many adventures, and apparently agitated by so many external events, posterity has perceived what actually filled it: the inner drama that detached Julian from Christianity, followed by an uninterrupted effort to demolish the faith and rebuild the cult of the gods. Once this idea entered his heart, it never left Julian. It accompanied him when he left Gaul, followed him on his march against Constantius, and inspired his every policy once he was sole emperor. It haunted him during his preparations for war against Persia, accompanied him in the crossing of Asia Minor that led him to his tragic destiny, and left the princeps dying without having realized his goal, crushed under his dream.

It is difficult to say what brought Julian to break with Christianity. Did his hatred of Constantius, whom he accused murdering his father, instinctively cast him into a religious party opposed to that of his family's persecutor? Or did the Arianism of the priests to whom his religious education had been entrusted[1] leave him with a false and incomplete idea of Christian doctrine and the faith's adherents? Everything leads us to believe that more direct influences attracted him to the old cult. His private tutor, the eunuch Mardonius, was a passionate admirer of Homer.[2] Early on, the *Iliad* and the *Odyssey* caused

---

[1] Ammianus Marcellinus, XXII, 9.
[2] Julian, *Misopogon*, ed. Hertlein, p. 453.

the young man to regard the gospel and the Bible with disgust. His extensive knowledge of Jewish and Christian books remained entirely external and never passed into his soul. From the start, he became accustomed to viewing their authors as barbarians. The prophets and apostles seemed vulgar to him, compared to the brilliant civilization of the Greeks. Mardonius was not only enthusiastic about poets: well-versed in philosophy,[3] he opened the eyes of his student to the beauties of Plato and Aristotle. The moral isolation in which Julian lived, in a distant castle of Cappadocia, with no companion his age other than his brother Gallus, left him defenseless in the face of impressions all the more vivid with nothing to distract him. When he received permission to study first at the schools of Constantinople, then in Nicomedia, Pergamum, and Athens, he was already a pagan in mind and heart, or at least a Hellenist.[4] The Christian practices he still observed, and which he prudently followed until 301,[5] masked a dead faith. In his *Letter to the Alexandrians*, written in 362, he himself fixed the time he began to attend the schools of the sophists—the date of his inner adherence to paganism—twelve years earlier, that is to say, in 350.[6] Contact with the neoplatonists lifted the last obstacle. One thing had long prevented Julian from taking the decisive step: he preserved from his early Christian education an almost insurmountable aversion to the plurality of gods.[7] Neoplatonic doctrine taught him to reconcile this plurality with the unity of a supreme Being, and to make this ancient fable into an idea less irreconcilable with reason. Degenerate as they had become, these doctrines thrilled his soul with a taste of the marvelous. Through initiations, recollection, and the practice of theurgy, Maximus of Ephesus revealed to him every occult aspect, every intoxicating and unhealthy illusion of paganism.[8] From that time on, Julian subscribed to it entirely, remaining Christian in appearance to the point

[3]Julian, *Against the Cynic Heraclius; Misopogon;* Hertlein, p. 301, 456, 414.

[4]*A rudimentis pueritiae primis inclinatior erat erga numinum cultum.* Ammianus Marcellinus, XXII, 5.

[5]Ammianus Marcellinus, XXI, 2.

[6]Julian, *Ep.* 51.

[7]Libanius, *Prosphon.* ed. Reiske, vol. I, p. 408; *Epitaph., ibid.,* p. 528.

[8]Eunapius, *Vitae sophist.* Maximus.

of affecting a monastic bearing in order to ward off the suspicions that had already arisen,[9] but pagan in reality, "a lion dressed in the skin of a donkey," according to words, more biting than proud, of his panegyrist Libanius.[10]

What was Julian's religion, then? It was nothing like the religion of ancient Rome, which was naturalistic in its origins but now quite formalistic and official, still speaking to the people through the pomp of ceremony and spectacle, yet in essence little more than a political cult in which the principal priests comprised so many aristocratic fiefdoms. The devout African who, in an inscription found in Numidia, describes Julian as "the restorer of the Roman religion,"[11] verges on misinterpretation. In Rome, they seem to have been the better judges. While taking satisfaction in seeing a pagan on the throne, the Roman aristocracy seems to have avoided compromising its cause. When Julian made his vehement case against Constantius before the senate in November 361, the assembly reminded the usurper of the respect due to the Augustus, the author of his fortune.[12] At no time in Julian's reign were there reports of a marked eagerness to serve him on the part of the senators. It appears that Roman paganism supposed him not to be its enemy, most likely, but in some respects a rival, and thus watched him proceed without interfering much in his actions. By presenting himself as the champion of "Hellenism," to use his expression—that is to say, of the intellectual, literary, and artistic religion of Greece— rather than of the official religion of Rome, Julian perhaps neglected the only force that would have lent strong support to his enterprise. In this, he showed little political sense.

Even in the belief that he served the Greek religion, however, he seems to have misread his own thinking. We find great differences between the anthropomorphism of the finished contours of Hellenism at the most beautiful epoch of its history, gracious and pure as the lines of the statues of Phidias or Praxiteles, and the vague, whimsical, almost elusive religion of Julian. We discern only with difficulty his

[9]Socrates, III, 1; Sozomen, V, 2.
[10]Libanius, *Epitaph.*; Reiske, vol. I, p. 528.
[11]*Corpus inscr. lat.,* vol. VIII, 4326.
[12]Ammianus Marcellinus, XXI, 20.

idea of the gods; perhaps he would have had trouble defining it himself. Sometimes he saw in them beings altogether distinct and personal, which appeared to him in every great crisis of his life, to the point that their features, according to Libanius, became as familiar as those of his friends. Sometimes the gods were confused in his eyes with the various nations that a supreme Providence had appointed them to protect. They shaped the temperament of each people in conformity to their own type; on this basis, Julian declared himself ready to worship even the God of the Jews. But more frequently the traditional divinities were transformed by him into purely intelligible concepts, floating ideas without a precise contour, nebulous realities that the philosopher's imagination forms and deforms in the service of the theory he constructs. He then borrowed from all sides: neoplatonism, the oriental mysteries, the gnostic systems. All this can be found in his praise of the Mother of the gods; his discourse in honor of the King-Sun is even somewhat reminiscent of Christian theology.

However, Julian's religion was far removed from purely philosophical dilettantism, for in it superstition played a very personal and vivid part. If this religion was linked above all to neoplatonism, the latter was a decadent form virtually devoid of the nobility and simplicity of its origins. In his desire to enter into a relationship with the gods, Julian was satisfied neither with the intellectual ecstasy of Plotinus, nor with the inner purification of Porphyry. Along with Jamblichus, he asked for something more exciting: a method by which to compel the gods according to the singular power of the word "theurgy," an almost mechanical procedure for attracting the heavenly powers to himself. He once described this state as a "bacchic frenzy," contrary to reason. Speaking pompously of the knowledge of God, scorning the uninitiated, the school to which Julian belonged understood knowledge as something entirely different from the strong and sober certainty achieved by faith. It was mingled with something experimental and sensitive, an effort, a trembling nervosity, a disordered mixture of the ambiguous, which no true worshiper has never experienced, and which is unknown to Christian ecstasy. In Jamblichus, Maximus, and Julian we find the modern "medium" far more than we do the philosopher.

2. The Reform of Paganism

Whatever Julian's opinion of the gods may have been, the first act of his religious reform was to reorganize their worship. He gave an example of this by fulfilling every sacred office himself, at the risk of exciting the ridicule of those who saw him carrying the wood, blowing on the fire, handling the sacrificer's knife, constantly questioning the entrails of the victims, and walking surrounded by the bacchantes and favorites in a shameful parade at certain pagan feasts.[13] But he made up for this ridicule and the excesses of his superstition[14] through the idea he had formed of the priesthood. As bizarre as the practice was, the theory was quite elevated. It seems that nothing so healthy and also right can be found in Julian's ideas. The priestly character, he says, merits respect and homage even when the man endowed with it shows himself unworthy of the sacred office. But the priest must make every effort to lead an exemplary life. In accepting this title, he is obligated to the highest virtues. He must have great devotion to the gods and a scrupulous exactness in his liturgical duties; he must be simple in life, clothing, and manners, observing continence and abstaining from evil reading, dishonest spectacles, taverns, and shameful occupations. Moreover, the priestly vocation depends upon neither birth nor fortune: "the most virtuous men, the most religious, the most humane, whether rich or poor, obscure or famous,"[15] must be called to the service of the altars.

Such, for Julian, was the priestly ideal. Perhaps nowhere else did the restorer of Hellenism show himself to be less Roman. Instead of Rome, which made the highest political personages members of the sacerdotal colleges and at the same time holders of the great religious offices, the priestly order was to remain almost without contact with the outside in the pagan church that Julian organized. He recommended that the priest abstain from public affairs, visit the magistrates only rarely, and seldom visit the agora and forum. Here emerges the

---

[13] Ammianus Marcellinus, XXII, 14; St Gregory of Nazianzus, *Oratio* V, 22; St John Chrysostom, *De S. Babyla adversus Julianum et Gentiles*, 14.

[14] Ammianus Marcellinus, XXV, 4.

[15] Julian, *Fragment of a Letter*; Ep. 49, 62; Hertlein, p. 380–391, 552, 583.

almost unconscious tactics of Julian. Through an involuntary homage to Christianity, he tried to transfer its virtues to the pagan world. The priest, as he portrayed him, was not the Latin priest who engaged in business, a civil servant who officially attended the games and spectacles as well as the theatre—where the love affairs of the gods were mocked—and the amphitheater, inundated with human blood.[16] Nor was he the oriental or Greek priest, more separated from politics, more isolated in his religious office, but often profligate and orgiastic. Julian wrote with his eyes fixed on the Christian priest, who was chosen independently of birth or fortune, and upon whom the laws of the Church imposed not only purity of life but also abstinence from secular office, evil companions, shameful occupations, and the spectacles.[17]

Forming an exemplary clergy for the gods was the basis of Julian's religious construction. Upon this foundation, following the example given fifty years earlier by Maximin Daia, he built an entire hierarchy in more or less exact imitation of the Christian hierarchy. The high priest of each province was a type of metropolitan, having "general stewardship of everything that concerns religion, authority over the priests of the cities and villages, and the right to judge the actions of each,"[18] a chief hierarch[19] corresponding directly to "the sovereign pontifex who presides over the cult of the gods"—in other words, Julian himself.[20] But for Julian it was not only a matter of reproducing the constitution of the Church from the outside; he also had to steal something of her spirit. Christianity's strength lies in obedience to the commandment of the Lord: "Go, teach all the nations." The Christian priest doubles as an apostle and a preacher. Under paganism, no one preached. Having neither fixed doctrine, nor certain morality, nor history, the cult could not be the object of regular instruction. However, this was what Julian tried to give it. He proposed establishing chairs of preaching—schools where lecturers and doctors in pagan theology would explain dogmas and morality. He also thought to recite a type of common prayer, with

[16]Prudentius, *Peri Stephanon*, X, 219–230.
[17]*Apostolic Canons*, 17, 18, 20, 42, 43, 54, 81, 83.
[18]Julian, *Ep*. 63.
[19]*Fragment of a Letter*; Hertlein, p. 382.
[20]*Ibid*.; cf. *Ep*. 62.

a litany of alternating melodies. Finally, he considered establishing an entire penitential system, with atonement in proportion to the faults of each.[21] Save for the preaching, which was tried,[22] it is not clear that these reforms were ever executed. But they complete the involuntary confession pried from Julian by force. Having decided to suppress Christianity, he recognized that he was unable to replace it other than by copying it.

He made this confession more openly still, and with great bitterness. What paganism lacked most of all was charity. Julian saw the Jews assisting their paupers and the Christians assisting the poor of every religion. He had been witness to the brilliant flowering in the fourth century that made hospitals and hospices rise from the ground next to the cathedrals. There was nothing like it among the pagans. Aside from official assistance, the poor could expect nothing from the worshipers of the gods. The latter possessed neither institutions of charity nor personnel trained to care for the sick and needy. "We worship Jupiter the hospitable, but we are more inhospitable than the Scythians," Julian writes to a pontifex.[23] His ill humor on the subject manifested itself in many ways.

> It is the indifference of our priests to the unfortunate that has suggested the idea of practicing charity to the impious Galileans[24]. . . .
> It would be shameful when the Jews do not have a single beggar, when the impious Galileans nourish both their own and ours, for our own to be deprived of the help we owe them. . . . Let us not leave to others the zeal of the good: let us be ashamed of our indifference.[25]

He thus exhorted his priests not only to give alms, visit prisoners, and succor their enemies,[26] but also to found institutions of public

---

[21]St Gregory of Nazianzus, *Oratio* IV, 111; Sozomen, *Hist. Eccl.,* V, 16.

[22]See Letter 607 of Libanius, to Acacius. (Wolf, *Libanii Epistolae,* Amsterdam, 1738, p. 291.)

[23]*Fragment of a Letter;* Hertlein, p. 374.

[24]*Ibid.,* p. 391.

[25]*Ep.* 49.

[26]*Fragment of a Letter; Ep.* 49; Hertlein, p. 371, 553.

assistance. "Establish numerous hospitals in every city," he writes to the high priest of Galatia, "so that strangers there may enjoy our hospitality—not only those of our religion, but all who have need of us. I have provided the necessary funds."[27] But Julian was ashamed of leaving the state to defray the costs of the pagan hospices, when the Christians sufficed on their own to cover theirs. "Teach the Hellenes to provide their part of the contributions," he adds, "and teach the Hellenic villages to offer their premises to the gods; accustom the Hellenes to these works of charity."[28] Paganism had to acquire an entire education on this point. It was rather late, perhaps, for such an undertaking, and no one could try it except by attending the school of the Christians.

If Julian sought to defeat Christianity on the grounds of piety, virtue, and charity—to supplant Christians by making the pagan religion produce fruits superior to theirs—he applied himself to an illusory goal, but at least he put excellent means in the service of a bad cause. Spiritualist that he was, Julian was not a man to follow this path, nor to neglect the more material and more rapid means of attaining his goal. His impatience demanded immediate results. In his letters, he complains that Hellenism's triumph does not come quickly enough. Such a princeps would have been incapable of following the policy inaugurated at the start of Constantine's reign by the Edict of Milan by keeping an even balance between the two religions. He would never have been satisfied, like Constantine, with lavishing favors upon his own cult while strictly observing the rules of justice towards the other.

At the same time, formed by the events of his youth to a cautiousness that sometimes bordered on hypocrisy, he would have been afraid of imitating Constans' behavior with regard to paganism by opposing the Christian cult and ordering the closing of churches, as his predecessor had ordered closure of the temples. His approach was entirely different. On several occasions, he declared that freedom of worship was allowed to the Christians (or, as he always called them, the Galileans).[29] Yet at the same time he took care to heap scorn upon them

[27]*Ep.* 49.
[28]*Ibid.*
[29]Ep. 7, 43, 52.

publicly. His books, like his correspondence, describe them in terms so outrageous that the copyists of later ages have not dared to reproduce everything.[30] Constantine's few disdainful words regarding the pagans were nothing compared to this torrent of insults. Letting his feelings be known too openly was virtually the equivalent of a declaration of war. This war was pursued by oblique means, which gradually pushed the Christians outside of common law. When over-excited pagan passions were given free rein and blood was shed as a result of popular riots, Julian tolerated or reprimanded it with marked apathy. He himself, under various pretexts, sometimes ordered true acts of persecution. We do not know how far his hatred would have carried him, had not the brevity of his reign prevented the principles proposed by him to produce their logical consequences.

3. The Pagan Reaction

Julian's first concern was the reestablishment of paganism in its place as the official religion. Sacrifices were once again offered by the magistrates in the name of the state, provinces, and cities; pagan images replaced the monogram of Christ on the standards. During the distribution to the soldiers, each one in approaching to receive the imperial gift had to burn incense before the idols or before the Eagles.[31] But Julian did not limit himself to this civil and military restoration of the old cult. Making paganism once again the state religion seemed insufficient to him, unless the official personages became pagans again at the same time. Officers were stripped of their rank, and the magistrates were ordered to choose between their offices and their faith.[32] This was an exercise of violence against the conscience for the benefit of paganism, which neither Constantine nor Constans had tried. We know that these emperors did not hesitate to appoint pagans to the highest offices. Julian himself, in a letter, addresses a distinguished citizen of the town of Batna who received Constans in his house several times,

---

[30]See the lacunae of the *Ep.* 51, 63, and of *Fragent. of a Letter,* in fine.
[31]Sozomen, *Hist. Eccl.,* V, 17; St Gregory of Nazianzus, *Oratio* IV, 64, 82–84.
[32]Socrates, *Hist. Eccl.,* III, 13, 22; IV, 1; Sozomen, V, 18; VI, 6.

praising him for having remained faithful to the gods in spite of the emperor's efforts to attract him to Christianity.[33]

Some of Julian's other measures showed how far he was from granting the two cults equal treatment, as Constantine had done. The latter had declared catholic priests exempt from municipal charges, and especially from the obligations of the curia. This was not awarding them a favor, but allowing them to partake of a privilege that members of the pagan clergy had enjoyed from time immemorial. Rendered virtually meaningless by two laws of 320 and 326, which restricted admittance to sacred orders to those who by birth or fortune were not designated curiales, this immunity had been gradually reestablished for bishops, priests, deacon, and other clerics by a law passed in 361 under Constans.[34] Julian made haste to suppress this "exemption awarded to the impious," in the words of Libanius,[35] while maintaining or reestablishing that advantage that the pagan priests had enjoyed.[36] A law of 362 recalled the the decurions [former magistrates] who had ceased being part of the city assemblies after entering the Christian clergy.[37] A short letter to the inhabitants of Byzantium shows this law applied by the forced reintegration of all "Galileans" into their senate.[38] We learn from another letter, addressed to the inhabitants of Bostra, that "the named clerics"[39] were likewise stripped of the legal powers awarded by Constantine in certain cases to the bishop and his advisors.[40] Julian went even farther: he withdrew the subsidies awarded to the clergy a short time ago by Constantine and Constans and obligated them to return the sums perceived as such. He compelled even the women assisted by the Church's charity—virgins and widows consecrated to

[33]Julian, *Ep.* 27.

[34]*Theodosian Code,* XII, I, 40.

[35]Libanius, *Epitaph. Juliani.*

[36]Sozomen, *Hist. Eccl.,* V. 3.

[37]*Theodos. Code* XII, I, 50; XII, I, 4. As an exception to his habits, instead of using the scornful expression *Galilaei* Julian here uses the word *christiani*, which as Godefroy has shown, is in this text the equivalent of *clerici*.

[38]Julian, *Ep.* 11.

[39]*Ton legomenon klerikon, Ep.* 52.

[40]*Theodos. Code,* I, XXVII, 1; and an appendix by Sirmond, 1 and 17. Cf. Humbert, art. *Episcopalis audientia,* in *Dict. des antiquités,* vol. II, 697.

God—to give back the stipends that Constantine had assigned to them from the yield on municipal contributions.[41]

Another measure, more justified in appearance, completed this cruel and insidious revenge. To compensate for the losses suffered by the temples under the two preceding regimes, the property of numerous churches was seized and their precious vessels confiscated. Julian went further: he decided that everyone who had participated in the destruction of a pagan sanctuary should rebuild it at his own expense, or at least pay the costs of reconstruction.[42] This sentence, among others, was imposed on the bishop of Arethusa.[43] In one remarkable circumstance, an entire city was convicted under this law. Caesarea, a metropolis of Cappadocia, had been almost entirely Christian since the reign of Constans. By common agreement, two temples that had became useless to the inhabitants were demolished; a third had just been knocked down. Julian removed the city's name of Caesarea, levied it with an enormous fine, increased its taxes, enrolled its entire clergy in the police troops, and threatened to destroy the whole city if the temples were not rebuilt.[44]

Despite the simplicity of his manners, Julian was in great need of money, either because of expenses involved in the restoration of the pagan cult, the pomp with which he surrounded it, and the immense consumption of the victims who were his sacrifices,[45] or because of the expedition he prepared against the Persians. He also took pleasure in imposing fines upon the Christians. Any pretext was enough to satisfy him. In order to punish the violence exercised by the Arians of Edessa against another heretical sect, he confiscated every church property in that city, distributing movable assets to the soldiers and awarding the real estate to his own domain.[46] This, Julian ironically wrote, was the best way to smooth over the road leading to the kingdom of heaven for

[41]Sozomen, *Hist. Eccl.*, V, 5. The historian puts forward as proofs the constraints awarded to the agents of the fiscus, and still existing.

[42]Sozomen, V, 5.

[43]Sozomen, V, 10; St Gregory of Nazianzus, *Oratio* IV, 88–90.

[44]Sozomen, V, 4; St Gregory of Nazianzus, *Oratio* IV, 92.

[45]Ammianus Marcellinus, XXV, 4.

[46]Julian, *Ep.* 43.

the Galileans.[47] Such a mixture of greed and mockery, as evidenced by this letter from the restorer of Hellenism, lends likelihood to the report of Socrates the historian about a war tax that would have been required especially from Christians, and would have brought great sums into the imperial treasury.[48]

4. The Edict on Education

As a general rule, Julian either tended to place the Christians outside the law or to create special legislation for them, which amounts to the same thing. His edict on public instruction is proof of this. Perhaps no act does less to honor Julian's memory. Every party, including the honest and moderate faction of pagan opinion, as well as the Christians, has judged it harshly. Ammianus Marcellinus, a faithful echo of the pagan faction, described it as "barbarian" and doomed it to "an eternal silence."[49] The Christian Socrates saw in it a true "act of persecution," designed to forbid his coreligionists "the study of the humanities."[50] Sozomen summarized it by saying that Julian forbade Christian children from reading Greek authors and attending schools kept by the pagans.[51] St Augustine states that Julian forbade Christians "to teach and learn the humanities."[52] In terms probably more precise,[53] Ammianus Marcellinus reported that Julian closed public teaching to rhetors and grammarians who did not follow the cult of the gods.[54] This was the apparent significance of the law of June 17, 362, which subjected every nomination for public professors to imperial approval,[55] and most especially the sense of the general edict that followed it—a long

[47] Ibid.

[48] Socrates, *Hist. Eccl.*, III, 13.

[49] Ammianus Marcellinus, XXII, 10.

[50] Socrates, *Hist. Eccl.*, III, 12.

[51] Sozomen, *Hist. Eccl.*, V, 18.

[52] St Augustine, *De civit. Dei*, XVIII, 52.

[53] Unless we suppose, as Bidez and Cumont (*Recherches sur la tradition manuscrite des letters de l'empereur Julien*, p. 14, n. 4) have done, that a third law forbade Christians to attend schools where classical teaching is provided, a law of which two fragments would have been preserved by St Gregory of Nazianzus, *Oratio* IV, 102, and Socrates, III, 22.

[54] Ammianus Marcellinus, XXV, 4.

[55] *Theodosian Code*, XIII, 111, 5.

and diffuse piece, although less incoherent than many of its author's productions.[56] Christian teachers were free to explain "Matthew" or "Luke" in church, but they were no longer to teach their listeners either as rhetors, grammarians, or sophists, nor to train them in the elocution, morality, or political science of the classical pagans: the poets Homer and Hesiod, the historians Herodotus and Thucydides, and the orators Demosthenes, Isocrates, and Lysias. In the examples cited by Julian, we observe the exclusively Greek tendency of his mind, which led him to include no Latin writer.

The alleged motive for this prohibition was that a teacher would be dishonest if he were to comment to his pupils on a book involving gods in which he himself does not believe—a notion so superficial that we find it difficult to believe it sincere. Reduced to such a narrow principle, the human spirit would be excluded from all cultural understanding, making it unlawful to inquire into foreign literature regarding the secrets of style, or to investigate those of thought through distant philosophers, or to look into the ancient annals regarding the science of history, or to use the laws of ancient peoples to understand the rules of comparative law. All intellectual progress would come to a halt and threaten to run up against a brick wall. This wall would be a religion as oppressive and crushing for the mind as the one Lucretius aspired to deliver to his contemporaries, *oppressa gravi sub religione* ["crushed beneath the weight of religion"]. Closing science, philosophy, and letters to any perspective other than the pagan one, while at the same time excluding the pagan ideal (which had held, and still held, such an important place in the world) from those students who did not subscribe to it with complete faith, was an exercise of the most atrocious tyranny upon the reasoning mind.

Apparently, Julian did not perceive these consequences, which reduced his system to an odious absurdity. However, he was concerned about the ammunition that even a literary study of mythology might lend to Christian polemics. For enlightened pagans, such studies had become scandalous. They tried by all means to overcome its unfortunate aspects. Julian himself, if piety had not restrained him, would

[56]Julian, *Ep.* 42; Hertlein, p. 544.

perhaps have been tempted to smile sometimes at the fables to which popular credulity still clung; we know of his lovely letter on the nymph Echo.[57] At least the spirit of the times and his own intellectual habits furnished him with the means to reconcile these mythological stories with reason and modesty. He drew a veil of subtle allegory, sometimes pedantic and complicated, over the most vile adventures. In this way he nearly succeeded in making the myth of Cybele and Attis edifying. But not everyone shared his filial piety for the gods, and it would have been difficult to expect it from Christian teachers. Everything leads us to assume that these masters—they were numerous, some even famous—did not attempt to conceal the oddities of literal meaning as they explained the poems of Homer and Hesiod in their schools. It is quite likely that they did not refrain from ridiculing and stirring up the mire of mythology in order to contrast the immorality of these fables with the purity of Christian doctrine and biblical morality. The historians' works provided material for lessons of a different sort, turned to the detriment of the same idolatrous customs and the glorification of Christian morals. This is what Julian refers to as "explaining the works of the authors, and rejecting the gods they worship," and again as "accusing the poets of impiety, foolishness, and error regarding the gods." This genre of commentary—a useful method in preaching and ecclesiastical catechesis—was most likely the one he wished to end.

However, amusing Christian pupils at the expense of mythology was not the sole outcome of the study of pagan letters. At the same time, such studies opened to them every treasure of ancient wisdom and discernment. The advice that Basil of Caesarea would later give his audience on the reading of profane writers was already in the mouths of Christian instructors. Ever since that time, the essence of their teaching can be summarized in this charming verse of Gregory of Nazianzus: "Scorn the ridiculous divinities of whom the poets speak, admire the beauty of the words; on the trunk of ancient letters, leave the thorn and pluck the rose."[58] Julian desired to snatch this very flower from those he considered his enemies. This obscure

---

[57] *Ep.* 54.
[58] St Gregory of Nazianzus, *Ad Seleucum,* 57–61.

and hidden goal of the edict was readily perceived by the shrewd historian Socrates.[59] Julian had not forbidden young Christians to attend pagan schools, as Sozomen erroneously stated. However, Julian knew that many Christian families, deprived of the teacher of their choice, would refuse to send their children to acquire learning from sources they judged to be poisoned. The emperor hoped to see new generations of the Church growing up in a kind of intellectual isolation, until gradually the whole population of the "miserable Galileans" relapsed into the ranks of the unlettered barbarians. Oblivious to the art of speaking well and to the rules of logic and science, ignorant of what was learned in the schools and those benefits that only classical culture could provide, the Christians would lose all influence over tender minds. No formidable adversary of the sophists, philosophers, and priests of the gods would ever emerge from their midst. Hellenism would no longer have rivals capable of turning its own weapons against it. Those rivals and old classmates, whose superiority Julian endured with impatience—the Basils, the Gregorys, nourished simultaneously by secular and religious literature, elegant writers, powerful orators—would die without leaving heirs![60] After one or two generations, who knew if one might still encounter Christian preachers able to quote a word from Epimenides, or cite for their audiences a verse from Euripides or Aratus, as in the example of St Paul?[61] The worshipers of Christ would by then have become a people apart, like the Jews: gloomy and strange, nourished only by their religious literature, separated from the brilliant world of Hellenism, no longer sharing its ideas nor understanding it, nor able to make themselves understood by it.

We have little information about the manner in which the Christians received Julian's edict. The most interesting pages on the subject are those penned by Socrates, to which I have already alluded, and half a century later than the event. One contemporary, Gregory of Nazianzus, expressed on the day after Julian's death the indignation he had

[59]Socrates, *Hist. Eccl.*, III, 16.
[60]St Gregory of Nazianzus explains that in his youth he enthusiastically attended schools of literature in order to become able to refute the sophists, "to escape the subtle knots of their argumentation" and give "false letters as aids to true letters." *De Vita sua*, 112–118.
[61]The reflection is by Socrates, *Hist. Eccl.*, III, 16.

felt at the news of an order that would deprive him of the fruit of so many labors and journeys undertaken in the quest of eloquence. He uttered this cry of the true artist enamored with ancient beauty: "They had wished to deprive us of the Hellenic language, considering us to be usurpers of someone else's wealth; all that remained was to deprive us of the arts of Greece under the same pretext!"[62] We know the proud attitude of the two most famous rhetors in Rome and Athens, Victorinus and Prohaeresius, who descended from their pulpits at once, even though Julian offered Prohaeresius the exceptional favor of continuing his teaching without being forced to abjure.[63] We also know the naïve illusion relied upon by two other professors, the grammarian Apollinaris and the rhetor of the same name. They believed it possible to counteract the order's disastrous effects by changing the Bible and the gospel into Greek verse, either in the form of an epic or tragedy, or into prose dialogues, in order to take the place of Homer, Aeschylus, and Plato for the Christian students. This testament of commendable good will, and also of an odd literary infatuation, did not survive the crisis that occasioned it. By the time Socrates wrote his *Ecclesiastical History*, the works of the two Apollinarii were no longer extant; the intelligent historian, delighted to see ancient literature once again an integral part of Christian education, thanked Providence that their attempts had proven unnecessary.[64]

5. Julian and the Jews

Julian's relationship with Judaism forms one of the most curious episodes of his history. The Jews did not take umbrage with the champion of Hellenism. Resistant to the civilization he preferred but never aspiring to supplant it, they received from him favor mixed with scorn. The scorn was for a people he judged inferior to the Hellenes in every respect, the favor for a people who rivaled Julian in their hatred of Christians. Julian's theory concerning national gods made him accept

---

[62]St Gregory of Nazianzus, *Oratio* IV, 100.

[63]Eunapius, *Vitae sophist.*; Prohaeres.; St Jerome, *Chron.*; St Augustine, *Confess.*, VIII, 5, 10.

[64]Socrates, *Hist. Eccl.*, III, 16.

even the god of the Jews. With the kind of contradiction that constituted the foundation of his theology, Julian sometimes recognized his name as that of the universal God;[65] at other times, by contrast, he deprived him of universal character and reduced him to the local divinity of a people and race.[66] Upon his return from the Persian expedition, he proposed to go worship him in Jerusalem and at the same time rebuild the city from its ruins.[67] We know that Julian conceived a still more extraordinary plan, that of rebuilding the temple destroyed by Titus. This enterprise commenced at great cost. What intention, exactly, lay behind this attempt? Was a desire to link himself to the Jews and honor their God his sole motive? Most likely there were others. By calling the Jews back to Jerusalem and making it their holy city again, which it ceased to be during the time of Titus and especially Hadrian, he provided Judaism with a center around which its scattered elements might gradually be rallied. In this way, he hoped to substitute a national character for the universal one that the diaspora had lent to the worship of Israel, and reduce it to nothing more than the religion of a minor people in Palestine. No matter how worrisome Jewish proselytism might be for a restored Hellenism, all fear of its influence on cultivated minds could henceforth be dismissed. Christianity itself would be affected indirectly. It would apparently lose its historic base, and no longer be able to tie its origins to the traditions of Israel. Who would recognize such a narrowly localized cult, from then on, as the precursor of one aspiring to universal domination?

Julian apparently wished to deliver an even more direct blow to Christianity. We know the gospel predictions concerning the temple at Jerusalem: "Not a single stone will be left on another," Jesus Christ tells his disciples.[68] Julian had certainly read those words. He was familiar with the gospels, which are frequently cited in the all-too-brief fragments that remain to us of his seven books against the Christians. One of his citations from Matthew[69] precedes by only a few verses the

---

[65] *Ep.* 25, 63.
[66] See the passages quoted by St Cyril, *Adv. Julianum*, IV.
[67] *Ep.* 25.
[68] St Matthew, XXIV, 2; St Mark, XIII, 2; St Luke, XXI, 6.
[69] St Matthew, XXIII, 27, in St Cyril, *Contra Julianum*, X; Neumann, *Juliani imperatoris librorum contra christianos quae supersunt*, p. 225.

text of this same gospel concerning the complete future destruction of the temple. What a triumph for Julian, to attribute a lie to Jesus Christ himself by showing that his prophecy never came to pass, or rather, to himself prevent the prophecy from being fulfilled! What an argument against the gospel! What a disaster for the Christian cause! Christian writers did not hesitate to ascribe these thoughts to Julian, and very likely they are not wrong. We know that the hopes of the emperor and the Jews were foiled. Even if we discard the testimony of Christian writers as overly partial,[70] it was nevertheless an enterprise undertaken at great cost, under the direction of a high magistrate, yet suddenly halted by an unknown force that no effort on the part of the engineers and workers could overcome. The pagan Ammianus Marcellinus, a contemporary, reported that balls of fire burst from the ground while they were hollowing out the foundations, driving away the workers and even consuming some of them. The project had to be abandoned.[71] Without giving details, Julian himself admits in a letter to having attempted to rebuild the Jews' temple, "in honor of the God worshiped there," without having succeeded.[72]

6. The Acts of Persecution

All of these acts were a knowing preparation for the war against Christendom. What remains to be seen is this war itself, and the part Julian played in it. Fifty years after the Edict of Milan, it was impossible to renew the old persecutions. Neither the rescript of Trajan, authorizing individual denunciations against Christians, nor the edicts ordering their official persecution, would have been applicable. Favored for half a century by the authorities, who had declared their support even when they struggled blindly in favor of schism or heresy, the Church had now spread everywhere. In certain provinces the Church comprised the majority of the inhabitants. Where its adherents remained a

---

[70]St Gregory of Nazianzus, *Oratio* V, 3–7; St John Chrysostom, *In Matth. Homilia* IV, 1; *Adv. Judaeos,* V, 11; *Contra Judaeos et Gentiles,* 16; Socrates, III, 20; Sozomen, V, 2; Theodoret, III, 20.

[71]Ammianus Marcellinus, XXIII, 1.

[72]*Fragment of a letter*; Hertlein, p. 379.

minority, they were still viewed as too considerable to be easily abused. We would hardly expect the Christian population, in the last half of the fourth century, to show the patience it had exhibited in earlier times. The faithful had seen Christianity on the throne; for them to endure the disdain and insults lavished upon them by Julian was already too much. The attitude assumed by Antioch's inhabitants towards the emperor and his entourage of sophists and hierophants showed how dangerous it was to wound popular sentiment where it was devoted to X and K, i.e., to Christ and the memory of the Christian principes Constantine and Constans.[73] Thus Julian never tried to ban Christianity, despite his hatred of it; he confined himself to attacking it in a thousand indirect ways. At the same time, however, he declared that he did not wish to apply coercion against it. "I vouch for the gods, I wish neither to massacre the Galileans nor molest them contrary to justice, nor make them submit to bad treatment. I only say that we should prefer to them people who respect the gods, in all circumstances."[74] Nothing prevents us from placing credence in the sincerity of these words. They do not come from a liberal, but seemingly from a man determined to observe at least a superficial tolerance. Julian probably believed himself capable of this, but he was too consumed by hatred to permit the composure needed for this policy.

For this reason the majority of indirect measures taken by Julian against Christianity, along with the excitement he stirred up in pagan passions, resulted in actual acts of persecution. At the beginning of his reign, when he recalled the Christians exiled by Constans on account of their religion, it seemed at first like a step toward equity.[75] His true intentions, however, soon appeared. Ammianus Marcellinus, generally well informed about these matters, says that Julian proposed to shatter the Christians' unanimity and awaken dissent. The historian adds that Julian knew that even ferocious beasts were less cruel to man than many Christians were toward one another[76]—unjust words, even after

---

[73]Julian, *Misopogon;* Hertlein, p. 460, 465.

[74]*Ep.* 7.

[75]Theodoret seems to echo this opinion, when he attributes the measure taken by Julian to a desire to gain the kindness of all. *Hist. Eccl.,* III, 2.

[76]Ammianus Marcellinus, XXII, 5.

the sad examples during the reign of Constans, but ones which seem to be Julian's in tone. We then see the leaders of the opposing parties enter: the Eunomians, who opposed the faith of Nicaea, versus the intransigent defenders of this faith; the philosopher Aetius against St Athanasius. The emperor showed his partiality at once. He opened his arms to the heretic Aetius, calling him to draw near through an affectionate letter and authorizing him to make use of the imperial post;[77] this favor, lavished on the bishops by Constantine and Constans, was reserved by Julian for philosophers. By contrast, Julian's anger exploded against Athanasius, who had scarcely been reestablished on the episcopal see of Alexandria. He contested his right to resume his ecclesiastical office. He was indignant because "this miserable one" had dared, while Julian reigned, "to baptize a few distinguished Greek women." He wrote to the people of Alexandria to inform them of Athanasius' banishment. In a second letter, or rather an edict to be posted, he severely reproached the people for their persistent attachment to this rebel, declaring that the bishop must not only leave the city, but quit Egypt. A rescript to the prefect of Alexandria threatened the magistrate with a hefty fine if "this Alexandrian, the enemy of the gods," was not expelled from the province within a short time. "The contempt of all the gods sorrows me greatly," he adds.[78] Thus the return of the exiles brought unexpected consequences a few months later: a renewed exile of Athanasius, or in other words, a formal act of persecution.

We may compare his harsh letters to this population and magistrate with the much milder reprimands addressed by Julian to cities where fanatics massacred Christians. This first took place in Alexandria, where the Arian bishop George, convicted of having destroyed temples under Constans, was tortured by the pagans before Athanasius' return. Julian reproached them for this heinous crime in a tone of gentle reprimand. "Fortunately for you, citizens of Alexandria, you committed this crime under my reign—under one who, out of reverence for the god (Serapis) and towards my uncle, my homonym,[79] who

[77] Ep. 31.
[78] Ep. 6, 26, 51.
[79] The count Julian.

commanded in Egypt and in your very city, wishes you to maintain brotherly love."[80] We may recall the enormous fine Julian imposed on the city of Caesarea on account of the destruction of a single temple. Neither the inhabitants of Gaza, nor those of Heliopolis and Arethusa, were punished for massacring Christians, including women and a bishop, with horrible refinements of cruelty.[81] The laments of the pagan prefect of Syria, who was ashamed and distressed by the excesses committed by the population of Arethusa, left Julian unmoved.[82] Having put some of the murderers in jail, the governor of Gaza was at the point of being tried and, it is said, condemned to death by Julian, to whom is ascribed these words: "Why was it necessary to act ruthlessly against men who have avenged their injuries and those of the gods on some Galileans?"[83] Other magistrates had a better grasp of the master's humor. The Christians of one province, complaining that a governor had harassed them without official approval, received this ironic reply from the emperor: "It is your role to suffer injuries patiently, for so your God has commanded."[84]

This talk of forgiveness does not excuse Julian from a sort of moral complicity in acts he had not ordered. Some violence exercised by the pagans in light of this impunity constituted a bloody revenge for the much less serious excesses committed by Constans against the temples, if not the population. Some of these savage scenes, however, appear to have been the direct consequence of Julian's measures. If Bishop Mark fell victim to a riot at Arethusa, it is because he refused to pay the damages due from those whom an imperial order had condemned for taking part in the ruin of a temple not long ago.[85] In certain towns with a population zealous for paganism, Julian gave the green light for

---

[80]*Ep.* 10. Ammianus Marcellinus seems to abandon his habitual impartiality when he depicts the emperor on the point of acting ruthlessly, restrained with difficult by his entourage, and addressing a letter of vehement reproaches and terrible threats to the Alexandrians.

[81]St Gregory of Nazianzus, *Oratio* IV, 87, 89; Sozomen, *Hist. Eccl.,* V, 9, 10.

[82]St Gregory of Nazianzus, *Oratio* IV, 91.

[83]Socrates, *Hist. Eccl.,* V, 9. St Gregory conveys this speech in more vivid form: "Is it such a great evil when a Greek kills ten Galileans?"

[84]Socrates, III, 11.

[85]St Gregory of Nazianzus, *Oratio* IV, 390.

other excesses. Even as he ordered the rebuilding of the temples, he enjoined the destruction of "the atheists' tombs," i.e., the sanctuaries of the martyrs. He admitted that attacks against the Christians followed this destruction: "A fervent zeal, a short-tempered ardor erupted against the impious, more than his will had commanded."[86] Even the measures he took to reestablish idolatry in the army led to the exile and condemnation of some Christian soldiers.[87] However, the sentences pronounced on these occasions were for insubordination and rebellion.[88] Care was taken to demonstrate only offences against common law in actions that, at other times, would have earned the condemned the honors of martyrdom.[89] By this tactic Julian concealed many violent deeds for which policy served as the pretext and religion the true cause. When, at the outset of his reign, he sought reprisals against Constans' friends and advisors (an act that the sincere Ammianus Marcellinus declared unworthy of a philosopher),[90] he punished them with either death or exile, finding them guilty of abusing power, extortion, or of having "stuffed themselves with the remains of temples."[91] The testimony of Gregory of Nazianzus[92] and some words of Libanius[93] and Julian himself[94] lead us to believe that among these people—not all of whom were irreproachable, but among whom, as Ammianus admits, there were also innocent victims[95]—the Christians were the first to be prosecuted.

[86]Julian, *Misopogon;* Hertlein, p. 466.

[87]*Oligoi . . . hoi kai dikēn eisparchthesan.* Sozomen, *Hist. Eccl.,* V, 17. Cf VI, 6; and St John Chrysostom, *In Juventinum et Maximinum,* 1; St Gregory of Nazianzus, *Oratio* IV, 82–84; *Passio SS. Bonosi et Maximiliani,* in Ruinart, p. 644.

[88] . . . *Hōs peri ta ethē Rōmaiōn neōterizonta; kai eis politeian kai basileia examartanontos.* Sozomen, V, 17.

[89]St Gregory of Nazianzus, *Oratio* IV, 53; VII, 11.

[90]Ammianus Marcellinus, XXII, 4.

[91]*Ibid.*

[92]Oratio IV, 61.

[93]*Tous peri ekeinon tous amuētous.* Libanius, *De vita sua;* Reiske, vol. I, p. 16.

[94]*Hoi tēn gnōmēn barbaroi kai tēn psychēn athesi.* Julian, *Ep.* 25.

[95]*Moderatos quidem, licet paucos, morumque probitate compertos.* Ammianus Marcellinus, XXII, 4.

7. The Results

What was the outcome of this policy? It is impossible to foresee what would have happened had Julian reigned more than two years. Gregory of Nazianzus accused the crowned champion of Hellenism with having greatly shaken Roman authority by declaring war on the Christian religion.[96] Here was a bold change of perspective! The reproach that the pagans, centuries earlier, had directed at Christianity as a danger to the moral unity and material existence of the empire, St Gregory now addressed to the renaissance of paganism, because the empire, although formerly pagan, had in fact become Christian in both constitution and number. This peril, if it was as great as the orator from Nazianzus stated, did not have the time to come to fruition, however; the wind quickly chased away the "small cloud" that seemed to conceal dangerous tempests in its womb.[97]

Apostasies were numerous. Through the leverage of military discipline, many serving in the army returned to paganism with as much ease, perhaps, as they had abandoned it; they replaced the labarum with images of the gods as painlessly as they had earlier substituted the labarum's "Chi-Rho" for those images.[98] There were also self-interested conversions among the populace, and Julian himself notes the boredom or clumsiness of those people who tried to sacrifice,[99] or else their excessive and suspicious haste.[100] There were more extraordinary renegades such as the sophist, a zealous Christian under Constans, who became a fervent pagan under Julian, and bemoaned his apostasy with loud ostentation under the following regimes.[101] Even among the clergy, there were some who yielded to fear or seduction: not only the strange bishop of Ilion who, having remained a secret pagan under Constans, hastily discarded the mask as soon as Julian

---

[96]St Gregory of Nazianzus, *Oratio* IV, 74. The inhabitants of Antioch also accused Julian of having "turned the world upside down." *Misopogon;* Hertlein, p. 465.

[97]An expression attributed to St Athanasius; Sozomen, *Hist. Eccl.,* V, 14.

[98]Julian, *Ep.* 38; St Gregory of Nazianzus, *Oratio* IV, 61–65.

[99]*Ep.* 4.

[100]*Ep.* 27.

[101]Socrates, *Hist. Eccl.,* III, 13.

appeared,[102] but other bishops and priests, whose stories history has preserved.[103] In the face of such weaknesses, contrary examples also abound. Among some who were more directly tested, we see resistance continue to the point of martyrdom. Others, including high functionaries and officers of elevated rank, displayed the tenacity to remain insensible to promises as well as threats in order to guard their faith.[104] Julian himself reported how little effect his exhortations to return to the cult of the gods produced on the senate of Beroe.[105] Common people showed similar firmness and, according to the words of a contemporary, repelled like a solid wall every attack of a powerless machine.[106] We must add that, during combat itself, Christianity rebuilt its forces and often regained its lost terrain. At least in Alexandria, thanks to the strong influence of Athanasius, Christians who went over to the enemy were replaced every day by pagans who entered the bosom of the persecuted Church.[107]

One result that Julian scarcely anticipated was the end of any divisions among the Christian population in the face of common danger. Under the hand of the persecutor, the wounds opened by the religious tyranny of Constans were closed.[108] There was undoubtedly a passing truce, rather than lasting peace, but it was enough to repair a good deal of evil and give the churches the strength necessary to resist paganism's assault.

In the end, Julian's efforts failed. From his attempt to restore paganism only one thing remained: the weakness produced by the aborted attempt. The day after his death, the pagan religion was weaker than it was on the day he mounted the throne. The words attributed to the wounded Julian ("You have won, Galilean!"[109]) are true, like every historic word. They were probably never uttered, but they spring from the

---

[102]A letter of Julian, published by Henning in *Hermes*, 1875, and carrying the n. 78 in the Hertlein ed., p. 603.

[103]*Chron. pasc. ad ann.* 302; Philostorgius, VII, 13.

[104]St Gregory of Nazianzus, *Oratio* IV, 65.

[105]*Ep.* 27.

[106]St Gregory of Nazianzus, *Oratio* IV, 65.

[107]St Gregory of Nazianzus, *Oratio* XXX, 32. Cf. Julian, *Ep.* 6.

[108]Sozomen, *Hist. Eccl.,* VI, 4.

[109]Theodoret, *Hist. Eccl.,* III, 20.

consciousness of the people. As early as 361, Julian himself predicted what would become of his reign by trying to paint that of Constantine under false colors. He compared the works of the first Christian emperor to the gardens of Adonis, which Syriac women formed in the morning by planting cut flowers in a vase.[110] Evening found them withered, because they had no roots. The same was true of Julian's works; like the gardens of Adonis, they lasted only a day.

There was no need to destroy what he had done; the building collapsed on its own. Elected in haste in the midst of the Persian disaster, Jovian needed only to speak a word for the soldiers to return to Christianity.[111] On every side, the apostates asked to do penance. Many temples closed voluntarily, rather than be closed.[112] Obedient to the advice of their leaders, the Christians abstained from reprisals.[113] They even asked that the laws of Constans prohibiting idolatry not be revived; a simple edict reestablished religious freedom.[114] This step was enough to put things back where Constantine had left them, with paganism ceasing to be the official cult, but remaining a permitted religion, while Christianity once again became the religion of the emperor and the majority of his subjects, destined to become, in the near future, the religion of the state.

---

[110]Julian, *Caesars*; Hertlein, p. 423.
[111]Socrates, III, 3; Theodoret, IV, 1; III, 22; Sozomen, VI, 3.
[112]Socrates, III, 24.
[113]St Gregory of Nazianzus, *Oratio* V, 37.
[114]Themistius, *Oratio* V; cf. Socrates, III, 25.

CHAPTER SEVEN

The Transition—
Valentinian, Valens, Gratian

1. Valentinian (364–375)

At certain moments in the life of a people, history presents a singular spectacle. Either it reproduces the features of former events and vanished personages—sometimes weakened or exaggerated—or it provides a distant outline of new situations and future heroes. This seems to have been the case with the reigns that followed Julian's. Valentinian offered a reflection of Constantine; Valens repeated and even exacerbated the faults and crimes of Constans; Gratian ushered in Theodosius and laid the groundwork for the changes that would occur under that princeps in the empire's relationship with the two rival religions.

Valentinian had confessed the faith under Julian,[1] and we might have expected that at least in the West—the region he had reserved for himself during the division of the empire with his brother, Valens—an era of Christian reaction would begin. It did not happen. Valentinian limited himself to confirming, through certain detailed measures, the freedom of religion hastily restored by his predecessor. He simply restored the Christians to the legal situation they had enjoyed before Julian.

The answer he gave at the beginning of his reign to the orthodox bishop of Heracleon, who had asked him to use his power on behalf of the true faith, encapsulates his religious policy in advance. "I am a layperson," he said. "I am not anxious to examine dogma. This is the business of the prelates."[2] He remained the lay repository of power, even when he legislated in favor of the Christians. No princeps acted less as the "bishop from outside." His first concern had been to erase the law through which Julian had forbidden the worshippers of Christ

---

[1] St Ambrose, *De obitu Valent.*, 55; *Ep.* 21; Socrates, IV, 2. Sozomen, VI, 6; Theodoret, III, 16; Rufinus, II. 2. Cf. Zosimus, IV, 2.

[2] Sozomen, VI, 7.

to teach classical literature. However, instead of opposing Julian's declamations against Christian teachers with his own declamations, and refuting the verbose order from the champion of paganism at length, he said everything in two lines, revealing his desire to be just and to conceal his personal preferences. "Anyone who by virtue of his morals and talent is worthy of instructing youth, will have the right to either open a school or to bring his scattered audience together again."[3] Here is the imperious brevity of the lawmaker of old. Constantine himself did not speak in such a manner when a religious interest was at stake.

A second act was dictated to Valentinian at the beginning of his reign, still less by his sentiments as a Christian princeps than by concern for order and public peace. Forbidden on several occasions by Constantine and Constans, the nocturnal sacrifices had resumed under Julian. The practice of magic had even been promoted through the example of this princeps and his most intimate advisors. In 364 and 365, two laws were promulgated against magical conspiracies and nocturnal sacrifices.[4] If these laws were necessary, they seem to have been applied with care. One of the leaders of the pagan party in Rome, Praetextatus, who was then proconsul of Achaia, held that the mysteries of Eleusis, celebrated during the night, fell outside the scope of the prohibition.[5] Historians have seen this concession by Valentinian as a weakness. We recognize it, more accurately, as a moderate expression of the emperor's thought—a determination to curtail abuses without harming the practice of the pagan cult, of which ceremonies as ancient and famous as those at Eleusis were part.

A few years later, Valentinian had the opportunity to show his liberal tendencies even more clearly. Like Constantine, but with greater clarity of expression, he declared in 371 that the regular haruspices were not included in the forbidden evil spells:

> I do not consider this art as criminal, nor any religious observance established by our ancestors. The laws promulgated by me at the beginning of my reign are proof; they accord to each the freedom to

[3] *Theodosian Code*, XIII, III, 6.
[4] *Ibid.*, IX, XVI, 7, 8.
[5] Zosimus, IV, 3.

follow the cult of his choice. I thus do not condemn the haruspices;
I only forbid them to be mixed with criminal practices.[6]

Simply reading Ammianus Marcellinus is enough to confirm that
the temples were open under Valentinian, and the oracles were freely
consulted. The pagan cult was freer than under Constans, while the
Christian cult, naturally, had recovered the liberty had taken from it
by Julian at every turn, even as he pretended to maintain it on the
whole. In this way the balance between the two was reestablished, as
it had been at the time of Constantine. However, Valentinian differed
from Constantine by refraining from demonstrating any trace of his
intimate beliefs, affections, or reluctances in religious matters, whether
in his discourses or in his laws.

Among the measures taken by Julian out of hatred for Christianity,
one in particular excited complaints. Under the reign of Constantine—
and, above all, under Constans—the property of numerous temples
had been confiscated and given to the churches, or even to individuals.
On more than one occasion, there had been abuses of power difficult
to justify under the law. Most likely, the princeps had sought to put the
site of an abandoned temple, where the cult was no longer celebrated, to
better use, since the buildings that formed part of the entitlement were
henceforth no longer utilized. As Julian began the process of restoring paganism even against the wishes of the population, reopening
the temples, and reestablishing the sacrifices (not only where fear had
interrupted them, but also where they had become obsolete), his first
concern was to annul his predecessors' endowments and return the
property taken from the pagan sanctuaries. When his death brought
paganism's artificial rebirth to an end, it seemed wrong to leave this
measure in place. In many cases the temples to which property had
been returned in this manner were those where the cult, already in
decline before Julian, had ceased of its own accord as soon as imperial
authority no longer gave it artificial life. A degree of expropriation in
the reverse sense was now required of the sovereign, even when it had
not been claimed by the Christians. If some of Constans' bequests had
been unfair, most of Julian's no longer had reason for being. However,

[6] *Theodosian Code*, IX, XVI, 9.

Valentinian's expected act did not allow for the raising of delicate questions. Was it necessary to ensure that temples that were still frequented retained the property recovered by them under the previous reign, and to limit the removal of such property to those temples rendered inoperable by popular indifference? Or should temple property now in the possession of those to whom Constans had given or sold it be transferred without distinction (aside from those courtiers who held them only as a favor), merely returning those that for a time had been the property of the churches?

Valentinian did not go to the trouble of ordering an investigation, which at least in the latter case would not have been difficult. By means of a curious legal fiction, he deemed every building that, as a concession in the opposing sense by Constans and by Julian, had by turns been taken away from or given back to the temples, to be property without an owner. "Every place," he stated, "and every estate that is presently attached to the temples, but which previously had been sold or given away by the various principes, will return to our private domain; such is my good pleasure."[7] He was acting as a judge, after the fable of the oyster and the two litigants [in which two men disputing over an oyster were awarded the two halves of the shell by the judge, who kept the oyster for himself—Ed.]. We may wonder what Valentinian's motive might have been. Historians depict him as greedy, while at the same time concerned about relieving a population overburdened by taxes.[8] This twofold sentiment, which is not contradictory, may suffice to explain his act. It would not be misleading, however, to adopt another interpretation of his thinking. If he had returned to the churches the remains of temples that Julian had taken from them, he would have seemed to favor one religion at the expense of the other. The fear of abandoning his neutrality, which he had made an absolute norm for himself, was probably the main reason for his conduct.

In allotting favors to Christians and pagans, Valentinian seems to have preserved the same equilibrium: if he leaned one direction, he tended toward the latter. Undoubtedly, on those occasions when

[7] Ibid., X, I, 8.
[8] Ammianus Marcellinus, XXX, 8, 9; Aurelius Victor, Epitome; Zosimus, IV.

concerns for his power or for the other cult's sensibilities did not seem to come into play, Valentinian took visible pleasure in awarding discreet benefits to his coreligionists. For example, he forbade any judicial proceedings on Sundays,[9] awarded an amnesty on the occasion of Easter,[10] excused Christian soldiers from guarding the doors of pagan temples,[11] prohibited the condemnation of Christians to the gladiatorial arena,[12] and exempted from the theatrical profession actors and actresses who had received baptism in a case of serious illness, as well as their daughters if they led honorable lives.[13] At the same time, however, Valentinian confirmed and expanded the privileges of provincial pontifices of the pagan cult, as Constantine had already done.[14] After the second year of his reign, he renewed the prohibition against curiales entering sacred orders unless they gave up their inheritance, at the very least,[15] and he abolished the exemptions Constans had awarded to clerics who were in business.[16] Soon, yielding to the mistrust to which agents of civil power are subject at all times, he restricted the churches' right of asylum.[17] He defied clerical encroachment almost to the point of insult; in a law addressed to Pope Damasus, he forbade the clergy to receive bequests from Christian women, unless they happened to be legitimate heirs.[18] "And thus," cries St Ambrose, "if a Christian woman leaves her fortune to the priests of a temple, her testament is good; if she leaves it to ministers of her religion, it is bad!"[19]

If, as we have said, Valentinian calls to mind Constantine, it is perhaps with a fear of resembling him too much. More Christian in his conduct, despite an excessive severity that often degenerated into cruelty,[20] he was afraid to appear as such, striving above all to give himself

[9] *Theodosian Code*, VIII, viii, 1.
[10] *Ibid.*, IX, XXXVIII, 3, 4.
[11] *Ibid.*, XVI, 1, 1.
[12] *Ibid.*, XL, xl, 8.
[13] *Ibid.*, XV, vii, 1, 2.
[14] *Ibid.*, VII, I, 75.
[15] *Ibid.*, XII, I, 59; XVI, II, 17, 19.
[16] *Ibid.*, XIII, 1, 5.
[17] *Ibid.*, XIV, III, 12.
[18] *Ibid.*, XVII, II, 20.
[19] St Ambrose, *Ep.* 18.
[20] St Jerome, *Chron. ad ann. 366;* Sulpicius Severus, *Dialog.*, II, 6; Ammianus Marcellinus, XXVII, 7; XXIX, 7; XXIX, 3; XXX, 8; Zosimus, VI, 1.

an impartial air. As often happens, in order to avoid any appearance of preferring his own, Valentinian shared his favors unequally, spreading his graces more abundantly on the natural adversaries of his true feelings. However, we cannot say that his reign was bad for the Church. Constantine was more detrimental to her, by busying himself too much with her affairs; Valentinian, faithful to the principles proclaimed from the first days of his reign, abstained as much as possible from interfering. "It is not up to me to be the judge among the bishops," he said.[21] In keeping with these ideas, he avoided declaring even his opposition to the heretics. Aside from a law against the Manicheans (who were once banned by the pagan principes themselves) and another law against the Donatists' repetitions of baptism,[22] we do not see him concerning himself with them. A follower of the faith of Nicaea, he did not trouble the Arians. In the matter of Auxentius in Milan, he even sided with a bishop affiliated with their sect.[23] In this case, however, he yielded to an excessive desire to reestablish the appearance of peace, rather than to a taste for dogmatizing. It was his only error of this kind. In general, as with the pagans, he remained faithful to his resolution of neutrality in his relations with Christians of differing opinions. The prudent Tillemont, asking if we should praise him for this, leaned towards the affirmative.[24] Two of the more daring church historians of the fifth century, Socrates and Sozomen, approved of him without reservation.[25] On his side, Ammianus Marcellinus conveyed pagan opinion in remarkable terms: "What constitutes the glory of his reign is that he stood firm in the middle of all religious diversity, troubling no one, nor obliging anyone to follow this or that cult. He did not use threatening laws to bend his subjects towards that which he himself worshipped, but left all parties in the same state he found them."[26] This assessment is not altogether accurate, since Valentinian did reestablish the balance between the religious parties distorted by Julian. The truth is that he put things back more or less at the point where Constantine had left them.

[21]St Ambrose, *Ep.* 13.
[22]*Theodosian Code,* XVI, V, 3; VI, 1.
[23]St Hilary of Poitiers, *In Auxentium.*
[24]Tillemont, *Hist. des Empereurs,* vol. V, p. 10.
[25]Socrates, IV, 4; Sozomen, VI, 6.
[26]Ammianus Marcellinus, XXX, 10.

2. Valens (364–378)

Only once did Valentinian seem to take much interest in a dogmatic question. He agreed to transmit the council of Illyria's decisions, which energetically proclaimed the faith of Nicaea, to the churches of the East. In communicating the profession of faith of the Illyrian bishops to the persecuted eastern catholics, he added an exhortation to deny Caesar's demands concerning God's domain—in other words, he enjoined them to remain firm champions of orthodox doctrine against the company of Arians, who were aided by the civil authorities.[27] His death, which followed almost immediately, prevents us from seeing how far Valentinian might have advanced along this road, and for several years the field of the East was left open, once again, to the contrary doctrine of his brother, Valens.

Valens reminds us of Constans, but from one side only. Constans had declared himself the enemy of pagans and catholics; under his reign, laws banning idolatry alternated with acts of persecution directed against the followers of the faith of Nicaea. Valens, however, did not attack paganism. If the pagans suffered under him in the East, it was only as a result of his political mistrust of anyone he suspected of using magic to determine the name of his successor. Since the magic arts were professed by the pagans, his harshness was directed against them in particular; several of Julian's old friends fell victim to it.[28] However, we cannot cite any law Valens directed against idolatry. Far from prohibiting it, he gave it complete freedom,[29] and even depended upon the partisans of the ancient gods in his struggle against the orthodox Christians.

Baptized by an Arian bishop (not at the end of his life, like Constans, but at the very beginning of his reign), Valens had reportedly sworn to convert every one of his Christian subjects to Arianism.

---

[27]Theodoret, *Hist. Eccl.,* IV, 8–9. Schiller, *Gesch. des roem. Kaiserrechts,* vol. II, p. 364, seems incorrect in contesting the authenticity of Valentinian's letter. The commentary on this letter by M. de Broglie, *L'Église et l'Empire romain au quatrième siècle,* vol. V, p. 28, also seems to distort the meaning.

[28]Ammianus Marcellinus, XXIX, 1; Zosimus, IV, 15; Eunapius, *Vitae soph., Max.;* Philostorgius, VII, 15.

[29]Theodoret, *Hist. Eccl.,* IV, 21; V, 20.

His first act was to drive from their sees those bishops who had been banished only a short time ago by Constans, and who had returned home under Julian. This move clearly indicated his intention to pick up again at the point where Constans had left things. But Valens, elevated to the throne by chance, had little in common with Constans except bad instincts. He was neither the son of a great man, nor heir to an unchallenged power, and hence his boldness was mixed with timidity. Upon encountering a man of strong will or great renown, his plans suddenly ground to a halt. Only after the death of Athanasius did he begin the persecution in Egypt.[30] In Cappadocia, the presence and eloquence of Basil—a man superior in everything, an intrepid bishop, an accomplished man of the world, an incomparable administrator who knew how to make himself adored by his people, to resist magistrates, and to speak to principes all at the same time— filled him with admiration and terror, and preserved that province almost entirely.[31] Where no obstacle of this sort stood in his path, however, neither virtue, nor respect for holy places, nor the interests of Christian civilization, were able to suspend his sectarian furor. As a result of his orders—or those of his ministers—we see once again the most horrible scenes from the old persecutions. Churches were invaded; bishops, priests, and deacons were exiled, sent to the mines, exposed to the beasts, beheaded, or burned; virgins were assaulted or massacred; believers were put to death, without even the children being spared.[32] Telling of the excesses that appalled and bloodied Egypt, Syria, Osroene, and every provinces of the Eastern Empire in turn would be dreary and monotonous. Dogmatic nuances themselves eventually faded away in a blind effort to bend every mind to the tyrant's will. "Why do you not align yourself in communion with the emperor?" the clergy at Edessa were asked. "Is he a bishop and at

[30]Socrates, IV, 13; Sozomen, IV, 12; St. Epiphanius, *Haer.*, LXVIII, 10; St Basil, *Ep.* 61.

[31]St Basil, *Ep.* 44, 58, 59, 68; St. Gregory of Nyssa, *In Eunom.*, I; St Gregory of Nazianzus, *Oratio* XLIII, 52–54; Socrates, IV, 23; Theodoret, IV, 19; Rufinus, II, 9.

[32]St Basil, *Ep.* 10, 71, 73, 185, 200, 220, 264, 273, 283, 297, 395, 405; St Gregory of Nazianzus, *Oratio* XX, XXII, XXV, XXXII; St Epiphanius, *Haeres.*, LXVII, 10; Socrates, IV, 14, 16, 17, 18, 21, 32; Sozomen VI, 13, 14, 18, 20; Theodoret, IV, 16, 19, 21, 22, 23, 27; Rufinus II, 5, 23; Orosius, VII, 33.

the same time emperor?" a priest replied.[33] It was no longer a matter of convincing or persuading, but of grinding every soul down to the same level. Material obedience was sufficient, without inner allegiance. Heresy was in the process of becoming what paganism had been: a religion of the state.

In certain places the coarse and ignorant mass of pagans seems to have furthered this purpose. When it was a matter of chasing Athanasius' accepted successor from Alexandria and replacing him with a heretic, not only was Christian blood shed in torrents, but also at pagan hands. When bishops and priests were exiled, their preferred place of internment was a Phoenician town inhabited exclusively by pagans. The governor charged with prosecuting the orthodox Alexandrians was a pagan. The magistrate commanding the soldiers who installed the usurper on the episcopal see was the same one who had burned a Christian church under Julian. "Hail, you are dear to Serapis!" the idolaters cried when the Arian bishop passed by.[34] Pagan opinion, however, does not seem to have been unanimous in support of Valens. Separating themselves from the violent and fanatical crowds of idolaters, certain distinguished pagans criticized the excesses committed against the catholics. Somewhat skeptical in their philosophy, these men were attached to paganism as the tradition of their ancestors and the religion of the educated. Inclined to believe that every cult possessed some good and addressed itself to the same Divinity, they too were in need of freedom of conscience and did not wish evil on their adversaries. Largely men of the world, they were accustomed to living on good terms with the Christians, and perhaps suffered sincerely at seeing them persecuted. This explains the intervention by which, it is said, the philosopher Themistius tried to get Valens to stop persecuting the orthodox. While remaining a fervent follower of paganism, for which he had advocated before Jovian ten years ago, he maintained courteous relations with the great figures of the Church. Constans, not long ago, had showered him with honors, giving him an eminent place in the senate of Constantinople. Gregory of Nazianzus was in familiar

[33]Theodoret, *Hist. Eccl.*, IV, 15.
[34]*Id.*, *Hist. Eccl.*, IV, 19.

correspondence with him.[35] Themistius believed he was authorized to raise his voice in favor of the catholics, if that is indeed the meaning and scope of his twelfth discourse.[36] With kindly skepticism, he made the emperor to understand that it was not surprising to find doctrinal differences among the Christians, since the diversity of opinions was infinite among the followers of Hellenism. God was pleased, he added, by this variety of human ideas; he loved to see his creatures struggling over who may best honor his majesty and confessing, by their efforts, how difficult it is to know the answer.[37] This weak reasoning impressed Valens, it seems, and led him to pronounce less severe penalties against the orthodox.[38]

3. Gratian (375–383)

While an idolater was honored in the East for pleading on behalf Christians, the imperial power in the West was breaking its official ties with paganism for the first time. What the all-powerful Constantine never dared do, and what the prudent Valentinian never even thought of trying, his son Gratian undertook with the audacity natural to youth, but also in a spirit of continuity that reveals a carefully considered decision. When the college of pontifices, in the days following his accession, near the end of 375, offered him the insignia of the supreme pontificate, he refused to accept them. "Such attire," he replied, "is not fitting for a Christian."[39] This was not a violation of the pagan cult's freedom, nor even of its privileges. The violence committed the following year against a sanctuary of Mithras by Gracchus, the prefect of

---

[35]*Theodosian Code*, IV, IV, 12; Themistius, *Oratio* IV; St Gregory of Nazianzus, *Ep.* 24, 38.

[36]See Tillemont, *Hist. des Emp.*, vol. V, p. 414; Chastel, *Hist. de la destr. du paganisme en Orient*, p. 161, note 1.

[37]Themistius, *Oratio* XIII, ed. Dindorf, p. 494 and 600.

[38]Socrates, IV, 32; Sozomen, VI, 36.

[39]Zosimus, IV, 36. This anecdote, already contested by Godefroy and Pagi, appears suspect to Tillemont (*Hist. des Empereurs*, vol. V, p. 138 and 705); M. Boissier (*Fin du paganisme*, vol. II, p. 299) shares these doubts. What causes hesitation, at least on the date, is that Ausonius, in his *Gratiarum actio pro consolatu*, written in 369, calls Gratian *pontifex*, and even *pontifex maximus* on two different occasions (Migne, *Patrol. Lat.*, vol. XIX, col. 642–643).

Rome, was the excessively zealous work of a new convert, and not in any way connected to Gratian's policy.[40] This policy was summed up by an announcement of the coming separation of paganism from the state.

In 382,[41] Gratian took another step in this direction. He had the statue of Victory before which pagan senators, upon entering the curia, were in the habit of burning incense and pouring a libation, removed from the senate chamber.[42] Ever since Constantine's conversion, this statue had taken on extraordinary importance in the public mind. The Victories decorated other monuments without causing any kind of scandal. In 367, under Valentinian, an official placed a statue of Victory Augustus on one of the bridges of Rome.[43] Victories even appeared on the emperors' money. The senate statue, however, had become anything but a vague and inoffensive metaphor in the eyes of pagans and Christians alike. Both parties recognized it as the symbol of paganism, whose official dominance it represented. Early on, we see a singular struggle waged around it. Constans had it removed at the time of his trip to Rome. After his departure, the senate's pagan faction—more powerful in terms of influence and wealth, if not in numbers—had it reinstalled. It is not surprising that Julian, and even Valentinian, let it stand. But Gratian could not do this without being inconsistent himself. As long as the statue of Victory presided over its deliberations, the senate would remain an officially pagan assembly, regardless of the facts. The removal of the statue would end all ambiguity. This action wounded the conscience of the pagan senators less than its maintenance, over many long years, had wounded that of Christian senators. By ordering it, Gratian broke the link uniting paganism to the state for a second time.

A third measure, also taken in 382,[44] made the break complete. Until Gratian, even the principes who legislated against paganism continued

---

[40]St Jerome, *Ep.* 107; Prudentius, *Contra Symm.*, I, 561–565. Cf. *Bull. di arch. crist.* 1870, p. 161.

[41]In his commentary on the *Theodosian Code*, IV, XXXV, 3, Godefroy traces this abduction to the year 376, the second of Gratian's reign. Tillemont accepts 382.

[42]Symmachus, *Ep.* X, 3; St Ambrose, *Ep.* 17, 18.

[43]*Bull. della comm. arch. com. di Roma*, 1892, p. 72, 367.

[44]This measure, calling to mind a law of Honorius, *Theod. Code*, XVI, X, 20, is certainly from 382, as established by Rossi, *Roma sotterranea*, vol. III, p. 603.

to support it. Constans not only acted as sovereign pontifex by nominating the priests, but also opened the public treasury for the benefit of the temples and sacred rites. Gratian was more logical; his religious policy was determined with the rigor of a theorem. Since the emperor henceforth refused to be the leader of the pagan religion (and since the latter's symbol had disappeared from the senate), all that remained was to make paganism into a private cult, free to flourish but no longer drawing life from official subsidies. This was accomplished through one or two orders whose text has been lost, but whose dispositions are cited in the writings of Symmachus and St Ambrose, and in a later law inserted into the Theodosian Code. These laws abolished the privileges and exemptions of the pagan priests, distributing between the public treasury and the territorial prefect's chest those sums devoted annually, up that point in time, to covering the cost of the sacrifices. The laws affected the stipends for appointments paid to the Vestals and various servants of the altars for maintenance of their imperial posts; returned lands possessed by the temples and priestly colleges to the treasury; and declared gifts or bequests of real estate made to the temples and their priests to be obsolete, authorizing only gifts of personal property on their behalf.[45]

Gratian was at Trier at the time he refused the pontifical robe,[46] and most likely left to his own devices. However, the acts which would, at the end of his reign, complete this first object lesson date from his time at Milan, where he was staying in the intimate company of St Ambrose. The latter, who was at once a man of Church and state, was its visible inspiration. He was the first bishop to find a place in the counsels of a sovereign. Constantine had successively placed his confidence in Ossius of Cordova, then Eusebius of Nicomedia; Constans had numerous court bishops in his retinue. However, these principes asked the bishops for advice only on religious matters. Under Gratian and his successors, Ambrose would have a very different status. Lacking any official title, he was consulted on drafting laws, at times acting

---

[45]Symmachus, *Ep.* X. 3; St Ambrose, 17, 18, 37; *Theodosian Code,* XVI, X, 20.

[46]See Goyau, *Chron. de l'empire romain,* p. 549. Several historians place this refusal in 382 or 383, which accords better with the silence of Ausonius in 379; see p. 253, note 3.

as intermediary between a senate faction and the imperial consistory, at times chosen as ambassador in desperate cases, and by turns a prudent adviser, skillful negotiator, master of crowds, and the protector of principes. With his experience as a former magistrate, the rigor and precision of his mind, his disdain of transactions and nuances, and his knowledge of the Roman aristocracy (to which he belonged through birth and relationship), Ambrose clearly saw the point at which present circumstances would bring about success with the pagan party. The old religion survived only on help from the state; it lived on its privileges. There remained enough faith in it to accommodate common law. Some of its most sincere and obstinate adherents attempted to do without official favors, such as the patrician whose inscription mentions "having built a shrine to Mithras without the help of the Roman treasury" and boasts "of preferring, with pious souls, disgrace to prosperity."[47] However, the "man capable of sharing his inheritance with the inhabitants of heaven," according to the beautiful expression of this same pagan, was rare among his coreligionists. The pagan opposition began to break up when members of the Roman aristocracy, who formed its most solid core, no longer retained the property and income of the high priests, which up until that point were the virtual hereditary privilege of the patrician families. Once the pagan clergy ceased to be among the state's major property owners, their ranks gradually thinned. These clerics were not resigned to live as Christian priests then lived, without any kind of consideration from the state.

The Church's strength lay in its sole requirement of freedom to exist, while paganism's weakness was that it felt mortally wounded the moment its situation as a privileged religion was threatened. In fact, Gratian did nothing more than take its privileges away. Faced with the broken alliance between the old cult and the state, he did not attempt to give Christianity complete revenge by achieving that intimate union between Church and state toward which later ages would tend. Not only was there no budget for the Christian cult under his reign, but even the more restrictive laws had not yet been repealed. On several points, Christian priests remained in a less favorable position than the

---

[47] *Corp. inscript. lat.*, vol. VI, 754.

ministers of the gods. For example, a curiale could not take clerical orders without surrendering his patrimony; in certain circumstances ecclesiastics could not receive bequests, including movable assets. Gratian did not think to remove these inequalities; the separation of religion and state—such as it was, until something better came along—was the sole outcome of his religious policy. But if he did not improve the material status of the Church, which the disinterested Ambrose would never ask of him, he gave it greater satisfaction through numerous laws that bear witness to his orthodox sentiments. In the eastern provinces, he cleared away all traces of the persecution of Valens;[48] he obliged the Donatists to restore the churches they had seized from the catholics.[49] In every part of the empire, he suppressed the propaganda of heresy;[50] he exempted the various orders of the clergy from personal responsibility[51] and moderated the tax of the chrysargyrum in favor of clerics who conducted business;[52] he freed the Christian daughters of actors from any hereditary connection to that profession.[53] A curious law of 383 punishes Christians found guilty of apostasy.[54] This law appears to contradict the principle proclaimed elsewhere by Gratian on freedom of worship, yet at the same time it reveals the attraction that the old religion still exercised over weaker minds. It thus helps us understand the measures taken in the preceding year to remove benefits and honors from the idolatrous priesthood, which held the ambitious and greedy captive and sustained an interested opposition by a considerable portion of the Roman aristocracy.

[48]Socrates, V, 2; Sozomen, VII, 1.
[49]Theodosian Code, XVI, VI, 2.
[50]Ibid., XVI, V, 5.
[51]Ibid., XVI, II, 24.
[52]Ibid., XIII, I, 11.
[53]Ibid., XV, VII, 4; cf. 8, 9.
[54]Ibid., XVI, VII, 3.

CHAPTER EIGHT

The Christian State—
Theodosius (379–395)

1. The Religious Policy of Theodosius

Gratian's tragic death in 383 had no effect on the religious policy he had inaugurated. Theodosius, who had been associated with the empire since 369, worthily maintained this policy and brought it to fruition.

Over the course of four years, until Maximus' defeat in 388, the Roman world would have three masters: the usurper Maximus in Gaul, Spain, and Britain; Gratian's younger brother, Valentinian II, in Italy, Africa, and the Danubian provinces; and Theodosius in the East. Although he was stained with Gratian's blood, Maximus professed Christianity. He gave little evidence of this, however, when he condemned the schismatic Priscillian to death, to the great indignation of St Martin and St Ambrose.[1] The young Valentinian II, on the other hand, was receptive to the latter's advice so long as the Arian furor of his mother, Justina, did not force him to engage in conflict with the catholics. In 384, when every religious law of Gratian was thrown into question by the pagan party's offensive resurgence, the fifteen-year sovereign lent a favorable ear to the bishop of Milan's pleas while ignoring the prefect Symmachus' elegant arguments in favor of the altar of Victory and the privileges of the idolatrous clergy.[2] In 392, fifteen days before his assassination, Valentinian repulsed yet another attempt by pagan senators who came to Gaul to plead their cause.[3] The latter now neared the point of desperation. In the East, Theodosius had already dealt paganism a deadly blow. Under his energetic hand, the policies of Gratian and St Ambrose would finally succeed in the West. The separation recently

[1]Sulpicius Severus, *Hist. sacr.*, II, 50; *Dialog.* III, 15; St Ambrose, *Ep.* 52.
[2]Symmachus, *Ep.* X, 3; St Ambrose, *Ep.* 17, 18, 57; *De obitu Valent.*, 19; Paulinus, *Vita Ambros.*, 26.
[3]St Ambrose, *Ep.* 57.

proclaimed between the state and the pagan cult marked the first stage; the destruction of this cult by means of an intimate alliance between empire and Church would be the logical conclusion.

The Spaniard Theodosius was one of those rare emperors baptized at the beginning of his reign. It seems that this circumstance gave his policy a more clearly Christian character. The laws he mandated in favor of the Church surpassed in number all those of his predecessors combined; there were several of them each year. Enthroned in the East, his first concern was to defeat Arianism. With regard to the Trinity, he ordered all those under obedience to him in 380 to follow "the faith that the Roman church has received from the apostle Peter," such as "professed by Pope Damasus and Peter, bishop of Alexandria, a man of apostolic holiness."[4] Laws against the heretics followed in 381, 382, 384, 388, 389, and 394, taking the churches of the Eunomians, Arians, Apollinarists, Macedonians, and Manicheans and giving them to the catholics, banning their assemblies, driving out their bishops and priests, confiscating the places where their offices were celebrated, and rescinding their testaments, declaring them unable to give or receive.[5] The large number of these laws, many of which repeat themselves, indicates that they were not carried out everywhere, but at the same time denotes the energetic effort of the orthodox princeps to reestablish catholic unity in the provinces ravaged by the heresies dear to Constance and Valens.

We observe with some satisfaction that he gave the Church no financial privileges, nor was he lavish in bestowing material blessings. He confined himself either to elevating the dignity of his ministers, paying homage to his discipline and cult, and favoring Christian morality. He thus forbade bishops to be called as witnesses;[6] prohibited criminal trials during Lent;[7] banned physical torture "during this sacred time consecrated to the soul's purification;"[8] and forbade trafficking in the relics of the martyrs.[9] He numbered Easter and Sundays among the legal feast

[4] *Theodosian Code*, XVI, 1, 2.

[5] *Ibid.*, XVI, 1, 3; V, 6, 7, 8, 13, 14, 15, 16, 18, 22, 23.

[6] *Theodosian Code*, XI, xxxii, 8.

[7] *Ibid.*, IX, xxxv, 4.

[8] *Ibid.*, IX, xxxv, 5.

[9] *Ibid.*, IX, vii, 7.

days;[10] forbade spectacles at the amphitheater and circus on Sundays;[11] promulgated an amnesty for the day of Easter;[12] forbade marriages between Jews and Christians;[13] forbade Jews from buying Christian slaves;[14] barred actresses and women of ill repute from appearing in public dressed as virgins consecrated to God;[15] prohibited women and children who professed Christianity from joining dancing troupes;[16] barred individuals from owning and exhibiting slave musicians;[17] and struck at shameful vices in the cities while reforming the penalties.[18]

These laws—along with the personal feelings Theodosius expressed on numerous occasions, his regular participation in the sacraments of the Church,[19] and a penance he humbly accepted at St Ambrose's command after the cruel suppression of the riot in Thessalonica[20]—paint a picture of an emperor determined to regulate his public and private conduct in all matters according to Christian ideals. At the same time, his energetic character—easily carried away, little inclined to half measures, and fond of quick solutions—reveals him to be one of the men least able to continue or understand the evenhanded religious policy inaugurated by Constantine, which Gratian's orders, despite their unfavorable leanings toward paganism, did not necessarily negate. In his legislative work, as in the acts of his government, Theodosius appears incapable of tolerating nuances in Christianity itself. With a precision of language not previously encountered, but in which the rigor of the Latin mind is recognizable throughout, he required his subjects to adhere to catholicism in its most definitive form, instructing them to imitate or obey men of the West and East who seemed to him to best represent Roman orthodoxy. We find this authoritarian manner all the more remarkable in a princeps who, far from aspiring to dominate the

[10] *Ibid.*, II, viii, 12.
[11] *Ibid.*, XV, v, 2.
[12] St John Chrysotom, *Oratio* VI.
[13] *Theodosian Code*, III, vii, 2.
[14] *Ibid.*, III, I, 5.
[15] *Ibid.*, XV, VII, 12.
[16] *Ibid.*
[17] *Ibid.* XV, vii, 10.
[18] *Ibid.*, ix, vii, vi; Socrates, *Hist. Eccl.*, V, 18.
[19] St Ambrose, *De diversis*, 3.
[20] Theodoret, *Hist. Eccl.*, V, 117; Paulinus, *Vita Ambros.*, 24.

Church, appeared in every circumstance as the most submissive of her children. With him, there was no intention of styling himself as bishop from outside, as Constantine too often did; the imperial authority was placed at the service of the catholic religion, without any afterthought. It was placed there entirely, however, and henceforth no regard for discretion and prudence would check the weight of his arm. Theodosius felt strong enough to abolish heresy and paganism at the same time. Having the power, he reckoned that he had the duty, and he marched toward this goal with a singularly straight and firm step.

It was not that he sought to destroy all dissent at once; at first his conduct was different towards heretics and pagans. We have just seen him treat the first group as rebels whom he must now bring back, in spite of themselves, to the unity against which they had revolted; hence the laws that struck repeated blows against them, from the first years of Theodosius' reign until the last. This series of laws does not indicate a progressive repression. From the beginning, the princeps' will was displayed without reserve: heresy must cease to exist, its assemblies were to be dissolved, its pastors to lose their titles and authority, its followers to be relegated to the outskirts of the cities and deprived of the right to dispose of their property, becoming somehow, as one law expresses it, "excluded from the communion of men." Theodosius showed less severity toward the pagans. His goal was the same: to destroy paganism so that the Christian religion alone, reestablished in all the splendor of its orthodoxy, reigned over the ruins of false cults. The means, however, seem less abrupt: paganism, instead of being overthrown in a single blow, was to be demolished piece by piece. Although during the first part of the struggle against idolatry Theodosius had the eastern provinces (where Christianity already dominated) above all in sight, there were still parties of pagans too strong for it to be prudent to push them to despair immediately. Moreover, they were not in revolt against catholic unity, like the Arians and the Manicheans; they played only an indirect part and were far removed from the religious troubles that desolated the East under Constans and Valens. They deserved the consideration due to peaceful subjects and sincere believers.

From the beginning of Theodosius' reign, however, we perceive that the two religions were not in an equal situation in his eyes. The laws of 381 and 383 (imitated in 383 by Gratian) deprived baptized Christians who returned to paganism through apostasy of their right to receive and dispose of property by means of a will. Even simple catechumens guilty of deserting the Church for the temple were punished, although to a lesser degree.[21] In other words, if a pagan was allowed to become a Christian—and if, as Symmachus writes, abstaining from the cult of the gods was honorable[22]—then a Christian, on the other hand, was not allowed to become a pagan. One of the two rival religions was declared legally inferior to the other.

Paganism was not yet forbidden, but every day the circle of restrictions tightened around it. Constantine had forbidden the secret practice of divination but declared official divination, as it was practiced in the temples by the haruspices, to be free.[23] Constans had prohibited any consultations on the future, in the harshest of terms, but he allowed the distinction posed by Constantine to continue.[24] Valentinian I forbade magical incantations and nocturnal sacrifices, but he made express reservations in favor of the haruspices.[25] In 381, Theodosius forbade any sacrifice to be offered in a temple, by day or by night, for the purpose of telling the future.[26] This law could be understood as applying only to sacrifices carried out with the special goal of divination. It suppressed almost entirely the freedoms left in this respect by Constantine, Constans, and Valentinian, but did not seem to get at the divinatory rites that also comprised an integral part of the ordinary sacrifices. A law of 385 was directed at these rites. The inspection of the liver and intestines of the victims by a priest or haruspex was forbidden under any circumstance, under threat of the most severe penalties.[27] The purpose of the law was not to prohibit the sacrifices themselves, or forbid the

[21] *Theodosian Code,* XVI, vii, 1, 2.
[22] Symmachus, *Ep.* 1, 51.
[23] See above, p. 111.
[24] See above, p. 130–31.
[25] See above, p. 160–61.
[26] *Theodosian Code,* XVI, x, 7.
[27] *Ibid.,* 8.

immolation of the victims, but to suppress one of the principal parts of the ceremony—the very one in which pagan superstition took the greatest interest. Indeed, in many places this prohibition put an end to blood sacrifice. The repugnant and expensive practice was discontinued as soon as it was no longer possible, without being punished, to read the future in the burnt offerings. The most obstinate sometimes concealed the practice under the guise of a banquet.[28] Most replaced it with an offering of incense burned in honor of the gods. This sign of devotion was tolerated as long as the temples remained open.[29] People continued to enter them freely and to cense their altars, but one of the most essential rituals of paganism was no longer celebrated.

Either between these two laws, or after the second, stands the Egyptian mission of Cynegius, prefect of the eastern praetorium. Aside from its political goal, this mission had a religious aim. If we are to believe the pagan Zosimus, the high magistrate was in charge of closing all Egyptian temples.[30] Socrates says the same thing.[31] It is unlikely, however. If Libanius' discourse in favor of the temples is later than Cynegius' mission, as many believe,[32] we see that at the time this discourse was written the temples were still open everywhere and the censing of altars was tolerated in place of blood sacrifice. Neither the law of 381 nor that of 385 prohibited entrance to these temples, nor ordered them to close. No particular event in Egypt made such an exceptional measure necessary. If the temples had been closed in part of the East by Cynegius, the law that Theodosius issued in 391 would have no reason for being. Thus it is necessary here, as in other instances, to correct the overblown statements of both the pagan Zosimus and the Christian Socrates. Cynegius probably received the order to close those temples that disobeyed the laws of 381 and 383 by practicing divination, or by seeking omens from the sacrificed animals.

Just a few years later, Theodosius felt authorized to take more radical steps. He had submitted to the penance imposed by St Ambrose

[28]Libanius, *Pro templis.*
[29]*Ibid.*
[30]Zosimus, IX, 37.
[31]Socrates, *Hist. Eccl.,* V, 16.
[32]Sievers, *Libanius,* p. 192, note 26.

after the unfortunate events in Thessalonica. Sojourning in Milan (from where, in reality, he governed the whole empire), he considered himself unable to offer sufficient pledges of his repentance and fervor. Every one of his acts of 391 bear the mark of this idea. Two laws struck the Christian apostates anew, degrading those of high rank and declaring them unable to recover the rights they had lost, even if they repented.[33] Another law forbade any gathering of heretics.[34] Symmachus, at that time consul, had once again requested the reestablishment of the altar of Victory; Theodosius, irritated, removed it a hundred miles from the imperial residence.[35] Dating from the same year are two laws forbidding not only burnt sacrifices, but even entrance into the temples and (if we take the wording literally) gazing at the statues formerly worshiped there.[36] Any magistrate or high-ranking person who believed he might override this ban would be punished with a fine calculated according to his rank.[37] This time the prohibition was absolute. Sozomen is not mistaken when he tells us that Theodosius forbade approaching places consecrated to the pagan cult,[38] and Zosimus translates the same legal terms when he reports the dangers of believing in the gods and lifting up one's eyes to worship them.[39]

With every public cult thus removed from the pagans, the emperor had no scruples about transferring temple properties. Accordingly, he made a gift of an old sanctuary of Mithras to Theophilus, bishop of Alexandria. During the process of transforming it into a church, the workers discovered some bizarre objects that were used at initiations. The bishop exposed them to public ridicule, and the pagans of Alexandria revolted. They withdrew into the large, splendid temple of Serapis that dominated the town. Transforming it into a citadel, they made sorties, seized Christians, and massacred many. The magistrates were unable to restore peace. The riot was calmed only though the

[33] *Theodosian Code*, XVI, vii, 4–5.
[34] *Ibid.*, XVI, v. 20.
[35] *De prom. et praed. Dei*, III, 38. Cf. Seeck, *Symmachus*, p. LVIII.
[36] *Theodosian Code*, XVI, x, 10.
[37] *Ibid.*, XVI, x, 11.
[38] Sozomen, *Hist. Eccl.*, VII, 16.
[39] Zosimus, IV.

intervention of Theodosius. An imperial rescript granted amnesty to the rebels, but ordered the destruction of every temple in Alexandria. The Serapion, which was the pride of the city and the center of Egyptian religion, perished; along with it fell the sanctuaries of Canopus, once the meeting place of licentious pilgrims.[40] Many other temples in Egypt, even those outside of Alexandria and its suburb, were probably involved in this destruction.[41]

Praising Theodosius' religious policy, St Ambrose credits him with having abolished all pagan ceremonies.[42] Sozomen adds that honoring the gods was no longer allowed, even in secret.[43] A law of 392 indeed delivered the final blow to paganism. It renewed the ban on sacrifices in the temples, including the act of offering libations, fire, and flowers to the spirits, lares, and penates [household gods]. It declared that every field or dwelling where incense was burned would be confiscated.[44] In the fourth century there were many such domestic sanctuaries. Idolatry had taken refuge there, as its last stand. Chapels to the Fortune of the house or family were built in the gardens.[45] Underground shrines of Mithras, dug beneath the outbuildings, rapidly became the center of a secret cult.[46] Theodosius closed these sanctuaries, just as he had closed the temples. Most likely, however, many of those hidden under the protective shadow of private life escaped his investigations, and were perpetuated despite the prohibitions.

[40]Socrates, V, 16, 17; Sozomen VII, 15; Rufinus, II, 20, 30. Was the famous library of Alexandria, kept at the Serapion, destroyed with it? See, for different meanings, Gorini, *Défense de l'Église*, vol.1, p. 64–102; Chastel, *Revue historique*, April–June 1876, p. 484–496; Alglave, *Revue scientifique*, June 19, 1875; Lefort, *Gazette hebdomadaire de médicine et de chirurgie*, n. 26, 1875; Drapeyron, *l'Empereur Héraclius*, p. 405–409.

[41]Rufinus, II, 28, says that all the Egyptian temples were then destroyed.

[42]St Ambrose, *De obitu Theod.*, 4.

[43]Sozomen, VII, 20.

[44]*Theodosian Code*, XVI, x, 12.

[45]*Bull. di arch. crist.* 1884–1885, p. 120, 139; *Bull. della comm. arch. com.*,1885, p. 36; 1880, p. 17; 1894, p. 291; *Revue historique*, 1887, p. 347.

[46]See the examples mentioned in the *Bull. della comm. arch. com. di Roma*, 1892, p. 355.

2. The End of Paganism

Thus ended the pagan cult—legally, at least, if not in reality. Paganism continued in many places, but under the law its end had already come. Every pagan act—private as well as public—became a criminal act after laws in 391 and 392. However, St John Chrysostom was able to successfully contrast Theodosius' conduct with that of the Church's former persecutors.[47] The reason was that during his reign intolerance towards the cult was allied with greater tolerance towards individuals. On this point, Theodosius followed the path laid out by his Christian predecessors since Constantine. He never troubled anyone for the sake of religion, nor did he distinguish between pagans and Christians in the distribution of favors and offices. Libanius, the most passionate champion of idolatry in the East, received numerous favors from him[48] and freely composed works filled with pagan sentiment. Themistius, already showered with favors under the preceding regimes, became prefect of Constantinople.[49] In the West Symmachus, the political leader of the pagan party, was prefect of Rome in 384[50] and consul in 391.[51] Pretextatus, who could be considered the religious leader of the pagan faction, became prefect of the praetorium in 384[52] and was chosen for the consulate in 385.[53] An equally illustrious pagan, Nicomachus Flavian, enjoyed sufficient favor with Theodosius to be appointed prefect of the praetorium in 389.[54] In that very year Albinus was prefect of Rome—the same person, perhaps, who had been pontifex, according to St Jerome and who shared the same sentiments and attitudes as Symmachus, according to Macrobius.[55]

---

[47]St John Chrysostom, *Hom. In S. Babylam,* 3.

[48]Libanius, *De vita; Pro templis;* Eunapius, *Vitae soph.,* 14. See Tillemont, *Hist. des Emper.,* Vol. V, 226.

[49]Themistius, *Orat.* XVII, XVIII. Cf. *Theodosian Code,* VI, iv, 12.

[50]*Theodosian Code,* I, vi, 9. See Seeck, *Symmachus,* p. liv–lvi.

[51]Symmachus, *Ep.* II, 62, 63, 64; V, 15; IX, 149, 153.

[52]*Theodosian Code,* VI, v, 2; *Code of Justinian,* I, liv, 5.

[53]Symmachus, *Ep.* X, 12; cf. Seeck, p. lxxxviii.

[54]*Theodosian Code,* IX, xl, 13; cf. Seeck, p. cxvii, note 579.

[55]*Corp. inscr. lat.,* Vol. XI, 3791; St Jerome, *Ep.* 107; Macrobius, *Saturn.,* I, 2, 15. Seeck, p. clxxix and clxxx distinguishes the pontiff of whom St Jerome speaks from the prefect of Rome; for an opposite view, see Tillemont, *Hist. des Emp.,* vol. V, p. 301.

The events that followed lead us to wonder whether the Christian emperor might have been unwise to place his confidence in so many pagan personages. In the East, where the cult of the gods had lost virtually all influence, there was little danger in elevating a Themistius or lending an indulgent ear to the flatteries and complaints of a Libanius. In the West, however, it was perilous to entrust the highest offices to members of the pagan aristocracy. This was soon made clear by the revolt of Eugenius, or rather by the outcry which it occasioned for the entire pagan party.

After assassinating Valentinian II in 392, the general Arbogast, whose barbarian origins prevented him from assuming power himself, gave the purple to the rhetor Eugenius.[56] Eugenius was a Christian, but circumstances made him a docile instrument of the pagan reaction. Nicomachus kept the office of prefect of the praetorium and became in reality the leader and organizer of the rebellion, which quickly assumed religious overtones. First Flavian presented Eugenius with the request rejected several times by Gratian and Valentinian. From this phantom of a sovereign he obtained the reestablishment of the altar of Victory, the restitution of temple properties, the freedom to sacrifice, and even the right of divination.[57] Public and private buildings constructed in Rome on the sites of suppressed temples were demolished.[58] Christians were led to apostasy by the bait of magistracy. The pagans of Rome prepared for the inevitable struggle with Theodosius as for a holy war. The city was crisscrossed by processions, which some of the nobility followed. The national gods and foreign divinities were successively honored. Flavian himself was initiated into the cult of Mithras and offered a sacrificial bull.[59] This pagan orgy lasted until 394; Theodosius' victory over Eugenius, in which Flavian and Arbogast

[56]Zosimus, IV, 53; Socrates, V, 25.

[57]St Ambrose, *Ep.* 57; Paulinus, *Vita Ambrosii,* 26.

[58]This is how Seeck understands verse 36 of the anonymous poem referred to in the following note (*Symmachus,* p. cxviii).

[59]See Rufinus, *Hist. Eccl.,* II, 33; and the anonymous poem discovered in 1867 by Léopold Delisle, *Bibl. de l'École des Chartes,* 1867, p. 297; *Revue archéologique,* vol. XVIII, 1868, p. 451–459; *Bull. di arch. crist.* 1868, p. 49–75. After the laws of Theodosius against the pagan cult, this disgusting ceremony had stopped; we no longer find taurobolic inscriptions in Rome after 300; *Corp. inscr. lat.,* vol. VI, 512.

perished, put an end to it. This proved to be the decisive blow. The pagan aristocracy made its last stand, and lost. Theodosius entered the eternal city, convoked the senate, exhorted the senators to quit the cult of the gods, and obtained from the assembly a vote officially abolishing paganism in Rome.[60] From that time onward, conversions increased among the aristocracy.[61] Those attracted to paganism based solely on ambition or self-interest no longer had reason to stay. No violence was used against anyone, however. The pagan senators kept their seats, their riches, and their honors. Theodosius publicly deplored Flavian's death. The children of Flavian and Arbogast retained possession of their property.[62] There were neither confiscations nor reprisals, nor bloodshed. The amnesty demanded by St Ambrose[63] was accorded without reservation. The gods alone paid the price, instead of men.

This truly Christian victory ended Theodosius' life. He died on January 17, 395, after dividing the empire between his two sons, giving the East to Arcadius and the West to Honorius. The great emperor's sons resembled him neither in intelligence nor character. Arcadius spent his life in the midst of court intrigues, submitting to an overbearing wife and his unworthy favorites. Sheltered behind the walls of Ravenna, Honorius remained unmoved by the taking of Rome by the Goths, and hardly seemed to feel the ills that befell the Roman world as soon as Theodosius' sword ceased to hold the barbarians at bay. However, both sons staunchly maintained the religious policy of their father. Despite the opposing interests that divided the two empires during their long, virtually simultaneous reign—and, more than once, reached the point of turning into fratricidal war—the agreement between the two on this matter seems to have endured. The significance of their legislative work is astonishing. These two sovereigns, equally soft and inept, never ceased from rendering decrees in favor of the Church and

---

[60]The voyage of Theodosius to Rome, attested by Zosimus and Prudentius, but contested by several modern erudites, has been put beyond doubt by the discovery of an inscription engraved on the pedestal of the statue of Nicomachus Flavian, which alludes to it very clearly: see De Rossi, *Ann. dell'inst. di corr. archeol.* 1894, p. 285–356; *Bull. di arch. crist.* 1868, p. 70.

[61]Prudentius, *Contra Symm.*, I, 410ff.

[62]St Augustine, *De civitate Dei*, V, 26.

[63]St Ambrose, *Ep.* 61, 62; Paulinus, *Vita Ambrosii*, 11.

against idolatry. Every year laws were sent from Constantinople and Ravenna confirming the privileges of the clergy, repressing heresy, and threatening paganism.

Certain nuances distinguish the work of the two principes. Both frequently attacked the heretics: Apollinarists, Eunomeans, and Montanists in the East,[64] Donatists and even Manicheans in the West.[65] Arcadius seemed less inclined than his brother to extend the rights of bishops and clerics,[66] while at the same time he showed unexpected favor toward the Jews.[67] Honorius, by contrast, confirmed or augmented ecclesiastical immunity on many occasions[68] and curbed the abuses and propaganda of the Jews.[69] In their conduct toward pagans, which was essentially identical, there are also differences in form. In the East, where paganism was much weakened, Arcadius struck more rapid and numerous blows. In 395, wishing to make it understood that a change in sovereign did not imply a change in policy, he renewed the laws instated by his father concerning sacrifices and idols.[70] In 396, he removed the exemptions that the pagan priests still retained.[71] In order to reach idolatry in its last refuges, he ordered the demotion of temples in the countryside in 399, wherever it could be done without an uproar.[72]

Encountering a cult in the West that still retained strong support among the aristocrats as well as the people, despite the revolt of 394, Honorius showed greater consideration. In 399 he renewed only the ban on sacrifices; he was careful, however, to order through the same law respect for the statues of the gods that adorned public buildings.[73] He also allowed the celebration of feast days and corporate meals on their customary dates, provided that no act of idolatry

[64]*Theodosian Code*, XVI, V, 25, 26, 27, 28, 29, 30, 31, 32, 33, 34, 36.
[65]*Ibid.*, 35, 40, 41, 46, 51, 52.
[66]*Ibid.*, IX, XL, 16, XLV, I, 16 ; XVI, II, 32, 33.
[67]*Ibid.*, XII, I, 165; XVI, 10, 11, 12, 13, 15.
[68]*Ibid.*, XI, III, 7; XVI, II, 29, 30, 47; *Justinian Code*, I, IV, 8.
[69]*Theodosian Code*, II, IV, 7; XVI, 11, 17.
[70]*Ibid.*, XVI, x, 13.
[71]*Ibid.*, 14.
[72]*Ibid.*, 16.
[73]*Ibid.*, 14.

was intermingled with it.[74] Not until 408 do we see him take action against the temples. This radical step included a confiscation of any income they might still possess; the appointment of every pagan sanctuary for some public service; the removal of any statues they contained; and a ban on celebrating meals and feasts on their premises or in their dependencies.[75] However, because of public disturbances, and perhaps also through the connivance of certain officials, these strict orders do not seem to have been carried out everywhere. At the beginning of 409, Honorius was obliged to remind the heretics, Jews, pagans, and, above all, the magistrates, that Theodosius' religious legislation had not been repealed.[76] If we are to believe Zosimus, he then promptly contradicted himself by giving everyone full freedom of religion.[77] Such a change, if it occurred, did not last long, for in 415 Honorius promulgated a new law against paganism, driving the provincial priests from the various county seats of Africa, reuniting with the princeps' domain all territories devoted to the practice of idolatry, and confiscating the revenues and buildings intended for the feasts and other expenses with a pagan cast. Finally, overlooking the reserves he himself set aside not long ago to benefit works of art, he ordered the removal of statues once honored with sacrifices from the baths and public buildings, out of fear that they might become an occasion for sin on the part of the people.[78]

When we consider this legislation as a whole, we realize that laws alone, no matter how absolute their terms, were not enough to put an end to paganism. The emperors were often only half obeyed, as witnessed by the frequent repetition of the same laws. Their orders did not always reach the far corners of their vast states. The old cult had too many partisans, open and covert, among the ranks of the officials for every tract directed against their gods to reach its goal. The force of inertia alone was enough to deaden many blows. In many places, undoubtedly, the laws forbidding idolatry were carried out. "Jupiter,"

---

[74] *Ibid.,* 17.
[75] *Ibid.,* XVI, x, 19.
[76] *Ibid.,* XVI, V, 46.
[77] Zosimus, VI. Cf. Tillemont, *Hist. des Empereurs,* vol. V, p. 574.
[78] *Theodosian Code,* XVI, x, 20.

writes St Jerome, "all locked up in his temple at Gaza."[79] Contemporary writings, and even inscriptions, depict pagans hiding idols threatened with destruction.[80] St Augustine speaks of statues, temples, and sacred groves destroyed by the order or with permission of the magistrates.[81] However, he reveals that the execution of these orders often remained incomplete, and he himself counsels against pushing them to the breaking point. We should topple idols belonging to individuals when such people, having become Christian, authorize their removal, he states, but we should abstain from disturbing those found on lands whose owners remain pagan.[82] The severity of the law yielded to the rights of private property, just as it stopped short before the wishes of a population too attached to the ancient cult, before buildings of artistic value and the objects they represented,[83] and even before financial interests. One hesitated to close a famous temple for fear of seeing the pagans abandon the city, leaving the latter no longer able to pay its taxes.[84]

The pagans very cleverly used the empire's disasters to turn public sentiment back to the gods. They read into the evils of war and invasion the hand of immortal gods irritated at seeing Rome unfaithful to the old religion under which its power had grown, and which had become inseparable from its fate and now hastened its fall. St Augustine would refute this thesis in *The City of God*. Even if it failed to stand up to reflection and an attentive study of history, there were anxious times when this theory seemed to make an impression on distraught minds, in spite of everything. We are told that in 408, when Alaric appeared for the first time at the gates of Rome, the prefect of the city and the entire senate offered a sacrifice.[85] On the whole, however, the

---

[79]St Jerome, *Ep.* 107, ad Laetam.

[80]St Augustine, *De consensu Evang.* I, 27, 28; Prosper, *De promiss. et praed. Dei*, III, 38; Orelli, *Inscript.* 3275, 3276. Cf. De Witte, in *Ann. dell Instit. di corresp. archeol.* Vol. XL, 1968, p. 195–2111; Palu de Lessert, in *Revue archéologique*, vol. II, p. 206–09; Edmond le Blant, *Acad. des Inscr.* September 26, 1800.

[81]St Augustine, *Ep.* 91. Cf. *Bull. di archeol. crist.* 1805, p. 4; a caricature found in a catacomb, representing a Christian who overthrows an idol.

[82]St Augustine, *Sermo* 61.

[83]*Theodosian Code*, XVI, x, 8.

[84]*Vita S. Porphyrii*, 6; in *Acta SS.*, February, vol. III, 652.

[85]Sozomen, IX, 6; Zosimus, V.

barbarians were unexpected accessories to the laws forbidding idolatry. The temples of Rome were still in possession of their treasures when, in that very year of 408, they had to melt one of their most precious statues to pay the city's ransom to the Goths.[86] Greece, too, had succeeded in preserving its temples in places where the cult had not been interrupted. The approach of the Goths destroyed them, shattering the idols, interrupting the sacrifices, and bringing the mysteries of Eleusis, which up until then had escaped all edicts, to an end.[87]

The main agent of idolatry's destruction, however, was the zeal of the bishops and Christian missionaries. This zeal seems exaggerated in some cases; Libanius' complaints are probably not entirely false.[88] Even among the saints, we see a tendency at times to use force when the people do not wish to destroy the idols or their temples.[89] But most of those whom history remembers do not deserve this reproach. They usually accomplished what they considered the salvation of society through the example of their own lives, without the help of the public authorities. If St Martin and his imitators had not braved death a hundred times to destroy rustic chapels and sacred groves, the West would have remained the refuge of the coarsest superstitions for centuries.[90] Likewise, if St John Chrysostom's monks had not launched an assault on the temples of Phoenicia and Lebanon, perhaps the obscene cults of the East would not have ceased.[91]

With Valentinian III, nephew of Honorius and author of a final law against the pagans,[92] the Western empire virtually came to an end. His successors were phantom emperors whom the barbarians dressed or divested of the purple. No legislation remains to be summarized, for strictly speaking, there were no more legislators. Yet the old cult was not a position to profit from this weakness on the part of the imperial

[86]Sozomen, Zosimus, *l. c.*; St. Jerome, *Ep.* 11, 16.

[87]Zosimus, V, 5, 6; Eunapius, *Vitae soph. Maxim., Prisc.* Cf. F. Lenormant, *Eleusina, in Dict. des ant.* Vol. II, 551.

[88]Libanius, *Oratio* II (Reiske, p. 167).

[89]Sozomen, VII, 15.

[90]Sulpicius Severus, *Vita B. Martini; Dialogus de virtutibus B. Martini.* Cf. Bulliot and Thollier, *La Mission et le culte de saint Martin. Étude sur le paganisme rural,* Paris, 1892.

[91]St John Chrysostom, *Ep.* 221; Theodoret, *Hist. Eccl.,* V, 9.

[92]*Justinian Code,* I, xi, 7.

power. The moment had passed when it might have easily ensnared the invaders' naïve souls by means of attractions at once crude and refined. At a time when the the barbarians were dividing up the western provinces and establishing themselves in Africa, Italy, Spain, Gaul, and Britain, paganism had neither temples nor priests, nor sacrifices, nor organizations of any kind. Pagans could still be found—rarely in the cities, more often in the countryside—but paganism was no more. Nothing stood in opposition to the Church, which alone remained standing in the midst of universal collapse, that might attract the new masters of Europe or flow into the Christian mold of the society that would be born from contact between the barbarians and the remaining Roman institutions.

Imperial power endured for many more centuries in the East. It carried on the struggle against paganism, but this fight was extinguished of its own accord for lack of fuel. In his law of 423, Theodosius II was concerned "with pagans who still exist, although we think there are no longer any more."[93] In 435, through another law, he ordered the destruction or transformation into churches of "every sanctuary, temple, and edifice of idolatry, if any remain intact."[94] During the fifth (and even the sixth) century, we find some laws in the East directed against the pagans,[95] and yet even there paganism was no longer. If it survived on its own, it was in the form of popular superstition for some, or, for a small number, in the form of philosophy. Europe recognizes no religion other than Christianity, and society, through its institutions, through its laws, through its morals, is altogether Christian.

---

[93] *Theodosian Code*, XVI, x, 22; cf. 23.
[94] *Ibid.*, XVI, x, 25.
[95] Marcianus, *Nov.* 3; *Justinian Code*, I, IV, 15, 19; v. 21; xi, 7, 8, 9, 10; x, 1, 2.

On the Relations of the Emperors with the Christians up to the Reign of Constantine

I. The expulsion of the Jews by Claudius (about 51)

Judaeos, impulsore Chresto, adsidue tumultuantes Roma expulit.

Suetonius, *Vita Claudii*, 25

"Since the Jews constantly made disturbances at the instigation of Chrestus [Christ], he expelled them from Rome."

Suetonius, *Lives of the Caesars, Volume II*, Loeb Classical Library No. 38, J. C. Rolfe, trans. (Cambridge, MA: Harvard University Press, 1914), 53

II. Nero and the Christians (64)

Ergo abolendo rumori Nero subdidit reos et quaesitissimis poenis adfecit, quos per flagitia invisos vulgus Christianos adpellabat. Auctor nominis eius Christus Tiberio imperitante per procuratorem Pontium Pilatum supplicio adfectus erat; repressaque in praesens exitiabilis superstitio rursum erumpebat, non modo per Judaeam, originem eius mali, sed per urbem etiam, quo cuncta undique atrocia aut pudenda confluunt celebranturque. Igitur primum correpti qui fatebantur, deinde indicio eorum multitudo ingens haud perinde in crimine incendii, quam odio humani generis convicti sunt. Et pereuntibus addita ludibria, ut ferarum tergis contecti laniatu canum interirent, aut crucibus adfixi, aut flammandi atque, ubi defecisset dies, in usum nocturni luminis urerentur. Hortos suos ei spectaculo Nero obtulerat et circense ludicrum edebat, habitu aurigae permixtus plebi vel curriculo insistens. Unde quamquam adversus sontes et novissima exempla

meritos miseratio oriebatur, tamquam non utilitate publica sed in sae-
vitiam unius desumerentur.

Tacitus, Annales, XV, 44

"Consequently, to get rid of the report, Nero fastened the guilt and
inflicted the most exquisite tortures on a class hated for their abomi-
nations, called Christians by the populace. Christus, from whom the
name had its origin, suffered the extreme penalty during the reign of
Tiberius at the hands of one of our procurators, Pontius Pilatus, and
a most mischievous superstition, thus checked for the moment, again
broke out not only in Judaea, the first source of the evil, but even in
Rome, where all things hideous and shameful from every part of the
world find their center and become popular. Accordingly, an arrest was
first made of all who pleaded guilty; then, upon their information, an
immense multitude was convicted, not so much of the crime of fir-
ing the city, as of hatred against mankind. Mockery of every sort was
added to their deaths. Covered with the skins of beasts, they were torn
by dogs and perished, or were nailed to crosses, or were doomed to the
flames and burnt, to serve as a nightly illumination, when daylight had
expired. Nero offered his gardens for the spectacle, and was exhibiting
a show in the circus, while he mingled with the people in the dress
of a charioteer or stood aloft on a car. Hence, even for criminals who
deserved extreme and exemplary punishment, there arose a feeling of
compassion; for it was not, as it seemed, for the public good, but to glut
one man's cruelty, that they were being destroyed."

Annals of Tacitus: Translated into English, with Notes and Maps, Alfred
John Church and William Jackson Brodribb, trans. (London: Macmillan and Co., 1876), 304–305.

Adflicti suppliciis Christiani, genus hominum superstitionis novae ac
maleficae. . . .

Suetonius, Vita Neronis, 16

"Punishment was inflicted on the Christians, a class of men given to a
new and mischievous superstition. . . ."

Suetonius, Lives of the Caesars, Volume II (LCL 38), 111.

According to Robert L. Wilken in *The Christians as the Romans Saw Them*, Yale University Press, 1984 (p. 50–51), the word "superstition" referred to beliefs and practices foreign to the Romans, which had penetrated the Roman world from surrounding lands. Thus, two important Roman historians concur in labeling Christianity as a "pernicious and mischievous superstition."

III. The Christians condemned under Domitian

Kan tō autō allous te pollous kai Phlaouion Klēmenta hypateuonta kaiper anepsion onta kai gynaika kai autēn syggenē heautou Phlaouian Domitillan echonta katesphaxen ho Dometianos. Epēnechthē de amphoin egklēma atheotētos hyp'es kai alloies ta tōn Ioudaiōn ethē exokellontes polloi katedixasthēsan kai oi men apethanon, hoi de tōn goun ousiōn esterēthēsan. Hē de Dometilla hyperōristhē monon es Pandeterian. Ton de dē Glabriōna ton meta tou Traianou arxavta katēgorēthenta ta te alla kai oia hoi polloi kai hoti kai thēriois emacheto, apekteinen.

Dio Cassius, Hist. Rom., LXVII, 14

"At this time the road leading from Sinuessa to Puteoli was paved with stone. And the same year Domitian slew, along with many others, Flavius Clemens the consul, although he was a cousin and had to wife Flavia Domitilla, who was also a relative of the emperor's. The charge brought against them both was that of atheism, a charge on which many others who drifted into Jewish ways were condemned. Some of these were put to death, and the rest were at least deprived of their property. Domitilla was merely banished to Pandateria. But Glabrio, who had been Trajan's colleague in the consulship, was put to death, having been accused of the same crimes as most of the others, and, in particular, of fighting as a gladiator with wild beasts."

Dio Cassius, *Roman History, Vol. 8: Books 61–70*, Loeb Classical Library No. 176, Earnest Cary and Herbert B. Foster, trans. (Cambridge, MA: Harvard University Press, 1925), 349 and 351.

IV. Letter of Pliny to Trajan on the subject of Christians

Plinius Trajano Imperatori:

Solemne est mihi, domine, omnia de quibus dubito ad te referre. Quis enim potest melius vel cunctationem meam regere vel ignorantiam instruere?

Cognitionibus de Christianis interfui numquam: ideo nescio quid et quatenus aut puniri soleat aut quaeri. Nec mediocriter haesitavi sitne aliquod discrimen aetatum an quamlibet teneri mihi a robustioribus differant, detur paenitentiae venia an ei, qui omnino Christianus fuit, desisse non prosit, nomen ipsum, si flagitiis careat, an flagitia cohaerentia nomini puniantur. Interim (in) iis, qui ad me tamquam Christiani deferebantur, hunc sum secutus modum. Interrogavi ipsos, an esent Christiani. Confitenetes iterum ac tertio interrogavi, supplicium minatus: perseverantes duci jussi. Neque enim dubitabam, qualecumque esset quot faterentur, pertinaciam certe et inflexibilem obstinationem debere puniri. Fuerung alii similis amentiae quos, quia cives Romani erant, adnotavi in urbem remittendos. Mox ipse tractatu, ut fieri solet, diffundente se crimine plures species inciderunt. Propositus est libellus since auctore multorum nomina continens. Qui negabant esse Christianos aut fuisse, cum poaeeunte me deos appellarent et imagini tuae, quam propter hoc jusseram cum simulacris numinum adferri, ture ac vino supplicarent, praeterea male dicerent Christo, quorum nihil posse cogi dicuntur qui sunt re vera Christiani, dimittendos esse putavi. Alii ab indice nominati esse se Christianos dixerunt et mox negaverunt, fuisse quidem, sed desisse, quidam ante triennium, quidam ante plure annos, non nemo etiam ante viginti quoque. Omnes et imaginem tuam deorumque simulacra venerati sunt (ii) et Christo male dixerunt. Adfirmabant autem hanc fuisse summam vel culpae suae vel erorris quod esssent soliti stato die ante lucem convenire carmenque Christo quasi deo dicere secum invicem, seque sacramento non in scelus aliquod obstringere , sed ne furta, ne latrocinia, ne adulteria committerent, ne fidem fallerent, ne depositum appellati abnegarent : quibus peractos moremsibi discedendi fuisse, rursusque ad capiendum cibum, promiscuum, tamen et innoxium ; quod ipsum facere desisse post edictum meum, quo secondum mandata tua hetaerias esse vetueram. Qou magis necessarium credidi ex duabus ancillis, quae ministrae dicebanture, quid esset veri et per tormenta querere. Nihila aliud inveni quam superstitionem pravam, immodicam. Ideo dilata cognitione ad consulendum te decucurri. Visa est enim mihi res digna consultatione, maxime propter periclitantium numerum. Multi enim omnis aetatis , omnis ordinis, utriusque sexus etiam, vocanture in periculum et vocabuntur. Neque civitates sed vicos etiam atque agros superstitionnis istius contagio pervagata est ; quae videture sisti et corrigi posse. Certis satis constat prope jam desolata temple coepisse celebrari et sacrfa solemnia diu intermissa repeti pastumque venire cictimarum, cujus rarissimus pastumque venire victimarum, cujus adhus rarissimus emptor inveneienbatur. Ex quo facile est opinari quae turba hominum emendari possit, si sit poenitentiae locus.

Pliny the Younger, *Ep.*, X, 96

"Pliny to Trajan:

It is my custom, Sire, to refer to you in all cases where I am in doubt, for who can better clear up difficulties and inform me?

I have never been present at any legal examination of the Christians, and I do not know, therefore, what are the usual penalties passed upon them, or the limits of those penalties, or how searching an inquiry should be made. I have hesitated a great deal in considering whether any distinctions should be drawn according to the ages of the accused; whether the weak should be punished as severely as the more robust, or whether the man who has once been a Christian gained anything by recanting? Again, whether the name of being a Christian, even though otherwise innocent of crime, should be punished, or only the crimes that gather around it? In the meantime, this is the plan that I have adopted in the case of those Christians who have been brought before me. I ask them whether they are Christians, if they say 'Yes,' then I repeat the question the second time, and also a third—warning them of the penalties involved; and if they persist, I order them away to prison. For I do not doubt that—be their admitted crime what it may—their pertinacity and inflexible obstinacy surely ought to be punished. There were others who showed similar mad folly, whom I reserved to be sent to Rome, as they were Roman citizens. Later, as is commonly the case, the mere fact of my entertaining the question led to a multiplying of accusations and a variety of cases were brought before me. An anonymous pamphlet was issued, containing a number of names of alleged Christians. Those who denied that they were or had been Christians and called upon the gods with the usual formula, reciting the words after me, and those who offered incense and wine before your image—which I had ordered to be brought forward for this purpose, along with the regular statues of the gods—all such I considered acquitted—especially as they cursed the name of Christ, which it is said bona fide Christians cannot be induced to do. Still others there were, whose names were supplied by an informer. These first said they were Christians, then denied it, insisting they had been, 'but were so no longer'; some of them having 'recanted many years ago,' and more than one 'full twenty years back.' These all worshiped your image and the god's statues and cursed the name of Christ. But they declared their guilt or error was simply this—on a fixed day they used to meet before dawn and recite a hymn among themselves to Christ, as though he were a god. So far from binding themselves by oath to commit any crime, they swore to keep from theft, robbery, adultery, breach of faith, and not to deny any trust money deposited with them when called upon to deliver it. This ceremony over, they used to depart and meet again to take food—but it was of no special character, and entirely harmless. They also had ceased from this practice after the edict I issued—by which, in accord with your orders, I forbade all secret societies. I then thought it the more needful to get at the facts behind their statements. Therefore I placed two women, called 'deaconesses,' under torture, but I found only a debased superstition carried to great lengths, so I postponed my examination, and immediately consulted you. This seems a matter worthy of your prompt consideration, especially as so many people are endangered. Many of all ages and both sexes are put in peril of their lives by their accusers; and the process will go on, for the contagion of this superstition has spread not merely through the free towns, but into the villages and farms. Still I think it can be halted and things set right. Beyond any doubt, the temples—which were nigh deserted—are beginning again to be thronged with worshipers; the sacred rites, which long have lapsed, are now being renewed, and the food for the sacrificial victims is again finding a sale—though up to recently it had almost no market. So one can safely infer how vast numbers could be reclaimed, if only there were a chance given for repentance."

Readings in Ancient History: Illustrative Extracts from the Sources, Vol. 2: Rome and the West, William Stearns Davis, ed. (Boston: Allyn and Bacon, 1913), 219–222.

V. Rescript from Trajan to Pliny (112)

Trajanus Plinio S.

Actum quem debuisti, mi Secunde, in excutiendis causis eorum, qui christiani ad te delati fuerant, secutus es. Neque enim in universum aliqid, quod quasi certam formam habeat, constitui potest. Conquirendi non sunt: si deferantur et arguantur, puniendi sunt, ita tamen ut qui negaverit se christianum ese, itque re ipsa manifestum fecerit, id est supplicando diis nostris, quamvis suspectus in preteritum, veniam ex paenitentia impetret. Sine auctore vero propositi libelli (in) nullo crimine locum habere debent. Name et pessimi exempli, nec nostri saeculi est.

Pliny the Younger, *Ep.*, X, 97

"Trajan to Pliny,

You have adopted the right course, my dear Pliny, in examining the cases of those cited before you as Christians; for no hard and fast rule can be laid down covering such a wide question. The Christians are not to be hunted out. If brought before you, and the offense is proved, they are to be punished, but with this reservation—if any one denies he is a Christian, and makes it clear he is not, by offering prayer to our gods, then he is to be pardoned on his recantation, no matter how suspicious his past. As for anonymous pamphlets, they are to be discarded absolutely, whatever crime they may charge, for they are not only a precedent of a very bad type, but they do not accord with the spirit of our age."

Readings in Ancient History, Vol. 2, 222.

VI. Rescript of Hadrian to Minucius Fundanus (about 126)

Minucius Fundanus

Epistolēn edexamēn grapheisan moi apo Serēniou Granianou lamprotatou andros, hontina su diedexō. Ou dokei oun moi to pragma azēteton katalipein, ina mēte oi anthrōpoi tarattōntai kai tois sukophantais xorēgia kakourgias paraschethē. An oun sahpōs eis tautēn tēn axiōsin hoi eparchōtai dunōntai diischurizesthai kata tōn Christianōn, hēs kai pro bēmatos apokrinesthai, epi touto monon trapōsin, all'ouk axiōsesin oude monais boais. Pollō gar mallon prosēken, ei tis katēgorein bouloito, toutose diaginōskein. Ei tis oun katēgorei kai deiknusi para tous nomous; prattontas, outōs diorize kata tēn dunamin tou hamartēmatos. Hōs ma ton Heraklea, ei tis sukophantias charin tiouto proteinoi, dialambane huper tēs deinotētos kai phrontize, hopōs an ekdikēseias.

Appended to Justin Martyr's First Apology, after the final chapter (48)

"To Minucius Fundanus,

"I have received the letter addressed to me by your predecessor Serenius Granianus, a most illustrious man; and this communication I am unwilling to pass over in silence, lest innocent persons be disturbed, and occasion be given to the informers for practising villany. Accordingly, if the inhabitants of your province will so far sustain this petition of theirs as to accuse the Christians in some court of law, I do not prohibit them from doing so. But I will not suffer them to make use of mere entreaties and outcries. For it is far more just, if any one desires to make an accusation, that you give judgment upon it. If, therefore, any one makes the accusation, and furnishes proof that the said men do anything contrary to the laws, you shall adjudge punishments in proportion to the offences. And this, by Hercules, you shall give special heed to, that if any man shall, through mere calumny, bring an accusation against any of these persons, you shall award to him more severe punishments in proportion to his wickedness."

From *Ante-Nicene Fathers*, Vol. 5, Alexander Roberts, James Donaldson, and A. Cleveland Coxe eds. (Buffalo, NY: Christian Literature Publishing Co., 1886), 186.

VII. Rescript of Marcus Aurelius to the legate of Lyon (177)

. . . Episteilantos gar tou Kaisaros tous men apotumpanisthēnai, ei de tines arnointo, toutous apoluthēnai.

Letter of the Christians of Vienne and Lyon to those in Asia and Phrygia, from Eusebius, *Hist. eccl.*, V, 1, 47

"For Cæsar commanded that they should be put to death, but that any who might deny should be set free."

Nicene and Post-Nicene Fathers, Second Series [hereafter NPNF[2]], Vol. 1, Philip Schaff and Henry Wace, eds. (Buffalo, NY: Christian Literature Publishing Co., 1890), 216.

VIII. Comment on the rescript of Septimus Severus

Judaeos fieri sub gravi poena vetuit, item etiam de christianis sanxit.

Spartianus, *Vita Septimii Severi*, 17.1

"He forbade conversion to Judaism under heavy penalties and enacted a similar law in regard to the Christians."

Historia Augusta, Vol. 1, Loeb Classical Library, No. 139, David Magie, trans. (Cambridge, MA: Harvard University Press, 1921), 409.

IX. Rescript of Alexander Severus (between 222 and 235)

Cum Christiani quemdam locum, qui publicus fuerat, occupassent, contra popinarii dicerent, sibi eum deberi, rescripsit « melius essse ut quemadmodumcumque illic dues colatur, quam popinariis dedatur. »

Lampridius, *Vita Alexandri Severi*, 49, 6

"And when the Christians took possession of a certain place, which had previously been public property, and the keepers of an eating-house maintained that it belonged to them, Alexander rendered the decision that it was better for some sort of a god to be worshipped there than for the place to be handed to the keepers of an eating-house."

Historia Augusta, Vol. 2, Loeb Classical Library, No. 140, David Magie, trans. (Cambridge, MA: Harvard University Press, 1924), 279.

X. Libellus [certificate] of sacrificing under Decius (250)

Tois epi thusiōn hērēmenois kōmēs Alexandrou Nēsou para Aurēliou Diogenous Sataboutos apo kōm ēs Alexandrou Nēsou, ōs Lob, oulē ophrui dexia. Kai aei Thuōn tois theois dietelesa, kainun epi parousin humeinkata ta prostetagmena ethusa kai tōn hierreōn egeusamēn, kai axiō humas huposēmiōsasthai Dieutucheite, Aurēliois Diogenēs epidedōka. Aurelios s ... r ... thuonta Mus ... nōnos ses ... La autokratoros Kaisaros Gaiou Messiou Kointou Traaivou Dexiou euse-bous eutuxous sebastou epeiph B.

"[1st Hand.] To the commission chosen to superintend the sacrifices at the village of Alexander's Isle. From Aurelius Diogenes, son of Satabous, of the village of Alexander's Isle, ages 72 years, with a scar on the right eyebrow. I have always sacrificed to the gods, and now in your presence in accordance with the edict I have made sacrifice, and poured a libation, and partaken of the victims. I request you to certify this below. Farewell. I, Aurelius Diogenes, have presented this petition.
[2nd Hand.] I, Aurelius Syrus, saw you and your son sacrificing.
[3rd Hand.] ... onos ...

[1st Hand.] The year one of the Emperor Caesar Gaius Messius Quintus Trajanus Pius Felix Augustus, Epeiph 2 [June 26, 250]."

J. R. Knipfing, "The Libelli of the Decian Persecution," *Harvard Theological Review* 16 (1923): 345–90, at 363.

XI. The first edict of Valerian (257)

Imperatore Valeriano quartum et Gallieno tertium consulibus thertio Kalendarum Septembrium Carthagine in secretario Paternus proconsul Cypriano episcopo dixit: *Sacratissimi imperatores Valerianus et Gallienus literas ad me dare dignati sunt, quibus praeceperunteos, qui Romanam religionem non colunt, debere Romanas caeremonias recognoscere. Exquisivi ergo de nomine tuo, quid mihi respondes?* Cyprianus episcopus dixit: *Christianus sum et episcopus. Nullos alios deos novi, nisi unum et verum Deum, qui fecit coelum et terram, mare et quae sunt in eis omnia. Huic Deo nos christiani deservimus, hunc deprecamur diebus ac noctibus pro vobis et pro omnibus hominibus et pro incolumitate ipsorum imperatorum.* Paternus proconsul dixit: *In hac ergo voluntate perseveras?* Cyprianus episcipus respondit: *Bona voluntas, quae Deum novit, immutari non potest.* Paternus proconsul dixit: *Poteris ergo secundum praeceptum Valeriani et Gallieni exul ad urbem Curubitanam profiscisci?* Cyprianus episcopus dixit: *Proficiscor.* Paternus proconsul dixit: *Non solum de episcopis, verum de presbyteris mihi scribere dignati sunt. Volo ergo scire ex te, qui sint presbyteri, qui in hac civitate consistunt?* Cyprianus episcopus respondit: *Legibus vestris bene atque utiliter censuistis delatores non esse; itaque detegi et deferri a me non possunt. In civitatibus autem suis invenientur.* Paternus proconsul dixit: *Ego hodie in hoc loco exquiro.* Cyprianus (episcopus) dixit: *Cum disciplina prohibeat, ut quis se ultro offerat et tua quoque censurae hos displiceat, nec oferre se ipsi possunt, sed a te exquisiti invenientur.* Paternus proconsul dixit: *A me invenientur.* Et adjecit: *Praeceperunt etiam, ne in aliquibus locis conciliabula fiant, nec coemeteria ingrediantur. Si quis itaque hoc tam salubre praeceptum non observaverit, capite plectetur.* Cyprianus episcopus respondit: *Fac quod tibi praeceptum est.*

Tunc Paternus proconsil jussit beatum Cyprianum in exilium depor-
tari. Cumque diu ibidem moraretur, successit Aspasio Paterno procon-
suli Galerius Maximus proconsul, qui sanctum Cyprianum episcipum
ab exilio revocatum sibi jussit praesentari. . . .

Acta pronsularia S. Cypriani, 1–2

"When the Emperor Valerian was Consul for the fourth, and Gallienus
for the third time, on the third of the Kalends of September, Paternus
Proconsul at Carthage in his council-chamber thus spoke to Cyprian
the bishop: 'The most sacred Emperors Valerian and Gallienus have
honored me with letters, wherein they enjoin that all those who use
not the religion of Rome, shall formally make profession of their return
to the use of Roman rites; I have made accordingly enquiry of your
name; what answer do you make to me?' Cyrpian the bishop spoke: 'I
am a Christian and bishop; I know no other gods besides the one and
true God, who made heaven and earth, the sea, and all things therein;
this God we Christians serve, to him we pray day and night, for ourselves, for all mankind, for the health of the emperors themselves.'
Paternus Proconsul said, 'Do you persist in this purpose?' Cyprian
Bishop answered, 'That good purpose, which has once acknowledged
God, cannot be changed.' Paternus Proconsul said, 'Will you then,
obeying the mandate of the emperors, depart into exile to the city of
Curubis?' Cyprian Bishop said, 'I go.' Paternus Proconsul said, 'The
letters, wherewith I have been honored by the emperors, speak of presbyters as well as bishops; I would know of you therefore, who they
are, who are presbyters in this city?' Cyprian Bishop answered, 'By
your laws you have righteously and with great benefit forbidden any
to be informers; therefore they cannot be discovered and denounced
by me; but they will be found in their own cities.' Paternus Proconsul
said, 'I am accordingly inquisitor in this place.' Cyprian said, 'Our rules
forbid any man to offer himself for punishment, and your ordinances
discourage the same; they may not therefore offer themselves, but they
will be discovered by your inquisition.' Paternus Proconsul said, 'They
shall be discovered by me,' and added, 'they further ordain, that no
conventicles be held in any place, and that the Christians shall not

enter their cemeteries; if any transgress this wholesome ordinance, it shall be capital.' Cyprian Bishop answered, 'Do as you have been instructed.'

Then Paternus the Pronconsul bade them lead away the Bishop Cyprian into exile. During his long abode in this place, Aspasius Paternus was succeeded by Galerius Maximus, who bade the Bishop Cyrian be recalled from exile, and brought before him. . . ."

The Treatises of S. Caecilius Cyprian, Bishop of Carthage and Martyr, A Library of Fathers of the Holy Catholic Church, Anterior to the Division of the East and West, Vol. 3 (Oxford: John Henry Parker, 1840), xix–xx.

Oudamēs de exestai oute humin oute allois tisin hē sunodous poieisthai hē eis ta kaloumena koimētēria eisienai

Trial of St Dionysius of Alexandria, in Eusebius,
Hist. Eccles. VII, 11, 10

". . . and it shall by no means be permitted you or any others, either to hold assemblies, or to enter into the so called cemeteries."

NPNF[2] 1:300.

XII. The second edict of Valerian (258)

Quae autem sunt in vero ita se habent, rescripsisse Valerianum ad senatum, ut eposcopi et presbyteri et diacones in continenti animadvertantur, senators vero et egregii viri et equites Romani dignitati amissa etiam bonis spolientur et si ademptis facultatibus Christiani (esse) perseveraverint, capite quoque multentur, matronae ademptis bonis in exilium relegentur, Caesariani autem, quicumque vel prius confessi fuerant, vel nunc confessi fuerint, confiscentur et vincti in Caesareanas posessiones desrcipti mittantur. Subjecit etiam Valerianus imperator oriationi suae exemplum literarum, quas ad praesides provinciarum de nobis fecit.

St Cyprian, *Ep.* 80, 1 (*ad Successum*)

"But the truth concerning them is as follows, that Valerian had sent a rescript to the Senate, to the effect that bishops and presbyters and deacons should immediately be punished; but that senators, and men of importance, and Roman knights, should lose their dignity, and moreover be deprived of their property; and if, when their means were taken away, they should persist in being Christians, then they should also lose their heads; but that matrons should be deprived of their property, and sent into banishment."

Translated by Ernest Wallis. ANF 5:408. In the ANF numbering, this appears as *Ep.* 81.

Galerius Maximus proconsul Cypriano episcopo dixit: *Tu es Thascius Cyprianus?* Cyprianus episcopus respondit: *Ego sum.* Galerius Maximus proconsul dixit: *Tu papam te sacrilegae mentis hominibus praebuisti?* Cyprianus episcopus respondit: *Ego.* Galerius Maximus proconsul dixit: *Jusserunt te sacratissini imperators caeremoniari.* Cyprianus episcopus dixit: *Non facio.* Galerius Maximus (proconsul) ait: *Consule tibi.* Cyprianus episcopus respondit: *Fac quod tibi praeceptum est. In re tam justa nulla est consultatio.*

"The Proconsul demanded, 'Are you Thascius Cyprianus?' Cyprian Bishop answered, 'I am he.' Galerius Maximus Pronconsul said, 'The most sacred emperors have commanded you to conform to the Roman rites.' Cyprian Bishop said, 'I refuse to do so.' Galerius: 'Take heed for yourself.' Cyprian: 'Execute the emperor's orders; in a matter so manifest I may not deliberate.'"

The Treatises of S. Caecilius Cyprian, xxi.

Galerius Maximus conlocutus cum concilio sententiam vix et aegre dixit verbis huiusmodi: "*Diu sacrilega mente vixisti et plurimos nefariae tibi conspirationis homines adgregasii et inimicum te diis Romanis et religionibus sacris constituisti, nec te pii et sacratissimi principes Valerianus et Gallienus Augusti et Valerianus nobilissimus Caesar ad sectam caeremoniarum suarum revocare potuerunt. Et ideo cum sis nequissimorum criminum auctor et signifer deprehensus, eris ipse documento his, quos scelere tuo tecum adgregasti: sanguine tuo sancietur disciplina.* Et his dictis decretum ex tabella recitavit: *Thascium Cyprianum gladio ani-madverti placet.* Cyprianus episcopus dixit: *Deo gratias.*

"Galerius, after briefly conferring with his judicial council, with much reluctance pronounced the following sentence: 'You have long lived an irreligious life and have drawn together a number of men bound by an unlawful association, and professed yourself an open enemy to the gods and the religion of Rome; and the pious, most sacred and august emperors, Valerian and Gallienus, and the most noble Caesar Valerian, have endeavored in vain to bring you back to conformity with their religious observances; whereas therefore you have been apprehended as principal and ringleader to those with whom you have wickedly associated; the authority of the law shall be ratified in your blood.' He then read the sentence of the court from a written tablet: 'It is the sentence of the court that Thascius Cyprianus be executed with the sword.' Bishop Cyprian said: 'Thanks be to God.'"

The Treatises of S. Caecilius Cyprian, xxi–xxii

Post hanc vero sententiam turba fratrum dicebat: *"Et nos cum hoc decollemur.* Propter hoc tumultus fratrum exortus est et multa turba eum prosecuta est. Et ita idem Cyprianus in agrum Sexti productus est et ibi se lacerna byrro exspoliavit et genu in terra flexit et in orationem se Domino prostravit. Et cum se dalmatica exspoliasset et diaconibus tradidisset, in linea stetit et coepit spiculatorem sustinere. Cum venisset autem spiculator iussit suis, ut eidem spiculatori viginti quique aureos darent. Linteamina vero et manualia a fratribus ante eum mittebantur. Postea vero beautus Cyprianus manu sua oculos sibi texit. Qui cum lacinias manuales ligare sibi non potuisset, Julianus presbyter et Julianus subdiaconus ei ligaverunt. Ita beatus Cyprianus passus est, ejusque corpus propter gentilium curiositatem in proximo positum est. Inde per noctem sublatum est cum cereis et scolacibus ad areas Macrobii Candidiani procuratoris, quae sunt in via Mappaliensi iuxta piscinas, cum voto et triumpho magno deductum est. Post paucos autem dies Galerius Maximus proconsul decessit.

"After sentence was pronounced, the whole assembly of the brethren cried out, 'We will be beheaded with him.' A great tumult arose among the brethren, and a crowd followed to the place of execution. He was brought forth into the field near Sexti, where having laid aside his upper garment, he kneeled down, and addressed himself in prayer to the Lord. Then, stripping himself of his dalmatic, and giving it to the deacons, he stood in his linen tunic, and awaited the executioner, to whom when he came Cyprian bade twenty-five pieces of gold be given. The brethren meanwhile spread linen cloths and napkins on the ground before him. Being unable to tie the sleeve of his robe at the wrist, Presbyter Julian and Subdeacon Julian performed this office for him. Then the blessed Cyprian covered his eyes with his hands, and so suffered. His body was exposed in a place nearby, to gratify the curiosity of the heathen. But in the course of the night it was removed, and transported with prayers and great pomp with wax tapers and funeral torches to the burying ground of Macrobius Candidianus the Procurator, near the fish ponds in the Mappalian Way. A few days after, Glaerius Maximus the Proconsul died."

The Treatises of S. Caecilius Cyprian, xxii

Passus est autem beatissimus Cyprianus martyr die octava decima Kalendarum Octobrium sub Valeriano et Gallieno imperatoribus, regnante vero domino nostro Jesu Christo, cui est honor et gloria in saecula saeculorum. Amen.

Acta proconsularia sancti Cypriani, 3–6

"Thus suffered the most blessed Martyr Cyprian, on the eighteenth day of the Kalends of October, under Valerian and Gallienus Emperors; in the kingdom of our Lord Jesus Christ, to whom be honor and glory forever and ever. Amen."

The Treatises of S. Caecilius Cyprian, xxiii

XIII. Rescript of Gallienus (260)

Autokratōr Kaisar Pouplios Likinios Galliēnos, eusebes, eutuchēs, sebastos, Dionusiokaikai pinna kai Dēmētrio kai tois loipois episkopois.

Tēn euergesian tēs emēs dōreas dia pantos tou kosmou ekbibasthēnai prosetaxa. Hopōs apo topōn tōn thrēskeusimōn apochōrēsōsi. Kai dia touto kai humeis tēs antigraphēs tēs emēs tō tupō chrēsthai dunasthe, ōste mēdena humin enochlein. Kai touto hoper kata to exon dunatai uph humin anaplērousthai, ede pro pollou uhper emou sunkechōrētai. Kai dia touto Aurēlios kurenios, ho tou megistou pragmatos prostateuōn ton typon touton ton hup'emou dothenta diaphylaxei.

Eusebius, Hist. eccl., VII, 13, 2

"The Emperor Caesar Publius Licinius Gallienus, Pius, felix, Augustus, to Dionysius, Pinnas, Demetrius, and the other bishops. I have ordered the bounty of my gift to be declared through all the world, that they may depart from the places of religious worship. And for this purpose you may use this copy of my rescript, that no one may molest you. And this which you are now enabled lawfully to do, has already for a long time been conceded by me. Therefore Aurelius Cyrenius, who is the chief administrator of affairs, will observe this ordinance which I have given."

NPNF² 1:302.

XIV. The judgment of Aurelian (272)

. . . *Mēdamōs ekstēnai tou Paulou tou tēs ekklēsias oikou thelontos, basileus evteuchtheis Aurēlianos aisiōtata peri tou prakteou dielēphe toutois neimai prostattōn ton oikon, ois an hoi kata tēn Italian kai tēn Rōmaiōn polin episkopoi tou dogmatos episteolaien.*

Hist. eccl., VII, 30, 19

". . . But as Paul refused to surrender the church building, the Emperor Aurelian was petitioned; and he decided the matter most equitably, ordering the building to be given to those to whom the bishops of Italy and of the city of Rome should adjudge it."

NPNF² 1:316.

XV. The last persecution–first edict (303)

... Hēplōto o' athroōs pantachou grammata, tas men ekklēsias eis edaphos pherein, tas de graphas aphaneis puri genesthai prostattonta, kai tous men timēs epeilēmmenos atimous, tous de en oiketiais, ei epimenoien tē tou Christianismou prothesei, eleutherias steriskesthai proagoreuonta. Kai hē men tēs protēs kath'hēmōn graphēs toiautē tis ēn dynamis.

Eusebius, *De martyribus Palestinae*, I, Cf. *Hist. Eccles.*, VIII, 2

". . . [L]etters were published everywhere, commanding that the churches be leveled to the ground and the Scriptures be destroyed by fire, and ordering that those who held places of honor be degraded, and that the household servants, if they persisted in the profession of Christianity, be deprived of freedom. [Rufinus adds (*Hist. eccles.* VIII, 2) that those who already were slaves would never be franchised.] Such was the force of the first edict against us."

NPNF² 1:342.

XVI. The second and third edicts (303)

Tous pantachose tōn ekklesiōn proestōtas eirktais kai desmois eneirai prostagma ephoita basilikon.

Eusebius, *Hist. Eccl.* VIII, 6, 8

"[A] royal edict directed that the rulers of the churches everywhere should be thrown into prison and bonds. . . ."

NPNF² 1:328.

Authis d'eterōn ta prōta grammata epikataleiphotōn, en ois tous katakleistous ean badizein ep'eleutherias , enistamenous di murlais kataxaivein prostextaxto basanois. . . .

Eusebius, *Hist. Eccl.*, VIII, 6, 10. Cf. *De martyr. Pal.* I

"And as other decrees followed the first, directing that those in prison if they would sacrifice should be permitted to depart in freedom, but that those who refused should be harassed with many tortures. . . ."

NPNF² 1:328.

XVII. Fourth edict (304)

Deuterou d'etous dialabontos, kai dē sphodroteron epitathentos tou
kat'hēmōn polemou, tēs eparchias hēgoumenou tēnikade Ourbanou,
grammatōn toutō prōton bailikōn peroitēkotōn, en ois katholikō pros-
tagmati pantas pandēmei tous kata polin thuein te kai spendein tois
eidōlois ekeleueto. . . .

Eusebius, De mart. Palestinae, III, 1

"In the course of the second year, the persecution against us increased
greatly. And at that time Urbanus being governor of the province,
imperial edicts were first issued to him, commanding by a general
decree that all the people should sacrifice at once in the different cities, and offer libations to the idols. . . ."

NPNF[2] 1:344.

XVIII. Fifth edict (306)

Deuteras gar toi kath'hēmōn genomenēs epanasteōs upo Maximiou,
tritō tou kath' hēmas etei diōgmou, grammatōn te tou turannou
touto prōton diapephoitēkotōn, hōs an pandēmei pantes apoxaklōs
met' epimelias kai spoudēs tōn kata poleis archontōn thusein,
kērukōn te kath' holēs tēs Kaiareōn poleōs andras ama gunaixi kai
teknois epi tous tōn eidōlon oikous ex hēgemonikou keleusmatos
anaboōmenon, kai pros touyois onomasti chiliarchōn apo graphēs
exastin anakaloumenon. . . .

Eusebius, De mart. Palestinae, IV, 8

"For in the second attack upon us under Maximinus, in the third year
of the persecution, edicts of the tyrant were issued for the first time,
commanding that the rulers of the cities should diligently and speedily see to it that all the people offered sacrifices. Throughout the city of
Cæsarea, by command of the governor, the heralds were summoning
men, women, and children to the temples of the idols, and besides this,
the chiliarchs were calling out each one by name from a roll. . . ."

NPNF[2] 1:346.

XIX. Sixth edict (308)

Athroōs d'oun authis Maximinou diaphoita kath'hēmōn pantachou grammata kat'eparchian, hēgemones te kai proseti ho tōn stratopedōn archein epitagmenos programmasi kai epistolais kai dēmosiois diatagmasi tous en hapasaus polesi logistas ama stratēgois kai taboulariois epesperchon to basilikon eis peras agein prostagma, keleuon hōs an meta spoudēs pasēs tōn men eidōlōn anaikodomoien ta peptōkota, pandēmei de pantas andras ama guvaixi kai oiketais kai autois hypomaxiois paisi thuein kai spendein, autōn te akribōs ton enagō n apogeusthai thusiōn epimeles poioivto, kai ta men kat'agoran ōnia tais apo tōn thusiōn spondais katamolunoito, prosthen de tōn loutrōn ephedroi katatassointo, hōs an tous en toutois apokathairomenos tais pammiarois polunoein thusais.

Eusebius, *De martyr. Pal.* IX, 2

"Immediately letters from Maximinus against us were published everywhere in every province. The governors and the military prefect urged by edicts and letters and public ordinances the magistrates and generals and notaries in all the cities to carry out the imperial decree, which ordered that the altars of the idols should with all speed be rebuilt; and that all men, women, and children, even infants at the breast, should sacrifice and offer oblations; and that with diligence and care they should cause them to taste of the execrable offerings; and that the things for sale in the market should be polluted with libations from the sacrifices; and that guards should be stationed before the baths in order to defile with the abominable sacrifices those who went to wash in them."

NPNF^2 1:350.

XX. The edict of toleration of Galerius (311).

Inter caetera, quae pro rei publicae simper commodis atque utilitate disponimus, nos quidem volueramus antehac, iuxta leges veteres et publican disciplinam Romanorum, cuncta corrigere, atque id providere, ut etiam Christiani, qui parentum suorum reliquerant sectam, ad bonas mentes redirent: si quidem quadam ratione tanta eosdem Christianos voluntas invasisset et tanta stultitia occupasset, ut non illa veterum instituta sequerentur, quae forsitan primum parentes eorumdem constituerant; sed pro arbitrio suo atque it iisdem erat libitum, ita sibimet leges facerent, quas observarent, et per diversa varios populos congregarent. Denique cum ejusmodi nostra jussio extitisset, ut ad veterum se instituta conferrent, multi periculo subjugati, multi etiam deturbati sunt; atque cum plurimi in proposito perseverarent, ac videremus, nec diis eosdem cultum ac religionem debitam exhibere, nec Christianorum deum observare, contemplatione mitissimae nostrae clementiae intuentes et consuetudinem sempiternam, qua solemus cunctis hominibus veniam indulgere, promptissimam in his quoque indulgentiam nostram credidimus porrigendam; ut denuo sint Christiani, et conventicula sua componant, ita ut ne quid contra disiplinam agant. Per aliam autem epistolam judicibus significaturi sumus qui debeant observare. Unde iuxta hanc indulgentiam nostram debebunt deum suum exorare pro salite nostra, et rei publicae, ac sua, ut undiqueversum res piblica praestetur incolumis, et securi vivere in sedibus suis possint.

Lactantius, De mortibus persecutorum, XXXIV

"Amongst our other regulations for the permanent advantage of the commonweal, we have hitherto studied to reduce all things to a conformity with the ancient laws and public discipline of the Romans. It has been our aim in an especial manner, that the Christians also, who had abandoned the religion of their forefathers, should return to right opinions. For such wilfulness and folly had, we know not how, taken possession of them, that instead of observing those ancient institutions, which possibly their own forefathers had established, they, through caprice, made laws to themselves, and drew together into different societies many men of widely different persuasions. After the publication of our edict, ordaining the Christians to betake themselves to the observance of the ancient institutions, many of them were subdued through the fear of danger, and moreover many of them were exposed to jeopardy; nevertheless, because great numbers still persist in their opinions, and because we have perceived that at present they neither pay reverence and due adoration to the gods, nor yet worship their own God, therefore we, from our wonted clemency in bestowing pardon on all, have judged it fit to extend our indulgence to those men, and to permit them again to be Christians, and to establish the places of their religious assemblies; yet so as that they offend not against good order. By another mandate we purpose to signify unto magistrates how they ought herein to demean themselves. Wherefore it will be the duty of the Christians, in consequence of this our toleration, to pray to their God for our welfare, and for that of the public, and for their own; that the commonweal may continue safe in every quarter, and that they themselves may live securely in their habitations."

Translated by William Fletcher. ANF 7:315.

XXI. The inscription of Aricanda (311)

An inscription discovered in the ruins of Aricanda, in Lycia, by the Bendorf mission. The Latin fragment, with additions by Mommsen, is from a rescript of Maximin Daia, relating to the supplication in Greek (engraved below it) of the peoples of Lycia and Pamphylia.

[Quamcumque munific]entiam, vol[etis pro hoc vestro pio proposito pet]ere iam nunc ho[c facere et accepisse vos credere li]cet impetraturi e[am sine mora, quae in omne aevum t]am nostram iuxta deos i[mmortales pietatem testabi]tur quam vero condigna pra[emia vos esse a nostra cl]ementia consecutos liberis ac po[steris declarabit].

"[Some witnessing] of munificence that you wanted to ask of us [after your pious petition], you may [believe] presently [we give to you and you have received], for you will obtain them [without delay, and forever]; they will prove our piety toward the [immortal] gods [and at the same time] show that you have received from our [clemency] just rewards for your sons and your posterity."

[Tois sōtērsin] pantos anthrōpōn ethnous kai genous [Sebastois Kaj]sarsin Galer. Oualer. Maximeinō kai [Kōnstanteinō] kai Oualer.

Likinianō Likinniō. Para tou [Lukiōn kai P]anphulōn ethnous dee-
sis kai ikesia. Ergois apo [dedōkotōn t]ōn theōn tōn homogenōn
humōn philanthrōpias [pasin hō theio]tatoi basileis ois hē thrēskia
memeletētai[autōn huper tē]s humōn tēn panta neikōntōn despotōn
[aiōniu so]tērias, kalōs echein edokimasamen kataphugein [pros tēn
atha]naton basleian kai deēthēnai tous palai [asebeis Xri]stianous kai
eis deuro tēn autēn noson [diatērounta]s pote pepausthai kai mēdemia
skaia tini kai [nē thrēskeia] tēn theois opheilomenēn parabainein.
[Tout' an eis] ergon aphikoito, ei humeterō theiō kai aiōniō [veu-
mati p]asinkatastaiē apeirēsthai men kai kokōlusthai [exousia]v tēs
tōn atheōn apechthous ep[i]tēdeuseōs, [pantas de t]ē tōn homogenōn
humōn theōn thrēskeia schola[zein huper] tis aiōniou kai aphthar-
tou basileias humōn, hyper [pleiston syn]rerein pasin tois hymeterois
anthrōpois prodēlon estin.

"To the saviors of all mankind, the august Caesars Galerius Valerius
Maximian, [Flavius Valerius Constantinus], Valerius Licinianus Kicin-
ius, a petition addressed by the people [the Lycians and the Pamphy-
lians]. The gods, your counterparts, O divine emperors, have always
filled with manifest favors those who take their religion to heart, and
they pray to God for the [perpetual] salvation of their invincible masters. We thought it good to have recourse to your immortal majesty,
and to ask that the Christians, who have long been [impious] without
ceasing, be repressed at last and no longer transgress, through their
new and evil [cult], the respect we owe the gods. This result will be
obtained if, by your divine and eternal [decree], their impious observances are forbidden and they are forced to practice the cult of the
gods, your counterparts, and to implore them for your eternal and
incorruptible majesty, which would obviously benefit the wellbeing of
all your subjects."

Mommsen in *Archeologisch-epigraphoschen Mitteilungen aus Oster-
reich, vol. XVI, 1893, p. 93–102, 108;* Supplement to vol. III of the Corpus
inscriptionum latinarum , n. 12, 132, p. 2056–2057; Duchesne, in *Bulletin critique, 1893, 157;* De Rossi in *Bullettino di archeologia cristiana,
1894, 54.* Cf. Eusebius, *Hist. eccl.* IX, 7 (2–15) 9 (4–6).

XXII. The Edict of Milan (313)

Cum feliciter tam ego Constantinus Augustusm, quam etiam efo Licinius Augustus apud Mediolanum convenissemus atque universa, quae ad commode et securitatem publicam pertinerent, in tractatu haberemus, haec inter cetera, quae videbamus pluribus hominibus profutura, vel imprimis ordinanda esse credidimus, quibus divinitatis reverentia continebatur, ut daremus et Christiianis et omnibus liberam potestatem sequendi religionem, quam quisque voluisset, quo quidquid divinitatis in sede caelesti nobis atque omnibus, qui sub potestate nostra sunt constituti, placatum ac propitium possit existere. Itaque hoc consilio salubri ac rectissima ratione ineundum esse credidimus, ut nulli omnino facultatem abnegandum putaremus, qui vel observationi Christianorum vel ei religioni mentem suam dederet, quam ipse sibi aptissimam esse sentiret, ut possit nobis summa divinitas, cujus religioni liberis mentibus obsequimur, in omnibus solitum favorem suum benevolentiamque praestare. Quare scire dicationem tuam convenit placuisse nobis, ut amotis omnibus amodo conditionibus, quae prius scriptis ad officium tuum datis super Christianorum nomine continebantur, et quae prorsus sinistrae et a clementia nostra alienae videbantur, nunc libere ac simpliciter unusquique eorum, qui eamdem observandae religioni Christianorum gerunt voluntatem, citra ullam inquietudinem ac molestiam sui id ipsum observare contendant. Quae sollicitudini tuae plenissime significanda esse credidimus, quo scires nos liberam atque absolutam colendae religionis suae facultatem iisdem Christianis dedisse. Quod cum iisdem a nobis indultum esse pervideas, intelligit dicatio tua etiam aliis religionis suae vel observantiae potestatem similiter apertam et liberam pro quiete temporis nostri esse concessam, ut in colendo quod quisque delegerit habeat liberam facultatem; quae (a nobis peracta sunt, ne ulli) honori neque cuiquam religioni auf (erri) alquid a nobis (videatur). Atque hoc insuper in persona Christianorum statuendum esse censuimus, quod, si eadem loca, ad quae antea convenire consuerant, de quibus etiam datis ad officium tuum literis certa antehac forma fuerat comprehensa, priore tempore aliquid vel a fisco nostro vel ab alio quocumque viden-

tur esse mercati, eadem Christianis sine pecunia et sine ulla pretii peti-
tione, postposita omni frustratione atque ambiguitate, restituantur.
Qui etiam dono fuerunt consecuti eadem similiter iisdem Christianis
quantocius reddant. Etiam vel ii, qui emerunt, vel qui dono erunt consecuti, si putaverint de nostra benevolentia aliquid, vicarium postu-
lent; quo et ipsis nostrum clementiam consulatur. Quae omnia corpori
Christianorum protinus per intercessionem tuam ac sine mora tradi
oportebit. Et quoniam iidem Christiani non ea loca tantum, ad quae
convenire consuerant, sed alia etiam habuisse noscuntur ad jus corpo-
ris eorum, id est ecclesiarum, non hominum singulorum, pertinentia,
ea omnia lege, quam superius comprehendimus, citra ullam prorsus
ambiguitatem vel controversiam iisdem Christianis, id est corpori et
conventiculis eorum reddi jubebis, supradicta scilicet ratione servata,
ut ii, qui eadem sine pretio, sicut diximus, restituerint, indemnitatem
de nostra benevolentia sperent. In quibus omnibus supradicto corpori
Christianorum intercessionem tuam efficacissimam exhibere debebis,
ut praeceptum nostrum quantocius conpleatur, quo etiam in hoc per
clementiam nostram quieti publicae consulatur. Hactenus fiet, ut sicut
superius comprehensum est, divinus iuxta nos favor, quem in tantis
sumus rebus experti, per omne tempus prospere successibus nostris
cum beatitudine publica perseveret. Ut autem hujus sanctionis benevolentiae nostrae forma ad omnium possit pervenire notitiam, prolata
programmate tuo hae scripta et ubique proponere et ad omnium sci-
entiam te peferre conveniet, ut hujus benevolentiae nostrae sanctio
latere non possit.

Lactantius, *De mortibus persecutorum*, 48.
Cf. Eus., *Hist. Eccles.* X, 5, 2–15

"When we, Constantine and Licinius, emperors, had an interview at
Milan, and conferred together with respect to the good and security
of the commonweal, it seemed to us that, amongst those things that
are profitable to mankind in general, the reverence paid to the Divinity merited our first and chief attention, and that it was proper that the
Christians and all others should have liberty to follow that mode of
religion that to each of them appeared best; so that that God, who is

seated in heaven, might be benign and propitious to us, and to every one under our government. And therefore we judged it a salutary measure, and one highly consonant to right reason, that no man should be denied leave of attaching himself to the rites of the Christians, or to whatever other religion his mind directed him, that thus the supreme Divinity, to whose worship we freely devote ourselves, might continue to vouchsafe His favour and beneficence to us. And accordingly we give you to know that, without regard to any provisos in our former orders to you concerning the Christians, all who choose that religion are to be permitted, freely and absolutely, to remain in it, and not to be disturbed any ways, or molested. And we thought fit to be thus special in the things committed to your charge, that you might understand that the indulgence that we have granted in matters of religion to the Christians is ample and unconditional; and perceive at the same time that the open and free exercise of their respective religions is granted to all others, as well as to the Christians. For it befits the well-ordered state and the tranquillity of our times that each individual be allowed, according to his own choice, to worship the Divinity; and we mean not to derogate aught from the honour due to any religion or its votaries. Moreover, with respect to the Christians, we formerly gave certain orders concerning the places appropriated for their religious assemblies; but now we will that all persons who have purchased such places, either from our exchequer or from any one else, do restore them to the Christians, without money demanded or price claimed, and that this be performed peremptorily and unambiguously; and we will also, that they who have obtained any right to such places by form of gift do forthwith restore them to the Christians: reserving always to such persons, who have either purchased for a price, or gratuitously acquired them, to make application to the judge of the district, if they look on themselves as entitled to any equivalent from our beneficence. All those places are, by your intervention, to be immediately restored to the Christians. And because it appears that, besides the places appropriated to religious worship, the Christians did possess other places, which belonged not to individuals, but to their society in general, that is, to their churches, we comprehend all such within the regulation aforesaid, and we will that you cause them all to be restored to the society or churches, and that without hesitation or controversy: Provided always, that the persons making restitution without a price paid shall be at liberty to seek indemnification from our bounty. In furthering all these things for the benefit of the Christians, you are to use your utmost diligence, to the end that our orders be speedily obeyed, and our gracious purpose in securing the public tranquillity promoted. So shall that divine favour which, in affairs of the mightiest importance, we have already experienced, continue to give success to us, and in our successes make the commonweal happy. And that the tenor of this our gracious ordinance may be made known unto all, we will that you cause it by your authority to be published everywhere."

ANF 7:320.

Bibliography

The original version of Allard's bibliography largely consists of nineteenth-century titles in French, along with primary sources in Latin. For the convenience of modern readers, the translator has inserted selected English translations of the original sources [in brackets] and also added more recent studies in English as equivalents or supplements to those on Allard's list of secondary sources.

1. Primary Sources

Acta primorum martyrum sincera et selecta, ed. Ruinart. Paris, 1689.
   [Fastré, Joseph A.M. *The Acts of the Early Martyrs,* series 1–5. Philadelphia: P.F. Cunningman, 1871–85.]
Acta Sanctorum quotquot toto orbe coluntur, published by the Bollandists, Antwerp and Paris, 1643–1894, January to November, vol. I–LX.
Ammianus Marcellinus, ed. Valois. Paris, 1681.
   [*Ammianus Marcellinus.* J.C. Rolfe, ed. and trans. 3 vols. Loeb Classical Library. Cambridge, Mass.: Harvard University Press, 1935–40.]
   [*The Roman History of Ammianus Marcellinus.* London & New York: Bell & Son, 1894.]
Analecta Bollandiana vol. I–XXVII. Brussels, 1882–1909.
The Apology and Acts of Apollonius, ed. Conybeare. London, 1894.
Apology of Aristides, ed. Rendel Harris and Armitage Robinson. Cambridge, 1891.
   [*Apology for the Christian Faith.* D.M. Kay, trans. Ante-Nicene Fathers 9.]
   [Harris, Helen B. *The Newly Recovered Apology of Aristides: Its Doctrine and Ethics.* London: Hodder & Stoughton, 1891.]
Augusta historia, Paris, 1620, ed. Peter. Leipzig, 1865.

[Syme, Ronald. *Ammianus and the Historia Augusta*, Oxford: Clarendon, 1968.]

[_____. *Historia Augusta Papers*. Oxford: Clarendon, 1983.]

[Barnes, Timothy D. *The Sources of the Historia Augusta*. Brussels: Latomus, 1978.]

Corpus inscriptionum graecarum, 4 vols. Berlin, 1828–1877.

Corpus inscriptionum latinarum, vol. I–XV. Berlin, 1863ff.

Corpus iuris civilis, ed. Krenger-Mommsen. Berlin, 1872–7.

Corpus iuris romani anteiustiniani, ed. Huschke, Leipzig, 1861.

Codex Theodosianus, ed. Godefroy. Leipzig, 1737–1743.

[Pharr, Clyde. *The Theodosian Code and Novels, and the Sirmondian Constitutions*. Princeton, N.J.: Princeton University Press, 1952].

Corpus scriptorum ecclesiasticorum latinorum, vol. I–XVIII. Vienna, 1867ff.

[Benson, Edward W. *Cyprian, His Life, His Times, His Work*. New York: MacMillan, 1897.]

[Faulkner, John Alfred. *Cyprian: The Churchman*. New York: Eaton & Mains, 1906.]

Doctrina duodecim apostolorum, ed. Funk. Tuebingen, 1887.

[Kraft, Robert A. *The Apostolic Fathers: Barnabas and the Didachē*. New York: Thomas Nelson, 1965.]

Dio Cassius, ed. Valois, Paris, 1634; ed. Dindorf, Leipzig, 1863–5.

[Dio Cassius *Roman History*. E. Cary, trans. and ed. Loeb Classical Library, 9 vols. London: Heinemann, 1914–27.]

[Millar, Fergus. *A Study of Cassius Dio*. Oxford: Clarendon Press, 1964.]

Eunape, ed. Boissonade. Amsterdam, 1822.

[Breebaert, A. B. "Eunapius of Sardis and the Writing of History." *Mnēmosynē* (1979): 360–375.]

[Penella, Robert J. *Greek Philosophers and Sophists in the Fourth Century A.D. Studies in Eunapius of Sardis*. Leeds: F. Cairns, 1990.]

Eutrope, ed. Zell, Stuttgart, 1829; ed. Dietsch, Leipzig, 1875.

Exempla inscriptionum latinarum, ed. Wilmanns. Berlin, 1873.

Hérodien, ed. Bekker. Berlin, 1826.

[*Herodian.* C.R. Whittaker, trans. 2 vols. London: Heinemann, 1969.]

Inscriptions chrétiennes de la Gaule, ed. Edmond Le Blant. Paris, 1856–1865.

Inscriptiones christianae urbis Romae saeculo septimo antiquiores, ed. J.-B. De Rossi. Rome, 1861–1888.

Inscriptionum latinarum selectarum amplissima collectio, ed. Orelli and Henzen. Turin, 1826 and 1856.

Juliani imperatoris librorum contra Christianos quae supersunt, ed. Neumann. Leipzig, 1874.

[*Julian's Works.* W.C. Wright, ed. and trans. 3 vols. Loeb Classical Library. London, 1949–54.]

Julien, ed. Hertlein. Leipzig, 1875–1876.

[Lactantius *De Mortibus Persecutorum.* J.L. Creed, ed. Oxford: Clarendon Press, 1984.]

Libanius, ed. Reiske. Oldenbourg, 1791–1797.

[Libanius *Selected Orations.* A. F. Norman, trans. Cambridge: Harvard University Press, 1977.]

Libanius *Lettres,* ed. Wolff. Amsterdam, 1728.

[*Libanius: Autobiography and Selected Letters.* A. F. Norman, trans. Cambridge: Harvard University Press, 1992.]

[Libanius *Selected Letters of Libanius: From the Age of Constantius and Julian.* Scott Bradbury, trans. Liverpool: Liverpool University Press, 2004.]

Liber Pontificalis, ed. Duchesne. Paris, 1886–1892.

[*The Book of Pontiffs.* Raymond Davis, trans. Liverpool: Liverpool University Press, 2000.]

[*The Book of the Popes.* Louise R. Loomis, trans. Merchantville, N.J.: Evolution Pub., 2006].

Martyrologium hieronymianum, ed. J.-B. De Rossi and Duchesne. Paris, 1894.

Opera Patrum apostolicorum, ed. Funk. Tuebingen, 1878 and 1881.

[*The Apostolic Fathers.* Robert M. Grant, ed. New York: Thomas Nelson, 1964–1968.]

Panegyrici (after Casaubon's *Pline le Jeune*), 1504, ed. Baehrens. Leipzig, 1874.

[*In Praise of the Later Roman Emperors: The Panegyrici Latini.* C.E.V. Nixon and Barbara S. Rodgers, trans. Berkeley, CA: University of California Press, 1994.]

Patrologiae cursus completus, ed. Migne. Paris, 1844ff.: 1st series, *Patrol. Latina,* vol. I–LXI; 2nd ser., *Patrol. Graeca,* vol. I–LXXXIV.

Pline le Jeune, ed. Lemaire, Paris, 1822; ed. Hardy, London, 1889.

[*The Letters of the Younger Pliny.* Betty Radice, trans. New York: Penguin Classics, 1963.]

[Sherwin-White, A. N. *The Letters of Pliny: A Historical and Social Commentary.* Oxford: Clarendon Press, 1966.]

Prudence, ed. Dressel, Leipzig, 1860.

[Palmer, Anne-Marie. *Prudentius on the Martyrs.* Oxford: Clarendon Press, 1989.]

[Peebles, Bernard M. *The Poet Prudentius.* New York: McMullen Books, 1951].

Sacrorum conciliorum nova et amplissima collectio, vol. I–VI, ed. Mansi. Florence and Venice, 1759.

Suétone, ed. Lemaire, Paris, 1828; ed. Roth, Leipzig, 1871.

[Wallace-Hadrill, Andrew. *Suetonius: The Scholar and His Caesars.* New Haven, Conn.: Yale University Press, 1983.]

[Suetonius, *Lives of the Caesars,* vol II. J.C. Rolfe, trans. Cambridge: Harvard University Press, 1914.]

Symmaque, ed. Seeck. Berlin, 1883.

[Symmachus *Prefect and Emperor: The Relations of Symmachus.* R.H. Barrow, trans. Oxford: Clarendon Press, 1973.]

[Haverling, Gerd. *Studies on Symmachus' Language and Style.* Goeteborg, Sweden: Acta Universitatis Gothoburgensis, 1988.]

Tacite, ed. Lemaire, Paris, 1819–1820; ed. Furneaux, London 1884–1891.

[Tacitus *The Histories.* New York: Penguin Classics, 1984.]

[Tacitus *The Annals of Imperial Rome.* New York: Penguin Classics, 1989.]

Themistius, ed. Dindorf, Leipzig, 1832.

[Vanderspoel, John. *Themistius and the Imperial Court*. Ann Arbor, Mich.: University of Michigan Press, 1995.]

Zosime, ed. Bekker, Bonn, 1837; ed. Mendelssohn, Leipzig, 1887.

[Goffart, W. "Zosimus, the First Historian of Rome's Fall." *American Historical Review* 76 (1971), 412–441.]

[*Historia Nova–New History*. Ronald T. Ridley, trans. Canberra: Australian Association for Byzantine Studies,1982.]

2. Secondary Works

What follows is a selection of works, which by definition is incomplete. A complete listing would require a separate volume. Note: The translator has inserted modern entries in brackets, as well as at the end of each section, to make the bibliography more relevant to the English-speaking reader.

A simple but helpful overview of Roman history and culture may be found in Thomas Greer, *A Brief History of the Western World*, Hartcourt College Publishers, 2002, ch. 3, pp. 108–161. See also Rostovtzeff, *Social and Economic History of the Roman Empire*, ed. P.M. Fraser, 2 vols., New York and London: Oxford University Press, 1957.

I. The Roman Empire

General History: Emperors of the First Three Centuries

De Champagny, F. *Les Césars*. 5th ed. Paris, 1876.

[Grant, Michael. *The Twelve Caesars: From Julius Caesar to Domitian*. New York: Scribner, 1975.]

———, *Les Antonins*. Paris, 1863.

[Garzetti, Albino. *From Tiberius to the Antonines: A History of the Roman Empire* A.D. 14–192. London: Routledge, 1974.]

———, *Les Césars du troisième siècle*. Paris, 1870.

De Ceuleneer, *Essai sur la vie et le règne de Septime Sévère*. Brussels, 1880.

De la Berge, *Essai sur le règne de Trajan*. Paris, 1897.

[Smallwood, E. Mary. *Documents Illustrating the Principates of Nerva, Trajan, and Hadrian.* Cambridge University Press, 1966.]

Duruy, Victor, *Histoire des Romains.* Paris, 1878–1895.

[Duruy, Victor. *History of Rome and the Roman People, from its Origin to the Establishment of the Christian Empire.* J.P. Mahaffy, trans. London: K. Paul, 1883–86.]

Gibbon, Edward. *History of the Decline and Fall of the Roman Empire.* Brown, 1967.

Goyau, *Chronologie de l'Empire romain.* Paris, 1891.

[Charlesworth, M.P. *The Roman Empire.* Oxford University Press, 1951.]

Gsell, *Essai sur le règne de Domitien.* Paris, 1894.

[Hardy, Ernst G. *Christianity and the Roman Government.* New York: B. Franklin, 1971.]

[Henderson, Bernard W. *Five Roman Emperors: Vespasian, Titus, Domitian, Nerva, Trajan, A.D. 68–117.* New York: Barnes and Noble, 1969, repr.]

Homo, *Essai sur le règne d'Aurélien.* Paris, 1904.

[Halsberghe, Gaston H. *The Cult of Sol Invictus.* Wiley-Blackwell, 1997.]

Lacour-Gayet, *Antonin le Pieux et son temps.* Paris, 1888.

[Lindsay, Jack. *The Ancient World: Manners and Morals.* New York: Weidenfeld and Nicolson, 1968.]

Lécrivain, *Études sur l'Histoire-Auguste.* Paris, 1904.

Merivale, *A History of the Romans under the Empire.* London, 1850–1852.

Noel des Vergers, *Essai sur Marc-Aurèle.* Paris, 1866.

[Birley, Anthony. *Marcus Aurelius: A Biography.* New Haven, Conn.: Yale University Press,1987.]

[Bussell, F. W. *Marcus Aurelius and the Later Stoics.* Edinburgh, 1910.]

[Farquharson, A. S. L. *Marcus Aurelius: His Life and His World.* Oxford: Basil Blackwell, 1952.]

Schiller, *Geschichte der römischen Kaiserrechts.* Gotha, 1881–1887.

Speigl, *Der roemische Staat und die Christen.* Amsterdam, Hakkert, 1970.

Additional Modern Sources

Charlesworth, M. P. *The Roman Empire.* New York & London: Oxford University Press, 1951.

Grant, Michael. *The Roman Emperors: A Biographical Guide to the Rulers of Imperial Rome, 31 BC–AD 476.* New York: Scribner's, 1985.

II. Roman Empire—Morals, Administration, Provinces

Arnold, *The Roman System of Provincial Administration to the Accession of Constantine the Great.* Oxford, 1906.

Audollent, *Carthage romaine.* Paris, 1896.

[Brown, P. R. L. "Christianity and Local Culture in Roman North Africa." *Journal of Roman Studies* 58 (l968): 85–95.]

Boissier, *L'Afrique romaine.* Paris, 1897.

[Frend, W. H. C. "The North African Dimension 370–430," in *The Rise of Christianity.* Philadelphia: Fortress Press, 1984.]

Chapot, *La province romaine proconsulaire d'Asie.* Paris, 1904.

[Magie, David. *Roman Rule in Asia Minor to the End of the Third Century.* Princeton, N.J.: Princeton University Press, 1950.]

[Coleman-Norton, P. R. *Roman State and Christian Church.* London: SPCK, 1966.]

Friedlander, *Civilisation et mœurs romaines d'Auguste à la fin des Antonins.* Paris. 1865–1874.

[_____. *Roman Life and Manners under the Early Empire.* 4 vols. London: SPCK, 1908–1913.]

Marquardt, *Römische Staatsverwaltung.* Leipzig, 1876–1878.

[Rawson, Beryl. *The Family in Ancient Rome: New Perspectives.* Ithaca, N.Y.: Cornell University Press, 1986.]

[Levick, Barbara. *The Government of the Roman Empire: A Source Book.* Totowa, N.J.: Routledge, 1985.]

Mommsen, *De collegiis et sodalitiis Romanorum.* Kehl, 1843.

Petit de Juleville, *Histoire de la Grèce sous la domination romaine.* Paris, 1875.

[Jones, A. H. *The Greek City from Alexander to Justinian.* New Haven, Conn.: Yale University Press, 1981.]

[Stevenson, George Hope. *Roman Provincial Administration Till the Age of the Antonines.* Oxford: Basil Blackwell, 1949.]

Wallon, *Histoire de l'esclavage dans l'antiquité.* 2nd ed., Louvain, 1879.

[Bradley, K. R. *Slaves and Masters in the Roman Empire: A Study in Social Control.* New York: Oxford University Press, 1987.]

[Westermann, W. L. *The Slave System of Greek and Roman Antiquity.* Philadelphia, Pa.: American Philosophical Society, 1955.]

Waltzing, *Étude historique sur les corporations professionnelles chez les Romains, depuis les origines jusqu'à la fin de l'Empire.* Louvain, 1895–1899.

Additional Modern Sources

Cantarelle, Eve. *Pandora's Daughters: The Role and Status of Women in Greek and Roman Antiquity.* Baltimore, Md.: Johns Hopkins University Press, 1987.

Cochrane, Charles N. *Christianity and Classical Culture.* New York: Oxford University Press, 1957.

Lintott, Andrew. *Imperium Romanum: Politics and Administration.* London: Routledge, 1993.

Macmullen, Ramsay. *Roman Social Relations, 50 B.C. to A.D. 284.* New Haven, Conn.: Yale University Press, 1974.

Malherbe, Abraham J. *Social Aspects of Early Christianity.* Eugene, Ore.: Wipf & Stock, 2003.

Smallwood, E. Mary. *The Jews under Roman Rule from Pompey to Diocletian.* Leiden: Brill, 1981.

III. Roman Empire: Public Law and Penal Law

Daniel-Lacombe, *Le droit funéraire à Rome.* Paris, 1886.

Mommsen, *Roemisches Staatsrecht.* Leipzig, 1877.

———, *Roemisches Strafrecht.* Leipzig, 1879.

Willems, *Le droit public romain*. Paris & Louvain, 1883.

Additional Modern Sources

Barnes, Timothy. "Legislation Against the Christians." *Journal of Roman Studies* 58 (1968): 32–50.

Corbette, Percy Ellwood. *The Roman Law of Marriage*. Oxford: Clarendon Press, 1930.

Epstein, L. M. *Marriage Laws in the Bible and the Talmud*. Cambridge, Mass.: Harvard University Press, 1942.

Flaceliere, Robert. *Love in Ancient Greece*. London: McFadden, 1964.

Rawson, Beryl. *The Family in Ancient Rome: New Perspectives*. Ithaca, N.Y.: Cornell University Press, 1966.

Wiedemann, Thomas E.J. *Adults and Children in the Roman Empire*. New Haven, Conn.: Yale University Press, 1989.

IV. Roman Empire—Pagan Religions

Translator's note: A very thorough clarification of the terms "pagan" and "pagan worship" may be found in A. A. Barb, "The Survival of Magic Arts," in *Conflict Between Paganism and Christianity in the Fourth Century,* edited by A.D. Momigliano, Oxford, 1963. Also, Robert Lane Fox, *Pagans and Christians* (Harper & Row, 1987, pp. 11–101) contains an excellent discussion of "paganism," which is not to be understood as an insulting term.

Beurlier, *Essai sur le culte rendu aux empereurs romains*. Paris, 1890.
[Millar, Fergus. *The Emperor in the Roman World, 31 BC–AD 337.* Ithaca, N.Y.: Cornell University Press, 1977.]
[Nash, Ronald. *Christianity and the Hellenic World*. Grand Rapids, Mich.: Eerdmans, 1981.]

Boissier, *La religion romaine d'Auguste aux Antonins*. Paris, 1874.
[Ogilvie, R. M. *The Romans and Their Gods in the Age of Augustus*. New York: W.W. Norton, 1969.]

Cumont, *Les religions orientales dans l'Empire romain*. Paris, 1906.
[Cumont, Franz. *Oriental Religions in Roman Paganism*. New York: Dover Publications, 1956.]

_____, *Les mysteres de Mithra.* Paris, 1903. [*The Mysteries of Mithra.* Cosimo Classics, 2008.]

_____, *Textes et monuments figurés relatifs aux mysteres de Mithra.* Brussels, 1896–1899.

[Campbell, Leroy A. *Mithraic Iconography and Ideology.* Leiden: E. J. Brill, 1968.]

[Speidel, Michael. *Mithras-Orion: Greek Hero and Roman Army God.* Leiden: E. J. Brill, 1980.]

Lafaye, *Histoire du culte des divinités d'Alexandrie hors de l'Egypte.* Paris, 1884.

Reville, *La religion à Rome sous les Sévères.* Paris, 1886.

Toutain, *Les cultes païens dans l'empire romain.* Paris, 1907.

[Ferguson, J. *The Religions of the Roman Empire.* Ithaca, N.Y.: Cornell University Press, 1970.]

Additional Modern Sources

Beard, Mary. *Pagan Priests: Religion and Power in the Ancient World.* Ithaca, N.Y.: Cornell University Press, 1990.

Cary, Max. *Life and Thought in the Greek and Roman World.* London: Methuen, 1940.

Ferguson, John. *The Religion of the Roman Empire.* Ithaca, N.Y.: Cornell University Press, 1970.

Halliday, W. R. *The Pagan Background of Early Christianity.* Liverpool: University Press of Liverpool, 1925.

Macmullen, Ramsay. *Paganism in the Roman Empire.* New Haven, Conn.: Yale University Press, 1981.

Mylonas, George. *Eleusis and the Eleusinian Mysteries.* Princeton, N.J.: Princeton University Press, 1961.

Ogilvie, R.M. *The Romans and Their Gods in the Age of Augustus.* New York: W. W. Norton, 1969.

Otto, Walter. *Dionysus: Myth and Cult.* Bloomington, Ind.: Indiana University Press, 1995.

Witt, R. E. *Isis in the Greco-Roman World.* Ithaca, N.Y.: Cornell University Press, 1971.

V. The Church at the Time of Persecutions

In this section, I mention neither the general histories of the Church, which are known by all, nor the critical studies on the acts of the martyrs, which lie outside the subject of this book. I only deal with works which have a more or less direct link to the state at the time of the persecutions.

Allard, *Histoire des Persécutions*. 3rd ed. Paris, 1903–1908.

_____, *Dix lecons sur le Martyre*. Paris, 1907.

[Frend, W. H. C. *Martyrdom in the Early Church*. Blackwell, 1965.]

[_____. *The Rise of Christianity*. Philadelphia: Fortress Press, 1984.]

Arnould, *De apologia Athenagorae*. Paris, 1898.

[Bernard, Leslie W. *Athenagoras: A Study in Second Century Christian Apologetic*. Paris: Beauchesne, 1972.]

Aubé, *Histoire des Persécutions de l'Église*. Paris, 1875–1885.

[De St Croix, G. E. M. "Why Were the Early Christians Persecuted?" *Past and Present* 26, (November 1963): 6–38.]

[Frend, W. H.C. "The Failure of the Persecutions in the Roman Empire." *Past and Present* 16 (1959): 10–30.]

[Janssen, L. " 'Superstitio' and the Persecution of the Christian." *Vigiliae Christianae* 33 (1971): 131–59.]

[Bell, H. Idris, and T. C. Skeat. *Fragments of an Unknown Gospel and Other Early Christian Papyri*. London: British Library, 1935.]

Battifol, *Anciennes Littératures chrétiennes*. Paris, 1897.

[Streeter, Burnett H. *The Primitive Church*. New York: Macmillan, 1929.]

[Turner, C. H. *Studies in Early Church History*. Oxford: Clarendon Press, 1912.]

Conrat, *Die Christenverfolgungen in römischen Reiche von Standpunkte der Juristen*. Leipzig, 1897.

Crivelluci, *Storia delle relazione tra lo Stato e la Chiesa*. Bologna, 1886.

Cruice, *Histoire de l'Église de Rome sous le pontificat de Victor, Zéphyrin, et Calliste*. Paris, 1898.

[Dill, Samuel. *Roman Society from Nero to Marcus Aurelius*. New York: Meridian Books, 1956.]

De Genouillac, H. *L'Église chrétienne au temps de saint Ignace d'Antioche*. Paris, 1907.

[Barnard, L. W. *Studies in the Apostolic Fathers and their Background*. New York: Schocken Books, 1966.]

[Grant, Robert M. *Ignatius of Antioch*. Camden, N.J.: Nelson, 1966.]

[*The Epistles of Ignatius of Antioch*. James A. Kleist, trans. Westminster, Md.: Newman Bookshop, 1946.]

[William R. Schoedel. *Ignatius of Antioch*. Philadelphia: Fortress Press, 1985.]

De Rossi, Giovanni Battista, *Roma sotterranea cristiana*. Rome, 1864–1877.

_____, *Bullettino di archeologia cristiana*. Rome, 1863–1894.

_____, *Nuovo Bullettino di archeologia cristiana*. Rome, since 1895.

Duchesne, L., *Histoire ancienne de l'Église*. Paris, 1907. [*The Early History of the Christian Church: From its Foundation to the End of the Third Century*. 3 vols. Claude Jenkins, trans. London: J. Murray, 1909–24.]

[Carrington, Philip. *The Early Christian Church*. 2 vols. Cambridge: Cambridge University Press, 1957.]

[Frend, W. C. H. *The Early Church*. Minneapolis, Minn.: Augsburg Fortress, 1965.]

_____, *Origines de culte chrétien*. Paris, 1907.

_____, *Fastes épiscopaux de l'ancienne Gaule*. Paris, 1891.

Freppel, *Les Pères apostoliques*. Paris, 1959.

[Bettenson, Henry, ed. and trans. *The Early Christian Fathers: A Selection from the Writings of the Fathers from St Clement of Rome to St Athanasius*. New York: Oxford University Press, 1956.]

_____, *Les apologistes chrétiens au second siècle*. Paris, 1860–1861.

[Grant, R. M. *The Greek Apologists of the Second Century*. Philadelphia, Pa.: Westminster, 1988.]

_____, *Origène*. Paris, 1907. [*Origen*. H. Crouzel, trans. Paris: Lethielleux, 1985.]

[Daniélou, Jean. *Origen*. W. Mitchell, trans. New York & London: Sheed & Ward, 1955.]

————, *Saint Irénée*. Paris, 1862.

[Lawson, John. *The Biblical Theology of St Irenaeus*. London: Epworth Press, 1948.]

————, *Tertullian*. Paris, 1864.

[Barnes, Timothy D. *Tertullian: A Historical and Literary Study*. New York & London: Oxford University Press, 1971.]

[Osborn, Eric. *Tertullian; First Theologian of the West*. Cambridge: Cambridge University Press, 1997.]

Gregg, John A. F. *The Decian Persecution*. London: William Blackwood & Sons, 1909.

[Rives, J. B. "The Decree of Decius and the Religion of Empire." *Journal of Roman Studies* 89: 135–154.]

[Keresztes, P. "The Decian *Libelli* and Contemporary Literature." *Latomus* 34. 3 (1975): 761–81.]

[Clarke, G. W. "Double Trials in the Persecution of Decius." *Historia* 22 (1973): 650–63.]

Guérin, *Étude sur le fondement juridique des persécutions dirigées contre les chrétiens pendant les deux premiers siècles de notre ère*. Paris, 1895.

[Keresztes, P. "The Emperor Hadrian's Rescript to Minucius Fundanus." *Phoenix* 21, University of Toronto Press, 1967: 120–29.]

[Lactantius *De mortibus persecutorum*. *On the Deaths of the Persecutors*. J. Moreau, ed. 2 vols. Paris : Sources chrétiennes, 1954.]

Guignebert, *Tertullien: Étude sur ses sentiments à l'égard de l'Empire et de la société civile*. Paris, 1901.

[Barnes, T. A. "Legislation Against the Christians." *Journal of Roman Studies* 58 (1969): 32–50.]

Hardy, E.G. *Christianity and the Roman Government*. London: Allen & Unwin, 1925.

[Barnes, Timothy. "Legislation Against the Christians." *Journal of Roman Studies* 58 (1968): 32–50.]

Healy, *The Valerian Persecution*. London, Boston, & New York, 1905.

Le Blant, *Les persécuteurs et les martyrs*. Paris, 1893.

[H. Musurillo, ed. and trans. *The Acts of the Christian Martyrs.* Oxford: Clarendon Press, 1972.]

[Bowersock, G. W. *Martyrdom and Rome.* Cambridge: Cambridge University Press, 1995.]

[Riddle, Donald W. *The Martyrs, a Study in Social Control.* Chicago: University of Chicago Press, 1931.]

Leclercq, *Manuel d'archéologie chrétienne.* Paris, 1907.

Lightfoot, *Apostolic Fathers (S. Clement of Rome, S. Ignatius, S. Polycarp).* London, 1889–1890.

Mason, *The Persecution of Diocletian.* Cambridge, 1876.

[N. H. Baynes, "The Great Persecution." *Cambridge Ancient History,* vol. 12. New York: Cambridge University Press, 1970.]

Neumann, *Der römische Staat und die allgemeine Kirche bis auf Diocletian.* Leipzig 1890.

Profumo, *Le fonte ed I tempi dell' incendio Neroniano.* Rome, 1905.

Rambaud, *Le droit criminel romain dans les Actes des Martyrs.* Lyon, 1895.

Ramsay, *The Church and the Roman Empire before 170.* London, 1894.

[Rives, J. B. "The Decree of Decius and the Religion of Empire." *Journal of Roman Studies* 89 (1999): 135–154.]

[Keretzes, P. "The Decian *Libelli* and Contemporary Literature." *Latomus* 34. 3 (l975): 761–81.]

Riviere, *Saint Justin et les apologistes du second siècle.* Paris, 1907.

[Barnard, L. W. *Justin Martyr: His Life and Thought.* New York: Christian Heritage, 1948.]

[Chadwick, Henry."Justin Martyr's Defense of Christianity." *Bulletin of the John Ryland's University of Manchester* 47 (1965): 275–97.]

Semeria, *Il primo sangue cristiano.* Rome, 1901.

[Sordi, Marta. *The Christian and the Roman Empire.* Norman, Oklahoma 1986].

Von Harnack, A., *Geschichte der altchristlichen Literatur.* Leipzig, 1893–1899.

———, *Die Chronologie der altchristlichen Literatur.* Leipzig, 1902–1904.

_____, *Die Mission und Ausbreitung des Christenthums in den ersten drei Jahrhunderten.* Leipzig, 1902. [*The Expansion of Christianity in the First Three Centuries.* J. Moffat, trans. New York: Putnam, 1905.]

Wieseler, *Die Christenverfolgungen der Caesaren bis zum dritten Jahrhundert.* Guttersloh, 1878.

Additional Modern Sources

Benko, Stephen. *Pagan Rome and the Early Christians.* Bloomington, In.: Indiana University Press, 1984.

_____. "Pagan Criticism of Christianity during the First Two Centuries." *Aufstieg und Niedergang der roemischen Welt,* II, *Principat* 23.2 (1980): 1055–1115.

Eusebius *The Ecclesiastical History and the Martyrs of Palestine.* 2 vols. Hugh J. Lawlor and John E. Oulton, trans. London: SPCK, 1927.

Glover, T. R. *The Conflict of Religions in the Early Roman Empire,* 3rd ed. New York: Charles Scribner's Sons, 1909.

Goodenough, Erwin. *The Church in the Roman Empire.* New York: Henry Holt and Company, 1831.

Markus, R. A. *Christianity in the Roman World.* New York: Scribner, 1974.

Nock, A. D. *Conversion: The Old and the New in Religion from Alexander the Great to Augustine of Hippo.* New York & London: Oxford University Press, 1933.

VI. The Christian Empire

Allard, *Julien l'Apostat.* Paris, 1900–l903.

[Browning, Robert. *The Emperor Julian.* Berkeley: University of California Press, 1976.]

[Fowdi, Athanassiadi. *Julian and Hellenism: An Intellectual Biography.* New York & London: Oxford University Press, 1981.]

_____, *Saint Basile.* Paris, 1899.

_____, *L'art paien sous les empereurs chrétiens.* Paris, 1879.

Aube. *De Constantino imperatore pontifice maximo.* Paris, 1861.

[Alfoldi, Andreas. *Constantine and the Conversion of Pagan Rome.* Oxford: Claredon Press, 1969.]

[Baynes, Norman H. *Constantine the Great and the Christian Church.* London: Oxford University Press for the British Academy, 1972.]

[Grant, Robert. *Augustus to Constantine: The Thrust of the Christian Movement in the Roman World.* New York: Harper & Row, 1970.]

[Jones, Arnold H. M. *Constantine and the Conversion of Europe.* London: English Universities Press, 1948.]

Baudrillart, *Saint Paulin de Nole.* Paris, 1906.

[Lienhart, Joseph. *Paulinus of Nola and Early Western Monasticism.* Cologne: P. Hanstein, 1977.]

Baunard. *Histoire de Saint Ambroise.* Paris, 1891.

[Dudden, F. Homes. *The Life and Times of St Ambrose.* New York & London: Oxford University Press, 1935.]

Beugnot, *Histoire de la destruction du paganisme en Occident.* Paris, 1835.

[Arnoldo Momigliano. *The Conflict Between Paganism and Christianity in the Fourth Century.* Oxford: Clarendon Press, 1963.]

Boisier, *La fin du paganisme.* Paris, 1891.

[Geffcken, Johannes. *The Last Days of Greco-Roman Paganism.* New York: North Holland Publishing, 1978.]

[O'Donnell, J. J. "The Demise of Paganism." *Traditio* 35 (1979): 69–80.]

Broglie, *L'Église et l'Empire romain au quatrième siècle.* Paris, 1856–1866.

Bulliot and Thollier, *La mission et le culte de saint Martin: Essai sur le paganisme rural.* Paris,1892.

[Stancliffe, Clare. *St Martin and his Hagiographer: History and Miracle in Sulpicius Severus.* Oxford: Clarendon Press, 1983.]

Chastel, *Histoire de la destruction du paganisme dans l'empire d'Orient.* Paris & Geneva, 1850.

Gardner, *Julian: Philosopher and Emperor and the Last Struggle of Paganism Against Christianity.* New York : G. P. Putnam & Sons, 1895.

Goyau, *Sainte Mélanie*. Paris, 1908.

Hatzfeld, *Saint Augustin*. Paris, 1897.

[Bonner, Gerld. *St Augustine of Hippo: Life and Controversies*. Philadelphia, Pa.: Westminster Press, 1964.]

[Brown, Peter. *Religion and Society in the Age of St Augustine*. New York: Harper & Row, 1972.]

[_____. *Augustine of Hippo: A Biography*. Berkeley: University of California Press, 1967.]

Héfélé, *Histoire des Conciles*, vol. I and II. Paris, 1869 and 1907.

Koch, *Kaiser Julian der Abtrunnige*. Leipzig, 1809.

Largajolli, *Della politica religiosa di Giuliano imperatore*. Plaisance, 1887.

Largent, *Saint Hilaire de Poitiers*. Paris, 1902.

[Newlands, G. M. *Hilary of Poitiers: A Study in Theological Method*. Bern: P. Lang, 1978.]

Lecoy de la Marche, *Saint Martin*. Tours, 1881.

Naville, *Julien l'Apostat et sa philosophie du polytheisme*. Paris, Neuchatel & Geneva,1897.

Negri, *L'imperatore Giuliano l'Apostata*. Milan, 1902.

Ozanam, *La civilisation au cinquieme siecle*. Paris, 1865.

Puech, *Saint Jean Chrysostome et les moeurs de son temps*. Paris, 1891.

Rampolla, S. *Melania giuniore senatrice romana*. Rome, 1905.

[Gerontius *The Life of Melania the Younger*. Elizabeth A. Clark, trans. New York: E. Mellen Press, 1984.]

Rauscher, *Jahrbuche der christlichen Kirche unter Kaiser Theodosius den Grossen*. Freiburg im Breisgau, 1899.

[Pharr, Clyde. *The Theodosian Code and Novels and the Sirmondian Constitutions*. Princeton, N.J.: Princeton University Press, 1952.]

Schultze, *Geschichte des Untergangs des griechisch-roemischen Heidentums*. Jena, 1892.

Thierry, Amedée, *Trois ministres des fils de Theodose: Rufin, Eutrope, Stilicon*. Paris, 1865.

_____, *Saint Jérôme, la société chrétienne à Rome et l'émigration romaine en Terre Sainte*. Paris, 1867.

[Kelly, J. N. D. *Jerome: His Life, Writings, and Controversies.* New York: Harper & Row, 1975.]

_____, *Saint Jean Chrysostome et la société chrétienne en Orient.* 2nd ed. Paris, 1894.

_____, *Recits de l'histoire romaine au cinquième siècle.* Paris, 1967.

Additional Modern Sources

Brown, Peter. *The World of Late Antiquity, AD 50–750.* New York: Harcourt, Brace & Jovanovich, 1971.

Glover, T. R. *Life and Letters in the Fourth Century.* Cambridge: Cambridge University Press, 1901.

Greenslade, S. L. *Church and State from Constantine to Theodosius.* London: SCM Press, 1954.

Jones, Arnold H.M. *The Later Roman Empire, 284–602.* Oxford: Blackwell & Mott, 1964.

Kaegi, Walter E. *Byzantium and the Decline of Rome.* Princeton, N.J.: Princeton University Press, 1968.

King, N. Q. *The Emperor Theodosius and the Establishment of Christianity.* London: SCM Press, 1954.

Macmullen, Ramsay. *Christianizing the Roman Empire.* New Haven: Yale University Press, 1984.

Pelikan, Jaroslav. *The Excellent Empire: The Fall of Rome and the Triumph of the Church.* San Francisco: Harper & Row, 1987.

Setton, Kenneth M. *The Christian Attitude Towards the Emperor in the Fourth Century.* New York: Columbia University Press, 1941.

Stark, Rodney. *The Rise of Christianiy.* San Francisco : Harper, 1997.

Van der Meer, Frederick, Christine Mohrmann, and Mary F. Hedlund. *Atlas of the Early Christian World.* London: Nelson, 1958.

Vasiliev, A. A. *A History of the Byzantine Empire, 324–1453.* 2 vols. Madison, Wis.: University of Wisconsin Press, 1958.

Willis, G. G. *Augustine and the Donatist Controversy.* New York: Sheed & Ward, 1931.